MENSWEAR

Suiting the Customer

Suzanne Boswell

REGENTS/PRENTICE HALL, Englewood Cliffs, New Jersey 07632

Library of Congress Cataloging-in-Publication Data

Boswell, Suzanne,
   Menswear: suiting the customer / Suzanne Boswell.
     p. cm.
   Includes index.
   ISBN 0-13-571423-0
   1. Tailoring. 2. Men's clothing. I. Title.
  TT580.B57 1993   92-22908
  646.4'02—dc20   CIP

Editorial/production supervision and
  interior design: **Janet M. DiBlasi**
Cover design: **Marianne Frasco**
Cover art: **Wanda Lundy**
Prepress buyer: **Ilene Levy Sanford**
Manufacturing buyer: **Ed O'Dougherty**
Page layout: **Robert Wullen**
Acquisition editor: **Elizabeth Sugg**
Marketing manager: **Robert Kern**
Photo editor: **Rona Tuccillo**

Illustrations by Wanda Lundy

*Dedicated to the memory of Joseph Cybick, Jr.,
teacher, mentor, and friend;
and to my students who consistently asked the questions
I needed to hear, and were an inspiring source
of boundless energy, humor, and spirit.*

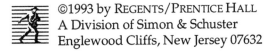©1993 by REGENTS/PRENTICE HALL
A Division of Simon & Schuster
Englewood Cliffs, New Jersey 07632

Printed in the United States of America

10 9 8 7 6 5 4 3 2 1

ISBN 0-13-571423-0

Prentice-Hall International (UK) Limited, *London*
Prentice-Hall of Australia Pty. Limited, *Sydney*
Prentice-Hall Canada Inc., *Toronto*
Prentice-Hall Hispanoamericana, S.A., *Mexico*
Prentice-Hall of India Private Limited, *New Delhi*
Prentice-Hall of Japan, Inc., *Tokyo*
Simon & Schuster Asia Pte. Ltd., *Singapore*
Editora Prentice-Hall do Brasil, Ltda., *Rio de Janeiro*

CONTENTS

PREFACE

This book has been written to educate those actively pursuing education in the area of fashion, style, fit, and quality, regardless of their age or gender. The reader may be a novice to the apparel industry or retail trade: a student of design, fashion marketing, a beginning sales associate, a young retailer. Conversely, he or she may be an adult with experience in the business, be that the retailer, designer, manufacturer, tailor, image consultant, or wardrobe consultant. The reader may *also* be an interested consumer, however.

The overall purpose of the book is to blend many aspects of the menswear business into one source. To my knowledge, there is no other single resource that addresses issues of relevance to the consumer, retailer, designer, and manufacturer as well as includes timely information on international trade and electronic data interchange.

The reader should come away with a heightened awareness of the impact menswear has always had on the entire fashion industry and a strong understanding of quality. The student should be challenged to see menswear in a new, exciting light.

All too often, students as well as the public perceive fashion to mean womenswear. Through this book, I hope to broaden that viewpoint for the reader. Fashion marketing students need to see the many options available to them by purposely choosing menswear as a career path. Frequently an individual "ends up" in this field by default rather than by design. As students become educated in this area, their options for career opportunities increase significantly, and the school offers a much broader perspective of the industry than previously addressed.

Many books on the apparel industry offer one chapter on menswear; the emphasis is usually placed on womenswear. Menswear sometimes seems like an afterthought. The same may be seen in the curricula of many schools. A service is done when a broader education is offered, resulting in increased career opportunities for the student. In developing and teaching this course, student response has been overwhelmingly gratifying. Most students had not given previous thought to the study of menswear, primarily because the concept had not been presented to them. On conclusion of the course, most students commented on a greater understanding of quality on the whole, and many seriously considered menswear, rather than just womenswear, as a viable avenue for future work.

Service, so critical and often lacking will be the key for organizations to survive through tough times. And emphasis has been placed here on assisting the consumer to make the very best purchase decisions possible. An outcome of this is a stronger, repeat customer base for the retailer or consultant.

The ultimate result of the book then is to produce a more informed consumer who is able to make wiser choices by recognizing value. This ultimate goal may best be achieved by working with an informed professional who assists him or her.

The title of the book, *Menswear: Suiting the Customer* places the emphasis and purpose of the book on the study of tailored garments: suits, suit separates, slacks, sportcoats, and furnishings. This is the area of greatest need in terms of education in the menswear field. One cannot neglect the importance of sportswear. Sportswear styles fluctuate much more radically, however, and are closer akin to womenswear in this respect. Therefore, the approach here is to investigate the *influences* on men's sportswear rather than specific styles or fit.

This book is organized into 12 chapters that are structured as follows:

Chapters 1–4: *Menswear industry*—an overview of media, designers, licensing, international issues, and trade associations.

Chapters 5–9: *Garment style, fit, and quality*—evaluation of tailored apparel, assistance of customer with garment fit and quality, selection of furnishings, formalwear choices, and an overview of sportswear influences.

Chapters 10–11: *Menswear fabrics and tailors*—fibers and fabric choices for menswear, garment care, options in special make apparel, selection of and work with tailors.

Chapter 12: *Development of the customer's wardrobe*—information from earlier chapters and put into practical application for the customer.

This book includes many illustrations throughout. The line drawings are stylized to clarify comprehension of design lines and garment fit. At the end of each chapter is a case study applying to the information in that chapter. Each case study is accompanied by several questions to encourage class discussion and independent thinking. In addition, at the close of each chapter is a list of terms specific to the chapter topic.

There are two glossaries in the book: the book glossary following the final chapter and a special fiber-fabric glossary that is part of Chapter 10.

A unique aspect of the book is Chapter 12, which includes a self-evaluating quiz to determine the man's personality expression, and best style and fit of apparel for the customer. This quiz may effectively be used by the student, the consumer, the wardrobe consultant, or the sales associate. It also includes charts for coordinating the wardrobe. This will be of special help to those who work with repeat clients.

An Instructor's Manual is available that includes tests and keys, case study comments, suggestions for class demonstrations, class projects, and field trips.

Suzanne Boswell is a professional speaker who is also available for informative seminars on self-presentation, business communications topics, or in-service training. Contact her directly at:

Suzanne Boswell Presentations
3767 Forest Lane, Suite 116-470
Dallas, Texas 75234

ACKNOWLEDGMENTS

It is only with the help and support of many others that a work such as this can exist. In gratitude for their assistance and support, I acknowledge Roman Alonso, Barneys New York; Jean Patrick Bonny, Gerard Soulaine/Paris; Ray Bushnell, Haggar Apparel Co.; Benetta Cook, Art Institute of Dallas; Miryam Drucker, Education Management corporation; Norman Oehlke, International Fabricare Institute; John Haller, Robert Talbott Inc.; Jimmy Haggar, The E. Magrath Apparel Co.; Eddie Janes, Milliken & Co.; Suzanne Kilgore, Mens Retailers of America; Leon Morrison, Tie-Coon Trading Co.; Marsha Parr, Haggar Apparel Co.; Stephen Schmidt, CSPI; Marvin Segal, Marvin E. Segal & Associates, Inc.; Bob Stern, Short Sizes Inc.; Joe Ventimiglia, J C Penney; and Debra Wallace Washington, Art Institute of Dallas.

I give very special thanks for the generous help, time, information, and feedback of my respected friends: Milton Hickman, Reed St. James, Division of Haggar Apparel Co.; Sylvan Landau, Dallas Market Center; and Ray Scott, Farah, Inc. I also acknowledge Wanda Lundy for her wonderful illustrations as well as her patience and friendship.

In addition, thanks to all the retailers who so patiently answered questions and offered advice; all my private clients who provided so much insight during consultations; the many educator-reviewers who offered valuable feedback and ideas that added immeasurably to the book; my adult audiences who gave me the impetus to pursue this endeavor; Bob and Jane Handly for their friendship, inspiration, and support throughout this project; and Brian, John, and Sarah Corcoran— you are in here.

Finally, I thank Herb for his constant support and unflagging encouragement through computer breakdowns, protracted anxiety, and many, many long days and nights!

CHAPTER 1
MALE CUSTOMER

"Know your customer" is the primary rule of any type of selling and a particularly important one in the selling of menswear. Before we can investigate the whys and wherefores of menswear itself, we must first consider the customer—his habits, likes, and dislikes, both in apparel and in shopping itself. A highly successful accessories retailer commented that the fashion business can be learned, appreciation for style can be learned, but there is a third most important element for success in the fashion business, and that is understanding and taking care of the customer.

The effective retailer, for example, must buy for the customer, follow up with the customer, display merchandise attractively for the customer, advertise for the customer, take complaints and returns—in short, make it easier and more pleasant for the customer to shop. To be successful one must pay attention to the customer, for he or she will tell you what is wanted. It is imperative to keep in touch with the customer's wants, needs, tastes, and desire for service.

AGE CATEGORIES AND SHOPPING HABITS OF MALE CUSTOMER

There are four factors that influence the customer in making garment choices: fashion, fit, quality, and price. Which of the four factors comes first depends on who the customer is. For some men, fashion styling is not a big factor, they would prefer to stay with the mainstream traditional look. And yet, that is still a fashion choice. The consumer of today is becoming more value conscious. He is looking more judiciously at what he is getting for his money. That ties quality in with price. Value is determined by the quality received for the price paid and the concept of value is very subjective. What is a good value for one man may not be a good value for another. We come full circle to understanding the customer and his needs.

Likes, dislikes, habits, life-styles, and income levels all change as we age, and those changes are reflected in a myriad of choices seen at retail. Once we understand the motivation of the consumer, we can *help* him make choices rather than *sell* him on buying. Let's look at today's average American man and how he changes in his approach to both the shopping process and his wardrobe choices.

Age 18–30

The young man often has a strong interest in shopping. This is a relatively new phenomenon that gained strength in the 1970s. Shopping became a date for adolescents—a way to rub elbows with their female counterparts in a low-risk environment. And retailers have observed that young men have tended to make more purchases when in the company of young women.[1] This brought about an interesting trend in retail stores. Many stores developed "unisex" departments catering to looks that both young men and young women could wear. This made shopping more attractive for those consumers and increased the sale of merchandise in those departments.

In his earlier years, the young man's budget might have only allowed him to shop at lower-end stores and department stores. As his income level rose, his choice of stores also changed. He is strongly influenced by women—mother, sister, girlfriends, perhaps wife. There's more open-mindedness in today's young man toward color and style in sportswear. His personality is still developing, and his closet may reflect a wide range of styles.

As he approaches age 30 a gradual shift in the wardrobe appears. His career is evolving and a greater percentage of wardrobe dollars is given to professional clothes and, depending on his personality type (see chapter 12), "dressy casual" for evening and weekend wear.

[1]Barbara Krupnicki, "Why Young Men Shop," *DNR the Magazine*, March 1985, p. 58.

Age 31–50

More men fall into this category than the other two age groups. These men also spend more money on clothing than the other two groups collectively. At the younger end of this age range, some men may have a tendency to spend beyond their means in an effort to send a message of affluence.

As the more conservative male consumer enters the "career years," however, he has less interest in shopping. His primary concerns now are his career and his family and friends. If married, his wife may do much of the shopping and she can have a major impact on wardrobe choices. Coordination of styles and garments may be difficult and time consuming for this man, and he often happily passes this responsibility on to his spouse with "Honey, what should I wear tonight?"

In retail purchases, he's more concerned with quality and value. As his income increases, he's more likely to frequent specialty stores and higher-end department stores for better choices and service. If he must shop, he wants the process to be quick and easy and as painless as possible. The faster and simpler the process, the better.

The married man's wardrobe will often have voids in styles. He'll have more clothing for work than for leisure, and his leisure clothes will be of the "garden variety"— blue jeans and T-shirts with very little in between.

Conversely, the single or divorced man may have some different concerns. Unless he has a natural bent for fashion, he may be frustrated on entering retail establishments. The time involved, overabundance of items to choose from, and confusion on quality are all perceived as problems by this man. The divorced man has a more trying time as he'd previously relied on his wife for help, and choices are more varied and complicated now. He may have a greater need for social interaction, yet no wardrobe for it. He typically feels uncertain and confused. More than any other type, this man has the greatest need and will respond the most to competent help.

Age 50 and Up

As he enters this age range, he typically is pretty set in his style preferences. We'll still see a predominance of clothing for career choices, but once he starts nearing retirement, he may become less concerned with business wear. If he's had to wear a suit and tie for years, he wants to relax the look now. More easy-care leisure wear filters in. He may hang on to his "old-friend" sportswear items that are in "perfectly good condition." Primary interest is with comfort and ease of wear.

If he becomes "newly single" at this age after many years of marriage, clothing choices and clothing coordination is made even more demanding. He may avoid shopping except when forced to and may find the process a very distasteful necessity. Many men of retirement age must be cost conscious and may prefer budget shopping.

Male Consumer and Fashion Professional

Although there are many variations, these are the basic tendencies in each age group. Most men do not enjoy shopping as much as women do. There is a strong need for reliable, knowledgeable, and competent sales help for the male consumer. They want value, and they want to work with someone they can rely on and trust. As a result, men will be valued, repeat customers to those who can help them with color, coordination, fit, and quality.

An added benefit in a sales associate is the ability to understand and balance the customer's budgetary considerations with his life-style and wardrobe needs. For this reason, *personal shoppers* have become more commonplace, especially for the executive man. Many specialty and major department stores offer this service for their clientele. For example, "Macy's Buy Appointment" offers personalized, one-on-one assistance in a private dressing area with garments coordinated and accessorized from all store departments. The personal shopper, a specially trained store employee, maintains records of the clients sizes, purchases, and style preferences.

There are also independent *wardrobe consultants* who offer more extensive services. They will determine the best color range and style for the client, evaluate his existing wardrobe, shop for the client at a variety of stores, and maintain records.

The most often used shopping assistant for the adult male consumer is a woman, and in many cases, that is his wife. She has tremendous impact on his purchases. She may shop without him for his shirts, underwear, accessories, and sportswear, and will accompany him on shopping trips for suits, sportcoats, and slacks. Quite often the gifts she buys for him are in the apparel category. When it comes to the tailored category of garments, however, the woman also needs guidance in making effective choices for the man. She was not raised or trained in the area of menswear fit, make, or quality.

What is important here is the need of excellent guidance for the average male consumer. A special sensitivity is required when assisting a man who is accompanied by a woman. It is as important to win the confidence of the female as well as the male consumer.

CASE STUDY

Gus Lindstrom is 53 years old. As a teenager, he had little interest in clothing other than wearing "the uniform" of his peers. On school days and weekends alike, he wore blue jeans, or khakis, with button-down shirts, and loafers. During medical school, he had neither time nor interest in clothing. His days and nights were spent either in class, studying, or on call at the hospital. As he dated, he found himself relying on his date's advice for what to wear to special events. His early career wardrobe, however, did not include any updated items since he was in high school.

Once he started his own medical practice, he found himself with a few obligatory suits mixed in with his old jeans and button-downs. He felt most at ease when wearing his lab coat over a pair of slacks. His life-style had changed, however, which resulted in many wardrobe challenges. Invitations to dinners, golf clubs, professional meetings, and increased social events often made him feel uneasy in determining what to wear.

When he married at age 34, his wife managed his wardrobe and made sure that he had a variety of styles that could take him into any business or social situation. Gus did not have to worry about clothing appropriateness.

At age 53, however, he and his wife divorced. No longer did he have someone he could rely on for guidance. And he had not developed the skill to coordinate his own wardrobe. To complicate matters, he started dating, which increased his anxiety in relation to appropriate dress for social functions. Ben decided he had to find a professional person to assist him in developing his existing wardrobe and in understanding how to shop for himself.

- Where could Gus go to locate those who could help him?
- What would the benefit be of hiring a wardrobe consultant versus working with a sales associate from a local store?
- What were the factors which led to his wardrobe problems at age 53?

TERMS TO KNOW

Define or briefly explain the following:

Unisex
Personal shopper
Wardrobe consultant

C HAPTER 2

MEDIA

AND MENSWEAR

The media unquestionably has had a major impact on the spread of fashion in modern history. In the past, people had to see and experience a new style before the style would be accepted and possibly spread. And it generally took a much longer time to get used to seeing a new style before it would be accepted and then adopted. That has changed tremendously today.

We've seen tremendous advances in the impact of electronic media on fashion. This is a major trend that will continue to have a huge impact on fashion at retail and the consumer's perception of style. Menswear, which traditionally is slow to change, will advance more rapidly now because of greater media coverage.

This process is very similar to what happens in the computer industry. As soon as a computer is purchased at retail, it is practically obsolete. Incredible advances made during the manufacturing process of that very computer will result in a new model that is faster and smaller, and offers a wider range of functions. So as we address the issue of fashion and electronic media, our data, likewise, will be outdated very quickly and advancements made very quickly.

Print media has become much more sophisticated and has followed the womenswear lead in blending elegance and worldliness into both advertising and editorial material. Slick, beautifully designed magazines now feature covers with well-known sports and media figures to reach and broaden the magazine's readership. Advertisers use *tear sheets* of their ads as counter displays in their stores. This increases the public's perception of the retailer's wide influence because of their affiliation with the print media. And, of course, it helps to highlight those goods the store wants to promote.

Fashion shows at retail stores now garner wider media coverage and a broader market through association with charity and social events. Where in the past, it might have been perceived as a feminine pastime, attending fashion shows has now become acceptable to many fashion-conscious males. Both men and women attend fashion shows where menswear and womenswear are shown.

Apparel advertising on television has had a huge impact on the spread of fashion today. The average person has much greater brand awareness and style than in the past. In addition, designers who lend their garments to television shows often receive recognition in the closing credits of the program. Some designers have high name recognition in connection with certain programs, such as Nolan Miller who designed the garments for the Dynasty series in the1980s and early 1990s. This even resulted in garments designed for sale at retail with the program affiliation clearly identified on garment hangtags. Fashion has had a major influence in the look and sophistication level of some television programs. In addition, many television talk shows incorporate "makeovers" for men as well as women. These television segments help to raise awareness to menswear styles and bring fashion to the masses in a highly dramatic manner.

There is no denying it, fashion is both a part of, as well as a form of, entertainment today. Wardrobe designers for both television and film very carefully craft the "look" for each character. They use apparel to help to get the actor's persona across to you and me. This is especially important in the 30-minute time frame of some television programs. That is a very short time within which to communicate the personality and character of a player to the viewer. Clothing plays a major part in letting us know quickly, for example, that the actor either cannot be trusted or is naïve and innocent!

PRINT MEDIA AND PUBLICATIONS

There are basically three types of publications within which fashion information is communicated: *consumer publications*, *trade publications*, and *dailies*.

Consumer Publications

These publications, most often magazines, speak in the consumer's terms. Their concern is to educate the consumer as to trends, quality, and what is available at retail. They also include editorial material that may be unrelated to fashion, and offer insight into other male-interest topics such as sports, travel, cars, business, investments, and world affairs. The mix of this information relates directly to the profile of the magazine readership. Some publications are known primarily for fashion, with a smaller percentage of editorial material devoted to other subjects, like Fairchild Publication's *M* magazine. Its readership is a sophisticated group, and the advertisers and articles indicate a worldliness with an emphasis on styles and subjects European.

GQ, or *Gentlemen's Quarterly*, also is primarily a fashion publication but with a different readership. It is directed more toward the mainstream man with a bent on upbeat, fashion-forward apparel. It often features film or sports celebrities on the cover that attract the attention of a broader audience than *M* might.

Esquire, conversely, takes a different approach to its reader. It has more editorial copy on nonfashion-related topics. Fashion is not its primary content, though each issue does address some fashion topics and apparel advertisers do support the publication. Like *Playboy*, periodically *Esquire* devotes large special sections in certain issues to menswear fashion trends.

There are many, many more fashion publications on the market today that reach very specific audiences. One look at the cover should give the browser a very good idea of the profile of the readership, the percentage of the publication devoted to

This advertisement was from the autumn-winter 1931–32 issue of the trade publication *The Progressive Tailor* (Tailoring Arts Publishing Co., New York, NY). This tailoring firm offered contract labor at varying prices based on the amount of workmanship in the garment (refer to chapter 3 for more information on garment grade and make).

menswear, and the sophistication level of the reader. What keeps a publication afloat is its advertisers, so by flipping through the pages, one can see that a men's magazine that puts little emphasis on fashion will have far fewer apparel advertisers.

Trade Publications

Trade publications are those which address business issues important to the fashion and garment industries including: manufacturers, retailers, designers, suppliers and so on. Within the menswear industry, the granddaddy of the trade publications is the *Daily News Record*, or *DNR*. Fairchild Publications produces this trade journal, just as it does *Women's Wear Daily*. Because *DNR* is the "bible" of the menswear industry, it is considered "must" reading for anyone in the business. The title sounds like a regular newspaper, but its content is based on news and trends in the menswear business. *DNR* is so important to the menswear industry, that it is sold at newspaper stands in New York, and it is delivered to manufacturers and retailers around the world daily.

This paper communicates the latest in style trends, financial and business news relating directly to the garment industry, and information on apparel manufacturers, mills, and suppliers. It also includes sections on manufacturing equipment for sale, want ads for open positions, and investment opportunities.

Some trade organizations produce publications to inform and educate their members. The National Association of Men's Sportswear Buyers, Inc. publishes a monthly membership newsletter on trends in men's sportswear, merchandising concepts for retailers, business subjects, and updates members in its upcoming functions. NAMSB also furthers its outreach by targeting its newsletter to educational institutions as well. In a broader perspective the National Retail Federation publishes the magazine "Stores" for its members and the industry. It addresses a wide range of topics of interest to retailers ranging from fashion and merchandising trends to business management.

Daily Newspapers

These publications, directed to the public, take a different viewpoint on fashion and the garment industry than either a trade journal or a consumer magazine. There are two major areas where the fashion industry is addressed. Many newspapers have a human-interest, or life-style, section. It is here where you usually find articles and photo editorials on fashion, most commonly womenswear. Periodically, however, menswear issues are addressed. Often the newspaper's source of fashion information will originate from Fairchild's publications. Larger cities may have a fashion editor who travels to the major design shows and reports on style trends. In addition, these same papers often produce a special section once a week devoted solely to fashion.

The business section of the newspaper covers retail trends, such as store openings, closings, and financial rankings of local and national retailers. Consistently reading these articles offers great insight into the retail market and reflects on the spending trends of the public. It is critical for anyone in the fashion-garment business to keep fingers on the pulse of the American public through following the business section.

Catalogs

Though these publications are created for the purpose of selling merchandise rather than educating the reader, they can provide that same result. Today mailing lists are often sold or rented to other mail-order companies, so once you are on a list, your mailbox may fill up quickly with catalogs. These catalogs are a good source of information on style trends and color directions during any season. By scanning the catalogs we receive, we can quickly get a pretty good perspective of trends at retail. Some catalogs design their publications to be as attractive and enjoyable to read as possible, choosing exotic locations for photography backgrounds. Others may include editorial material of an educational nature that softens the appearance of a hard sell and encourages the reader to peruse the catalog more thoroughly. Catalogs, like that of the retail store Banana Republic, create a very authentic aura through type of paper used, quality of drawings, and extensive information on the history and uses of the garments. Other publications cross over from catalog to magazine and blend the best of both, like the publication *NM, as Magazine* which had been produced by Neiman Marcus. Of course, Neiman Marcus has received worldwide publicity from its Christmas catalog, which offers items from the heights of luxury to the exotic to the outrageous.

The life-style of the average business person today may preclude extensive shopping trips to the mall. The ease of shopping in the comfort of home with coffee in hand becomes more and more attractive to the public. In addition, catalog companies and stores that sell by mail order offer the consumer the ability to purchase by credit card by calling a toll-free 800 number. They make it as easy as possible for us to spend our money! Major concerns the consumer should have in making mail-order garment purchases are both quality and fit. The inability to feel the fabric and see the construction is a drawback. Judging fit by how it looks on the model in the photograph may be unrealistic in choosing the garment for yourself— are you built just like that model? It is important to deal with reputable mail-order firms that have reasonable returns policies.

Increased postal rates are having an impact on the lifeblood of catalog companies. Not only is it becoming more expensive to mail the catalogs, but increased postal costs have encouraged some catalog customers to calculate their purchases more carefully.

BROADCAST MEDIA

Television

More than any other single medium, television has had the largest part to play in the spread of fashion and the speed of style change. Before 1950, most homes received their daily news via radio and newspaper. Radio, lacking visual communication, had little impact on fashion. Newspaper photos were often outdated, and advertising illustration provided the strongest form of visually showing style changes. A new style in New York might take months to affect style in New Mexico, if ever. Clothing styles were highly regionalized, and often lacked in worldly sophistication. Theater and movies had more impact on the public than anything else. Yet, production time for those forms of entertainment required lengthy lead times for styles to be seen and ultimately accepted (refer also to chapter 4).

Then came television and the world would never be the same again. New styles were instantly broadcast across the country. Live television in the 1950s and today's live evening talk shows result in a forced open-mindedness toward new fashion styles. It's unavoidable. The world is fascinated by the medium, we are fascinated by the entertainers and everything about them. As we see new style, it may, at first, appear shocking or displeasing to the eye. Each time we see it, however, we become more used to it. We may not *like* it, but we get used to it. At that point, it is a part of the accepted style of the day. Television speeds this process immensely. Millions of men and women across the United States watch sports broadcasts on the weekends. Sports announcers and even coaches are communicating much more strongly now than in the past in terms of clothing and appearance. Heywood Hale Broun, the sportscaster, made sometimes shocking visual impact in terms of his bright plaid jackets. It was for effect, however, and helped him to stand out from the rest of his peers. Pat Riley, former coach of the Los Angeles

Lakers, cut a dashing figure on the sidelines with his well-coordinated furnishings and fashionable style. As the male viewer sees his role models sporting fashionable looks, then "style" becomes more acceptable to the mainstream man. And so through television, we now see more fashion items being worn in the heartland of America as well as in the high-fashion metropolitan areas.

Fashion Programming

As the world has become smaller because of television, we have the opportunity to see international fashion shows. Cable television offers, for example, top-quality fashion programs like "Style with Elsa Klensch." In "Style" we can travel to the couture shows in Milan, Paris, and New York; hear designers talk about their lines; and learn more about fit and fabrics. This can bring about a greater understanding of design and a familiarization with specific designers. Often these same designers may have ready-to-wear lines available in local boutiques or department stores. Therefore the viewer may take the concepts seen at the highest levels of fashion and modify them to his own world.

Shopping networks on cable television often offer apparel for sale. This format provides the ease of shopping at home via catalog with one big benefit. In this format, the consumer can see how the garment moves if a model is wearing it, and more information as to fiber content, care instructions, and fit may be provided. As in ordering garments by mail, however, size and fit may be sacrificed because of the inability to try on the merchandise before purchase.

VIDEO

Television has produced a somewhat jaded public. The fast pace and high-stimulation factors of television can make other forms of communication somewhat boring. We are used to bright lights, vivid colors, exciting music, and we are now used to being entertained. So what happens when we enter the retail store? We may see some unusual visual displays. Often *counter cards* may be displayed at point of purchase. These stand-up display cards frequently feature advertisements, or tear sheets, from newspapers or magazines. If we're lucky, we may get some enthusiastic and helpful sales associate to create interest in what's in stock.

But what was your reaction the first time you walked into a store that had a television monitor and a fashion video running? Didn't you stop and watch for at least a few moments? Didn't it manage to get your interest and hold it? If you saw an outfit you liked on the screen, didn't you want to see it, touch it, feel it? In-store videos are having an enormous impact on the consumer today. Initially, the concept began in womenswear. Created for upscale, fashion-forward departments or for the teenage set, these videos are now entering the mainstream. They are used as a tool to get the customer into the department, interest him in the stock, and educate him as to style and fit as well. Many of the glitzier shows look much like music videos and look like they could have been lifted from MTV.

A big benefit of this medium to the retailer is the use of videotape versus live models. Videotape allows the retailer to entertain, educate, and sell to the consumer nonstop. He does not have to deal with live models or a fixed fashion show time. The monitor is selling for him constantly. The longer the customer is in the department the more likely he is to buy. Some retailers may use these videos in conjunction with a special event and may even offer refreshments to encourage consumers to linger.

Video Catalogs

With the advent of up to two video cassette recorders in many homes today, the video cassette is now being used for shop-at-home purchases. Some creative marketers have seen the impact of the video on the consumer and put their catalog in cassette form. Now the consumer can choose what type or line of apparel interests him, and at his leisure, he can make selections from the video. The benefit of this over the television fashion show is that he can stop action, back up, and take a longer look at certain items. His choices can then be called in to the catalog company by a toll-free 800 number. Sometimes there is a minimal charge for these videos, with a rebate if the video is returned. The catalog company would probably prefer that the consumer pass the video on to others, however, making it much more profitable in the long run.

Educational Videos

Some fashion videos are created purely as educational tools for the consumer. Their purpose is to train or educate the viewer in a specific area. Advertisements are not typically included, though reference may be made to other products that are on the market and might be of interest to this same viewer. For example, *Esquire* magazine produced a video tape on professional style called "Dressing Well as a Part of Career Success." It did an excellent job of educating the viewer in appropriate style, fit, quality, make, and color choice.

This type of video is very attractive to many as it is often thought of as preferable to reading a book on the subject. Again, the viewer has the benefit of stop-action and replay of the tape. In addition, it builds on the high-stimulation needs which have affected so many areas of our lives. The public and the consumer enjoy learning and shopping in this manner.

FASHION SHOWS

Consumer Productions

As the concept of fashion spreads among mainstream men, more stores are offering opportunities for men to see apparel not only displayed, but shown in the form of fashion shows. The idea of attending a fashion show is not readily accepted by many mainstream men. Retailers who present such shows are challenged in getting the largest attendance possible. Many offer refreshments, may include women's fashions also, encouraging couples to attend, and may offer promotional items such as door prizes or drawings at the end of the show.

Periodically, a magazine like *GQ* will conduct a regional or national tour of stores. They will conduct a fashion show that results in promotion of both their publication as well as use of stock from the participating retailer. Such productions may receive well-publicized advance promotion through the magazine as well as on a local level through print media and with mailers to the retailer's credit customers. Some of these events are considered quite exclusive, where the store may be open only to those who respond to an invitation.

Often a fashion show will be conducted in conjunction with a charity function with proceeds of the event becoming charitable donations. The retailer benefits by receiving the publicity through the charity, and establishes community goodwill by affiliation with charitable and nonprofit organizations. Those who pay to attend such events are often the target market of the retailer who hopes for increased sales as a result of the show. These events may be part of a luncheon or dinner, and both menswear and womenswear may be included in the fashions modeled. Frequently, members of the nonprofit group become the models, and increase interest in both the event and the items shown.

Industry Productions

Garment manufacturers and trade organizations also offer cutting edge information on trends and style through their own fashion shows. The Men's Fashion Association in New York produces major fashion shows and press previews for print and broadcast media. Information on the latest menswear styles is communicated throughout the United States and the world via the fashion press. The National Association of Men's Sportswear Buyers, Inc. produces four major shows each year for their members and the trade. In addition, NAMSB produces video news releases, videotapes of fashion shows, and fashion news. Often organizations gain greater strength through affiliation with each other on projects like this to reach broader audiences. The Men's Apparel Guild in California, known as MAGIC, plans two major shows for retailers a year. MAGIC is considered one of the most important menswear industry shows in the United States, attracting buyers from international markets. Organizations like National Retail Federation Cotton, Inc., Men's Fashion Association, and National Association of Men's Sportswear Buyers Inc., want to communicate in every way possible what is happening in their industries, and how both the public and the trade can benefit. This communication may come in the form of print media and promotional newsletters, or in meetings and shows where the latest concepts can be seen.

CASE STUDY

Esquire magazine produced a series of video cassettes under the title the "Esquire Success" series. This series included individual cassettes on the subjects of professional style, persuasive speaking, wine advisor, and several business topics. Their approach in marketing the series was unique. The videos were made available through ads in their own publication as well as others. The consumer could purchase a single topic selection or several.

In the video on professional style, an *Esquire* editor was interviewed as to interpretation of style. Highly respected and well-known experts from various fields of fashion and retail were included in interviews and demonstrations. In addition, there were interviews with three "real people" who had raised their own perspective of style to help themselves in their careers.

At the close of each video was a short promotional clip for the other topics in the series. The reputation of *Esquire Magazine* helped to lend credibility to the tape series and, of course the series was well promoted in their publication.

- How did *Esquire* spread its influence and possibly increase its readership through this video series?
- What was the purpose of having the three interviews with average businessmen rather than celebrities?

TERMS TO KNOW

Define or briefly explain the following:

Consumer publications
Trade publications
Dailies
Video catalog
Tear sheet
Counter card

C H A P T E R 3

MENSWEAR
DESIGN AND
MANUFACTURING

The garment industry in the United States finds its roots in New York City. Though the Southwest and the West Coast both play important parts in the design and production of menswear, New York City still leads the way because the industry was born there. As of 1991, more than 200,000 people were employed in New York's fashion industry, with most of the companies located along a strip of midtown Manhattan on 7th Avenue, sometimes referred to as *Fashion Avenue*[1]. The goal of the industry is to find out what the customer wants and to give it to him at a profit. As simple as that sounds, this is a very complicated and competitive business.

The public often only sees the glitzy, glamourous, and fast-track sides of the business. In reality, that front is backed up with high pressure, hard work, frustration, sweat, and lots of guts! Designers and manufacturing plants must be flexible and able to adjust to the whims of the consumer and the economic climate of the country. Changes in designs often must be made immediately or risk sacrificing the line to a retail trade that has changed direction. Those people responsible for the styling of a design line must have their ears constantly to the ground, listening for new trends. There is a bit more stability to the menswear industry than the womenswear industry though. This is especially true for the classification of tailored apparel, because change is slower than in furnishings or sportswear.

But to say that the menswear industry is different from the womenswear industry would be a gross understatement. Though there are similarities, there are many more differences. This is especially true when we look at the design and manufacturing of garments. Obviously, fabrications and styles are different. But manufacturing methods, time frames, and marketing are also very different. The purpose of this chapter is not to define and delineate all aspects of design and manufacturing for the marketing student, but to make clear the different approaches taken by menswear and womenswear manufacturers to reach the same objectives—design and production of quality, salable, and stylish merchandise.

STYLE ORIGINS

Before we can look at the actual manufacturing of garments, we must investigate where the ideas for those styles begin—what are the sources of inspiration to the designers. Where do their ideas come from, and how do they move from conception to completion?

As we've already seen, the media has an enormous part to play in the transference of style ideas from one person, place, or time to another. In addition to the impact of the arts, television, movies, theater, and world events have an impact on fashion. Wars that involve our troops or affect our economy in any way will also affect our fashion. At times of political or economic upheaval, many industries will feel the pinch, and the garment industry is no different. So the impact may be related to emotional responses, reflected, for example, in the popularity of camouflage-colored sportswear during times of war. Or the results may be for practical reasons. For example, less fabric was used during involvement in World War II when much of the piece goods production was relegated to the military. At that time, fewer cuffed pants were worn because of the additional fabric required to produce the cuff.

Often the political climate of the day will dictate the predominant proportion seen at that time. Lapel widths and pant-leg silhouettes may be the barometers of the conservativism or liberalism of the period. During late 1960s to early 1970s, wide lapels and full, flared pant legs were quite popular. Everything else in the outfit matched their proportions. And these garments reflected a general magnani-

---

[1] Susan Enfield, "Inside Fashion," *Harper's Bazaar*, October 1991, p. 119.

mous attitude of the wearers. As times became more conservative politically, however, the leg silhouette and lapel width narrowed, and again reflected general attitudes of the country.

The saying "everything old is new again" relates strongly to fashion. There is very little which is a totally unique style, never before seen. Most of the styles today have their roots in earlier fashion. Stylists "borrow" concepts seen before and may put them together in unusual combinations to put today's stamp on them. For example, the "stovepipe" pant leg has been popular throughout history. It was seen in the very earliest of men's pants, prior to ever considering putting a crease in the pant (the crease just makes the pant a lot easier to press). Once pants started to be pressed with a creaseline, that became the norm because of the ease of pressing the pant leg in that manner. So the reemergence of a "tubular" leg later seemed new! In the extreme styles of the l960s this "stovepipe" leg was called an "elephant leg" pant. In the early 1990s the style started to emerge once again in some very high-fashion European pants, yet in a silhouette more in line with the proportions of the day.

There are few true classics—garments which can be worn over decades without showing in some way an influence of the date of their birth. The man's trench coat may have the same styling details as that of the 1950s yet the older coat may be shorter, less full, have a higher lapel breakline, and so on. These details will hint at its age. If you think you can put a garment in storage and be able to wear it again some time in the future, that's a real long shot. Most styles just never come back in exactly the same way, nor do they, because of textile technology, come back in the same fabric. Unless the wearer has the panache and personality type to pull off wearing eclectic styles, the older garment probably won't work for him.

The best of those few styles that have stood the test of time have come from the 1930s. Tailored apparel of that period had an elegance of style and fabrication that still influences today's designers strongly. The lines of the 1930s as well as the 1940s can be seen in sophisticated clothing and sportswear at retail today. By looking at old photos or film clips of the Duke of Windsor, Fred Astaire, and Cary

Personalities of the 1930s like Fred Astaire showed great style and wit in their apparel. Astaire often wore patterned socks to draw attention to his fancy footwork. The Bettmann Archive.

Grant, one can see the importance of silhouette, fine fabrics, creative use of accessories, and wide use of texture to make a confident and cosmopolitan statement.

The designers on the cutting edge of forward fashion certainly take the greatest risk in promoting "new" looks. Many of the world's top designers, as well as the "underground" avant-garde designers, produce forward items that are modeled at fashion shows in cities like Milan, Paris, New York, Rome, and Los Angeles. They receive both notoriety and acclaim for their daring; however, many of the styles shown never reach the point where they are worn by the masses. These garments are typically out of reach of the average consumer because of their cost. Such couture garments may be one of a kind and primarily handmade, with special orders placed by individuals for purchase. In reality, very few garments are sold in this price range, and major designers usually have a *ready-to-wear* line reserved for the masses. This line may take some of the proportions and design elements of the more expensive garments, but make them more palatable and affordable for the average man. Different fabrics and construction methods will be used to hold down costs, and the styles will often not be as outrageous as the couture line.

And so the spread of fashion filters down toward street level, where a style is seen worn by the average man on the street. When a major designer produces a look that is fresh, acceptable, appreciated, and attractive to the consumer, the mass manufacturers jump on the bandwagon and start to produce *knock-offs*. Knock-offs are copies of popular styles and are typically lower priced than the style being copied. Costs are reduced by using less expensive fabrics, and eliminating some of the fit or design details seen in the original garments. By this time in the fashion cycle, the original designer has moved on to other styles. The designer may no longer want to be associated with garments that are found in discount stores or commonly seen on the street.

A trend among some of the world's top designers today is knocking off themselves! That is, they may take their top-of-the-line concepts and translate them into styles at a lower price point. This can be effected in two ways. In the true *diffusion concept* the designer may add other lines, give them different labels or names, and price them differently. For example, the great Italian designer, Giorgio Armani offers several lines: Giorgio Armani Couture, Giorgio Armani, Mani, and A/X Armani Exchange. Each line represents a different style, fit, price point, and often a different customer. The latest addition, the A/X line, is casual sportswear that includes jeans, certainly a departure from the typically tailored Armani.

One of the Pierre Cardin line labels is even entitled "Diffusion," clearly communicating the concept. In this way, the designer may reach new markets. In *price point spread*, the designer may retain one line name and just widen price point spread within that line. This method allows the designer to be represented in different stores and reach new customers while still maintaining the integrity of an individual line.[2] That is, the designer may retain the higher price points with high-end retailers, while offering lower price points under the same name to other retailers. (See the segment on Halston in the following section on licensing in this chapter.) Some designers may start out with a wider price point spread and ultimately move into name diffusion to reach larger markets.

The mass manufacturers who reach middle America have many challenges in meeting the needs and interests of the consumer. In styling they must look at what is realistically happening at retail—what's selling, and what other designers are doing. They must consider what is happening at the high end of apparel, as well as considering the direction womenswear is taking. They must follow the media, be aware of what's happening in movies, theater, television, and, most important, they must constantly read everything available on trends and consumer needs. In addition, the fiber mills often give direction to the manufacturers as to what colors and fabrics are popular.

This brings us full circle, with the forerunner designers always creating new looks to show the public, trying to create the need and desire for change. And their influence filters down to the masses, where it ultimately fades out as newer looks fill the pipeline.

Fashion historian James Laver's theory on the evolution of a fashion is referred to as "*Laver's Law*," and he purports that the way we look at a style changes with the years that precede and follow its popularity. His research shows that the same costume will be regarded differently as it is placed historically:

A Style Is Considered

Indecent	10 Years before its time
Shameless	5 Years before its time
Daring	1 Year before its time
Smart	Style has reached acceptance by the public
Dowdy	1 Year after its time
Hideous	10 Years after its time
Ridiculous	20 Years after its time
Amusing	30 Years after its time
Quaint	50 Years after its time
Charming	70 Years after its time
Romantic	100 Years after its time
Beautiful	150 Years after its time

Though you may relate to some of this concept as being more focused on womens-wear than menswear (we don't often refer to menswear as "beautiful"), the concept is sound as to the evolution of a style and the public's responses.

How might this concept affect the public's perceptions of incoming styles? Consider the flare leg which was so popular during the 1960s. The leg silhouette straightened in the late 1970s, and our eyes became used to the narrower cut. At that point, the flare leg looked silly and disproportionate. At 20 years after the popularity of the flare, anyone wearing the style would be seen as a subject of ridicule. As we enter the 30-year mark, the flare pant is starting to be shown at the very highest level of avant-garde—perhaps counterculture—fashion. It will not filter down with great acceptance to the masses because we are still in rather conservative times politically and economically. Its hint at reappearance will indicate that the style will return. However, seldom does a style return in exactly the same manner as before. It will take on the influence of the day, yet the roots of the style will be evident.

DESIGN AND MANUFACTURING TECHNIQUES

In the world of design the terms *stylist*, *designer*, and *patternmaker* are not synony-mous. This is frequently misunderstood by the public. In some large, mass-manu-facturing companies, the stylist may study the market, come up with the initial renderings, and pass the drawings on to a designer or patternmaker to initiate construction of the garment.

[2]Robert Parola, "Designer Sportswear Diffusion? Confusion Reigns," *Daily News Record*, July 15, 1991, p. 10.

The terms designer and patternmaker take on different meanings depending on the company. One company may opt to call the person who makes the patterns the designer. In another company, the designer may take the role of the stylist described previously and may then pass initial concepts on to a patternmaker. There are fewer variables in relation to the term patternmaker; definition is inherent in the name. This is the person who drafts the garment patterns but is usually not responsible for inception of style ideas. In short, do not assume you know the responsibilities of the individual based on their title alone.

Often we hear the word designer used as applied to a particular quality level of apparel, as in "designer sportcoat" or "designer tie." These are usually higher-end, better-quality items. There may be a designer's name used in the labeling and marketing of the line of apparel or furnishings. But, in fact, the term "designer" as used here may be rather a misnomer. In fact, any garment that hangs on a rack in a retail store is technically a "designer" garment—it was designed by someone! In many cases, however, the individual whose name appears on the garment label may never see the actual garment produced. It may, instead, have been created by assistant or staff designers to represent the overall look of the designer. The actual "name" designer in some cases might give final approval to designs created but may never have put pencil to paper in creation of the style for mass-distribution merchandise.

There are many differences between the design approaches of the avant-garde designer and the mainstream mass-manufacturer designer. The fashion-forward, high-end designer has much wider parameters in style, fabric, and construction details. This designer can afford to put more detail into garments because his customer demands it and can afford it. The mass manufacturer has tighter parameters in terms of construction and garment costs. Yet this customer still wants style and serviceable garments. Therefore, the garments produced in large quantities for middle America may retain some of the look of high-end merchandise, but lack the finer fabrics and the construction detail of their higher-priced counterparts.

Any mass manufacturer that produces in very high quantity may well have the capability to produce more highly engineered garments today, producing a uniformity of look with reduced expense. The term *highly engineered* indicates that more sophisticated, specialized machinery does specific sewing or pressing operations. The equipment is expensive and requires high-production quantities to justify the costs involved. In the highly engineered plant, there are often tight quality-control procedures. Time and motion studies of plant employees may be conducted by engineers to maintain high efficiency and productivity. This manufacturing advantage also encourages high incidence of similar styling in certain frequently produced details of garments. For example, the barrel cuff that is so common in shirts is very standard in style, regardless of fabric or other style treatments in the garment. It is therefore cost effective to have automated machinery sew this part of the garment. It is then produced with consistent quality and at high speed, resulting in lower cost and higher production efficiency.

PRODUCT LICENSING

The dictionary defines "license" as a formal permission to do something. And that is exactly what the concept of licensing is in the garment industry. It is a formal, legal agreement between a designer or company and a manufacturing organization whereby the manufacturer may produce garments and offer them for sale under a brand name. This is a very widespread business practice that came into full bloom in the 1960s and 1970s. During that time, there was a burgeoning popularity of "designer" clothing, much of which sported the designer's logo, prominently and permanently a part of the garment. Most of this merchandise, as well as many brand-name garments today, are produced by *licensees*.

The licensee is the manufacturer who will produce the finished garments and has signed a licensing agreement with the owner of the brand name, or the designer, to use that name to sell the garment, and possibly to use the brand logo or trademark on the garment itself. The *licensor* is the organization that has contracted with the manufacturer to make a product under the licensor's brand name. The contract will have stipulations set forth by the licensor as to how this relationship will be transacted and for how long a period it will be in effect.

What are the benefits to the licensor and licensee? The licensee may want to "grow" his business by the increased volume resulting from affiliation with a highly recognizable brand name. There are manufacturing operations or contractors who exist solely to provide production facilities to make licensed garments. This manufacturer benefits by increased production volume and resulting profit increases. Typically, the brand name immediately opens doors for distribution at retail. The licensor, through use of a contract manufacturer, has vastly increased volume potential, and can produce a fully coordinated product line if desired. The licensor will maintain certain controls over design, distribution, and quality of goods produced, though the amount of control and designer input varies widely depending on how the contract was written.

Another benefit to a design organization in entering a licensing agreement is the ease with which it can inject a new look into their offerings. A consumer who has been a faithful follower of a very staid and conservative line might become interested in a slightly more forward look coming out of Europe. Rather than lose market share to imports, an American firm may enter a licensing agreement with a European designer. This will allow the American company to broaden its look and maintain its customer base. The manufacturer, who is incurring a major production debt, will make the majority of profit, with a royalty as a percentage of sales going to the designer. Royalty percentages vary greatly; however, 3, 4, or up to 10 percent of the wholesale cost of the garment are not uncommon.

A major question to be asked here is: Who actually does the designing of the garments? Let's consider the magnitude of production output for a designer like Pierre Cardin. Cardin was one of the very earliest to master the licensing of his name, and it was done in quite a widespread manner. The Cardin name/logo is seen on shirts, pants, coats, suits, ties, accessories, shoes, underwear, sleepwear, eyeglasses, and luggage; the list goes on and on. Can Pierre Cardin himself choose every color and fabric, sketch every single style in each garment category? Of course not, it would be physically impossible for one person to do that. Each major designer has a staff of assistants who create the designs in the style representative of that designer. For ready-to-wear lines, the designer may have very little part to play in the production of these items. He is certainly at the helm of the operation and directs the style approach to be taken, but cannot himself implement the actual styling of every garment. Many designers own no manufacturing plants at all for their ready-to-wear lines. This same designer has complete input and participation in the creation of the upper-end couture line he may create. A much greater hold is maintained in this arena. They usually produce their couture garments in their own operations.

The challenge with this diffusion of production is to ensure that garments made by different licensees maintain the same level of quality standards and that the entire merchandise line coordinates; shirts made by one licensee should work with ties produced by another, and these items should also coordinate with the suits produced by another manufacturer.

An example of licensing is an agreement between Calvin Klein and GFT USA Corp., which occurred in 1991. Calvin Klein, licensor, contracted with GFT USA Corp., licensee, to produce a collection of men's clothing, sportswear, and furnishings. This production contained two price point levels and was produced in the GFT factories in the United States and Europe. Previously Klein's sportswear and clothing were licensed to Bidermann Industries Corp. That agreement lasted 8 years after which Klein bought the license back.[3]

There is another aspect of licensing that has an important impact in relation to the agreement between the licensee and licensor. If the manufacturer has a sales staff that sells to retailers, which retailers will carry the merchandise? The designer may stipulate in the licensing agreement the type of store to carry this line. For example, the designer may only want the line carried in upscale specialty stores. But the sales staff may wish to increase the sales volume by including department stores. This would create conflict between the two retailers. The specialty store desires some exclusivity in the lines carried, and the same merchandise appearing in a local department store could dilute the elite air of the specialty store. Such a clash could result in the line being dropped from one of the stores. For this reason, designers evaluate closely the retailers that will carry their merchandise.

During the 1970s Halston licensed his name for production and sale of a lower-priced line of womenswear to J C Penney. This was an opportunity for the Halston name to reach millions of women via a mass merchandiser. His couture line, however, was being offered in his own Madison Avenue boutique as well as in the most exclusive specialty stores nationally. There was an incredible uproar in the garment industry about such action. By using the Halston name in both lines, he seemed to degrade the integrity of his couture line. Would his faithful couture customers continue to buy if the Halston name was prominently placed in Penney's? Some of the specialty stores were outraged at such licensing and dropped the Halston line. After the brouhaha quieted down, Halston had lost only a few stores, and vastly increased his name recognition and profit share.

Celebrity sponsorships are somewhat akin to designer licensing. In the celebrity sponsorship, a well known personality, such as basketball superstar Michael Jordan, may "sell" his name to a manufacturer like Nike. He then becomes the sponsor for the manufacturer, and appears in print and media advertisements. Such sponsorship by no means infers that the celebrity participates in the design of the item or line—only that he or she endorses the product. Celebrities, particularly sports figures, benefit tremendously by the hefty *endorsement fees* that accompany such agreements. By association with these personalities, manufacturers gain higher profile, increased sales, and higher profits. Brand recognition increases as the sports figure wears the product, such as tennis players sporting logos on their shirts as they compete and are viewed world-wide on television. This concept has declined somewhat in menswear today with the exception of active sportswear. Celebrity sponsorship is more readily seen today in womenswear, though now associated with mid-to lower-end manufacturers and retailers. For example, the American actress, Jaclyn Smith, sponsors a womenswear line under her name through the K Mart stores.

Endorsements are being seen on many different levels. Even local retailers have seen the advantages of mutually beneficial associations with well-known personalities. This has been seen on network television for years, where a store may dress the host of a game show and in return receives recognition in the credits at the close of the program. Some retailers offer apparel to local sports or newscasters because of the exposure to be obtained. For example, the Kent Shop, a men's specialty store in Dallas, provides on-camera clothing and postgame sportswear to Richie Adubato, coach of the Dallas Mavericks. In return the store has exclusive rights for personal appearances and to use Richie's voice and image in print and electronic media[4] (refer to chapter 9 for more information on sportswear licensing).

---

[3] "It's Official! GFT Is Now Calvin Licensee," *Daily News Record*, June 24, 1991, p. 6.

[4] Stan Gellers, "Much Ado about Adubato," *Daily News Record*, June 24, 1991, p. 6.

QUALITY IN MANUFACTURING

The nature of smaller design firms, or high-end companies, is to produce fewer garments. Conversely, the larger mass manufacturers produce in higher quantities. There are pros and cons to these realities. The smaller quantities produced in one style are often referred to as *short runs*. A short run means that the style in question is being run down the manufacturing line for a short time, and fewer garments produced. A *long run* is one that is produced in higher quantities, and the style is in a long production run. What is considered a short run or a long run depends on the manufacturer. What is a long run for a small company may actually equate to a short run for a larger manufacturer.

A style that is being manufactured in a short run by a mass manufacturer will not produce the same quality level as that of a long run. The longer a style is manufactured the better the quality becomes. Manufacturing and pressing techniques improve with experience. This is particularly true when a style is being made in a highly engineered plant. What are the benefits to the consumer and the retailer? They are higher quality and consistency of quality as well as lower prices. The length of the run makes less quality difference in garments produced by a higher-end manufacturer, especially those that incorporate hand operations in their work. Most of these organizations maintain very tight controls over each manufacturing operation.

Production of short runs often requires more consistent and persistent quality checks to avoid consumer-retailer returns of seconds or defective goods, and ultimately the tarnishing of the manufacturer's reputation. The resulting benefit of a short run to the retailer or consumer is that the style is fresh. The consumer will not see as many others wearing the same garment on the street. At the same time, he may pay more for these garments because the start-up costs of manufacture are not spread out the way they are in a long run.

An important aspect of quality in apparel is the *wear test*. As a consumer, you do not want to be the person performing the wear test for the manufacturer! In the ideal situation, a manufacturer conducts a test of the garment's fabric strength, seam strength, and comfort before the garment is ever produced for shipment to retailers. Garments are worn, tested for comfort, and washed or dry cleaned to ensure that there is no excessive shrinkage and that care labels are appropriate.

Sometimes the manufacturer makes assumptions about the garment and produces and ships it before conclusive testing can occur. Retailers, relying on the reputation of the manufacturer, sell the merchandise and then are at the mercy of the consumers, who have become unwittingly the "wear testers"! Who maintains the responsibility in this situation, the retailer or the manufacturer? The retailer, to maintain the goodwill of the consumer, will normally accept a return on the defective merchandise, but the item should then be immediately returned to the manufacturer and restitution made to the retailer.

There is absolutely no way that a manufacturer can avoid making a defective item periodically. As long as human beings are involved in manufacturing there will be mistakes. Even machines break down and produce defective merchandise. Sometimes, there is a defect in the piece goods that may not be apparent in the manufacturing process. In that case the garment manufacturer would expect restitution from the piece goods mill. It is critical that, no matter the cause, the manufacturer be notified immediately by the retailer so that any further problems may be caught and corrected in the manufacturing process. It is also imperative that consumers bring problems to the attention of the retailer. The retailer must determine if similar items are still in stock, and the retailer must identify those vendors with whom they are experiencing quality difficulties.

INTERNATIONAL MARKETPLACE

Our world is getting smaller and smaller. Sophisticated communication technology brings us in immediate contact with our neighbors on the other side of the globe. Miles are negligible, and time has shortened with high technology communication linkage.

The world is becoming more democratic and countries are realigning to establish themselves as independent republics. The tearing down of the Berlin Wall, and the breakup of the former Soviet Union and the European Community in 1992, all are historic milestones that have had an impact on world economics and most certainly on world trade. These events do not ensure any stable, long-range economy wherein we can predict international trade practices. They do point toward the world embracing more of a free market, however. Organizations like the United States Apparel Industry Council exist to deal with United States and foreign governments. Their purpose is to promote the interests of mutual trade, to deal with the customer, and to provide pro-business input to trade negotiations and regulations.[5] The leaning toward democratization around the world will open up more channels of distribution between the United States and other countries.

Because the United States represents freedom around the world, garments that bear the label "Made in the USA" hold great appeal for citizens in many repressed countries. Though foreign governments produce roadblocks and red tape for American imports into their countries, the citizens typically are quite eager for the opportunity to buy our products.

There are two major types of imports to be addressed here: (1) imports of piece goods that will be used in the production of finished garments within United States borders and (2) imports of finished garments that have been manufactured outside the United States. These finished garments may also have been made with foreign-made piece goods. In addition, we will see that American manufacturers and retailers may both be players in the international market in relation to these imports.

The United States as well as most industrial countries wish to increase their production levels by exporting goods they have manufactured. Imports of raw goods or finished products are often purchased when such merchandise is not available domestically at the desired quality level or price. For example, Italy presently leads the world in production of fine worsted-wool yardage. A large percentage of the piece goods used in the United States are produced offshore. Piece goods may be imported to the United States and finished garments constructed inside United States borders. An American company may purchase piece goods from Italy and have the finished garments manufactured in Yugoslavia, then import these garments for sale in the United States. Conversely, the United States is well known for its manufacture of denim and blue jeans. There is a great interest and demand for such garments in the Eastern Bloc countries. A pair of American blue jeans today could sell in Russia for four times what an American would pay for the same garment.

Because of the high cost of manufacturing garments in the United States, many companies have gone *offshore* for production. This means that the manufacturer, with either imported or domestic piece goods, has the garments cut and sewn in overseas markets. Minimum-wage standards, union rates, and general costs of doing business in the United States have encouraged many garment manufacturers to seek less expensive areas of manufacture.

In menswear more than 75 percent of sportswear manufacturers have contracted their production offshore. Close to 90 percent of outerwear is made

[5]Pat Baldwin, "Among Apparel Firms, Supporting Free Trade, the Feeling is Mutual," *The Dallas Morning News*, July 22, 1991, p. 1D.

outside of the United States. In the mid-1980s about 75 percent of tailored apparel sold in the United States was manufactured here; the trend has reversed, and almost 65 percent of this classification is now produced offshore. These percentages indicate a major reversal in the direction of the United States garment manufacturing industry.

Europe, particularly Italy, has held the spotlight in recent years for eminence in overall quality and creative styling of tailored clothing. Along with its production of fine-quality fabrics the attraction of purchasing European-made tailored clothing is more for style than price. American sportswear manufacturers, however, have gone offshore in large part for price. Quality is not the factor quite so much as the reduced costs in manufacturing sportswear outside of the United States.

The manufacturing methods used to construct apparel are often referred to as the *make* of the garment. Apparel from companies that maintain high-quality manufacturing standards or are from countries that consistently provide the consumer with high-quality garments are said to offer excellent "make." Conversely, poor-quality merchandise may be said to be of inferior "make."

Private Label merchandise offered by the retail trade is often manufactured offshore. Several major retailers produce their own lines of apparel and sell these garments under a name available only through their own retail stores. For example, Macy's produces a shirt line labeled as "Club Room." It has been designed by Macy's and made primarily overseas. The benefits to the retailer are: a greatly increased profit margin, control over design and quality, and better prices for the consumer because there is no middle man.

The smaller retailers may offer their own lines, but these garments will most probably be made in the United States by contract shops. Contracting offshore is an extremely complicated business; negotiations with foreign governments and businesses are extremely complex. Only the major retailers that produce in very large quantities and have the clout to negotiate letters of credit with financial institutions can maneuver in this arena. This is a constantly changing situation of chasing the low-labor-cost countries. Once determination of the source country and company is made, a signed agreement does not ensure a successful outcome. There are always unforeseen risks, and these problems are made more difficult when they occur so far from home. Natural disasters like monsoons and cyclones can occur. Language differences can profoundly complicate matters. Political upheaval, coups, foreign-labor groups, and strikes can all slow production and possibly bring it to a grinding halt.

It is imperative that any organization that desires to enter this aspect of international business understand three important concepts. (1) They must understand which countries are best sources of merchandise—which countries produce the type of fabrics and finished garments in the quality and at the price the American manufacturer or retailer wants. (2) They must understand that each country has quotas on exports—can the preferred source country fill the requirements of the American company and remain within their quota? (3) They must understand the timing differences related to imports. There are very long lead times involved in such production. It may take up to 15 months from the initial contract date until the garments are seen in the United States. This can cause undue complications if a store has a special promotion or if an ad is planned around imported merchandise.

INTERNATIONAL PRODUCTION

Let's look at the countries that play the most significant part in this international trade. As you will see, some are more notable for their piece-goods quality, and others for the style and quality of their finished goods. Many American companies have gone offshore to take advantage of lower labor rates, increased production capabilities, and a wide range of piece-goods qualities. Likewise, many of the following countries have also spread their interests through purchase of fabric and production of finished goods in other areas.

Western Europe

Italy. The United States market is a very important one to the Italians; they monitor the trends of the American consumer, and they are constantly trying to match the needs of the market to their products.

The Italians are the undisputed leaders in production of fine piece goods and Italy is the dominant country in quality menswear. The Biella region of Italy, located at the foot of the Italian Alps, produces the most expensive and finest worsted-wool fabrics in the world. The top international designers all use piece goods from this area. The Italians also produce top-quality, finely-spun cottons out of Como and Turino. Italy is certainly the major source for yardage and construction of fine finished menswear.

The style and cut of Italian garments are unique to that country. This styling is currently more oversized and makes a more forward statement than many of the traditional American cuts. The look has certainly had an impact on United States manufacturers, and some Italian influence has reached even the most conservative companies here.

Manufacturers may import Italian piece goods for apparel manufacture in the United States or they may utilize a manufacturing source in another country that may not result in quite as much of a forward look.

France. France has maintained its position as the leading country for apparel designers, and almost every successful European men's and women's designer is based there or has its main office in Paris. It is the hub for worldwide fashion design.

Though France is certainly the leading country in womenswear, it runs second to Italy in the production of menswear. In an effort to increase awareness for menswear in France the leading womenswear designers are putting more emphasis on their menswear collections. Some designers who previously only offered womenswear have added menswear to their lines. Today, France is better known for its men's sportswear than for tailored clothing. In sportswear, garments lean toward a more forward, cutting-edge look. In tailored clothing, garments stay closer to the classic looks than Italian styles. There is less oversizing; one does not see the very broad shoulders and full chests as in apparel from Italy. Piece-goods production is not at the level of quality as that produced in Italy.

Germany. The German garment industry produces high-quality fabrics and well-constructed garments. Yet they cannot compete on the same scale as the Italians. They produce very fine viscose fabrics as well as cotton and wool. The cotton and wool fabrics tend to be on the coarse side, however, which makes them relatively heavy in weight. The main production of German fabrics is for their domestic use; hence, the heavy weight is appropriate for the climate. The garment styling is less fashion oriented and therefore, perhaps, accepted in more conservative business offices around the world than the Italian styles. The center of the menswear industry in Germany is Cologne.

Eastern Europe

Yugoslavia. Yugoslavia produces woolen fabrics that are of average quality. A great amount of fabric is imported from neighboring countries to produce sportswear. Yugoslavians are famous for producing heavyweight, hand-knit sweaters. They produce well-made garments in tailored clothing, sportswear, and outerwear; outerwear being their largest apparel export item. They produce many private label lines and offer good quality at better prices. For textiles, Yugoslavia and Poland are highly competitive in pricing. With gaining independence, Yugoslavians may no longer have state support, however, which could result in upward pricing.

Poland. The main industry is manufacturing of both coats and slacks. Polish fabric production is best known for inexpensive corduroy, which they export in finished sport coats and slacks.

Czechoslovakia. Since the overthrow of the government, Czechoslovakians have increased their effort to export piece goods. They produce good-quality polyester-viscose blends as well as polyester-viscose-wool blends. This will be a country to look at seriously for piece-goods and finished-goods production as the European Community becomes stronger.

Hungary. Hungary specializes in polyester-worsted blends in piece-goods production. It has huge production capacities to make these fabrics and is putting more emphasis on production of garments within the country for export. Hungary has important mills that produce polyester blend textiles, much of which is exported. A good deal of their piece goods is shipped to Germany and Korea for garment production.

United Kingdom

England, Scotland, and Ireland. Historically, the United Kingdom has been synonymous with fine-quality wools. Northern Ireland and Scotland produce large quantities of woolen textiles. Harris tweeds are handwoven in the Outer Hebrides, Scotland. The Shetland Islands off the coast of Scotland produce the high-quality Shetland wool. These woolens are a heavier weight appropriate for the cold, damp weather experienced in the United Kingdom. Currently, fewer woolens are being exported from the United Kingdom for several reasons. As world weather conditions have changed, and many countries have experienced a warming trend, these fabrics have become too heavy for frequent usage. Society has produced such highly sophisticated climate-controlled environments that there is less need to protect ourselves from the elements as in the past; the exception is industrial cities in northern climates where there is a lot of walking, like New York, Chicago, and Boston. In addition, because of the high cost of apparel today, many consumers prefer to purchase garments in all-year weights whenever possible, resulting in more of a year round wardrobe. Therefore, there is less exporting of heavy woolen piece goods than in the past.

London has been renowned for its *Savile Row bespoke*, or custom-tailored, suit. Savile Row, as well as Bond Street, in London are legendary for their "old school" custom tailor establishments which offer top-quality clothing and furnishings. Styling of these garments has traditionally been very conservative, and would be appropriate in most any board room internationally. In most recent years, English-make clothing has taken a back seat to that of the Italians. English styling is quite understated today. In the 1960s their sportswear and clothing were in the forefront of fashion in conjunction with the Beatles and England's dominance in music. Regardless of any radical fashion changes in England, the Savile Row look has always remained conservatively constant.

The Orient

For years the Orient has been the stronghold of competitively priced piece goods and finished apparel. Escalating labor rates, however, have allowed manufacturers in Southeast Asia and India to gain strength. In fact, many Far Eastern piece-goods mills and garment manufacturers now produce offshore as well, enabling them to take advantage of the lower labor rates and increasing technology of Southeast Asia.

China. The Chinese were the first to raise the silk worm and to manufacture natural fiber, and China is still a major exporter of silk to the world trade. It is the most important garment industry product from this country. China has made dramatic strides in the last several years with finished-goods production. Generally, the Pacific Rim has become less competitive because of increased labor charges. However, China, because of its overpopulation and huge work force, has kept costs down and has become a major player in world finished-goods production.

Hong Kong. Hong Kong remains the most competitive country throughout the Far East and, without exception, every garment manufacturer that produces men's pants in Hong Kong has offshore factories in Southeast Asia. Hong Kong is the hub for all menswear business, whether that business is conducted in Southeast Asia or Hong Kong.

Fabrics produced in Hong Kong are much more varied than those produced either in Korea or in Taiwan. The flexibility in production capabilities enables the manufacturer to produce any level of quality fabric in any construction.

Most of the business that is done in Southeast Asia is put together through the offices in Hong Kong. It is now becoming an important design influence. In the area of menswear, it has always been known for its tailored apparel, and still has a large and steady international trade in custom clothing (see Chapter 12 for additional information). They are known for their production of knitwear and blue jeans. United States manufacturers as well as designers from all over the world use facilities there for production of their merchandise.

Japan. "Apparel accounts for more than half of the finished goods that Japan exports to the United States."[6] Japan produces expensive but very fine textiles, including high-quality cottons, shirting fabrics, polyester, and silk. Much of its textile production is used in the womenswear market. The cost of doing business today in Japan is prohibitive, and it is not a dominant country for menswear.

In terms of menswear garment styling, it is known more for its sportswear than clothing. Styles are often interpreted in drab colors and are extremely forward fashion. Only a small percentage of Japanese produced sportswear is sold in the United States, primarily in very upscale, high-fashion specialty stores and boutiques.

Korea. Korea is known for its sportswear production rather than tailored apparel. In relation to finished apparel, Korea is more known for its contract work for export rather than its own creative designing. It is better known, however, for production of fine cottons for international export. It has become the most expensive of the Far Eastern countries in which to have finished goods made. The labor rate has increased appreciably, and the synthetic and natural fiber piece goods carry a very high import duty.

Taiwan. As opposed to Korea, Taiwan is somewhat more competitive pricewise both in fabric and garment production. Taiwan is known for its production of textiles, primarily polyester-rayon or polyester-cotton blends and exports a high percentage of synthetic textiles internationally. Like Korea, Taiwan is improving its finished-apparel quality and as a result is involved in more contract work

[6]Elaine Stone and Jean Samples, *Fashion Merchandising: An Introduction*, 4th ed. (New York: McGraw-Hill, 1985), p. 294.

for export. It has an important knitting industry.[7] The quality of the garment production has dramatically increased in the past years, but it is struggling to be competitive because of the staggering reduction of the work force in the factories.

Southeast Asia

Southeast Asia has become an increasingly strong force in piece-goods and finished-goods production in recent years. A good percentage of garment manufacturers from Korea, Taiwan, Hong Kong, and even China have opened plants in Southeast Asia. The countries involved include the Philippines, Malaysia, Singapore, Indonesia, Bangladesh, Sri Lanka, and Thailand. With increasing costs of manufacture in the Orient, and extremely low labor rates in these Asian countries, garment manufacturers have also gone offshore for reduced cost of production.

Indonesia is the fastest growing in terms of production of the Southeast Asian countries. Indonesia also produces a very high quantity of high-quality finished garments, particularly in the sportswear category.

India

The apparel industry in India is one of the most flexible in the world. It is very willing and desirous of working with foreign organizations. Its capabilities are endless in piece goods of cotton, rayon, or blends. And, of course, this is the birthplace of Indian Madras cotton. The quality of fabrics in India, for the most part, is as good as that of Hong Kong or Taiwan. They have high import quotas to the United States and there is little restriction on the number of garments being shipped into the United States. Finished-goods prices are extremely competitive for United States manufacturers.

South and Central Americas

During the 1970s inflation became a serious problem in doing business with Japan. As a result, many manufacturers and designers sought other sources for their production. Latin America, South America, and the Caribbean became attractive, close-by sources for American companies. They are also good sources for well-constructed, traditional, tailored clothing.[8]

South and Central Americas are a good source of fiber and fabrics as well as finished garments. South America produces a high quantity of various woolens for international export. Both South and Central Americas offer excellent quality, styling, and value in sportswear and clothing for international trade. Their tailored apparel offers especially high quality at excellent prices.

Brazil has the largest worsted and worsted-blend mill that exports to the United States. The quality of the piece goods produced rivals that of Italy. Uruguay produces excellent woolens. Argentina's main fabric production is denim.

Chile, Peru, and El Salvador have become major influences in the last years in fabric production. They produce polyester and rayon-yarn-dyed fancies in large quantities, as well as yarn-dyed fancies in 100% cotton. Importance of production in these areas has risen in direct correlation to Japan's production decline because of Japan's high production costs.

MAJOR AMERICAN AND INTERNATIONAL DESIGN FIRMS

American Design Firms

Traditional American menswear finds its roots in British clothing and the sack suit. This is a very traditional, old-school look often associated with the full-cut

[7]Ibid.
[8]Ibid.

Brooks Brothers suits. The American man has typically desired comfort in his apparel. Then the European invasion of the late 1960s and 1970s occurred. The man who was trim was able to wear these stylish, close-fitting, and highly expressive clothes. American and European designers both came to the conclusion that to garner a larger share of the market, they would have to incorporate the fashionable look of the European apparel, while adjusting fit to accommodate the build and desire of comfort for the American man.

With the 1990s came a new look from Europe that was to make dramatic changes in the approaches of the most traditional American manufacturers and retailers. The European oversized fit now became more attractive to the American traditionalist. The sack-coat roots of the Brooks Brothers suit were similar to that of some of the new European imports. This has resulted in the staunchest manufacturers making changes and incorporating more of the European look. This revolution still goes on today as American manufacturers and designers fight for retail floor space and the consumer's dollar.

Joseph Abboud has made a very strong name in fine American apparel. His style is traditional with an updated classic look. Abboud takes traditional styles, uses unusual fabrications, adds some international flavor, yet remains mainstream enough to be well-accepted by the American man.

Jhane Barnes, a rising star in menswear, is known for exceptional fabrics and unusual detailing in her forward, though not extreme, styling. She reaches a wide market through price point spread rather than the diffusion concept.

Bill Blass has been a name familiar to mainstream consumers since the1970s. At that time, he modified the sack-type, traditional coat cut to include a closer fit similar to the European styles. These modifications made him popular with the American man who wanted the stylish look of European apparel with the comfort of traditional clothing. Blass apparel is today available at mid-price points in department stores across the United States.

Brooks Brothers is a retailer, and a very important one in the history of American menswear. But the organization also produces its own line of apparel for their stores. Historically, Brooks Brothers has offered the most conservative clothing for the traditional man. Colors were somber, styles were staid, and fabrics were sensible. These garments were suited to upper-echelon, corporate types who inherited the family business or wanted to look like they had! In the late 1980s Marks & Spencer, a British retailing firm purchased Brooks Brothers. Brooks business had decreased with the competition of European styles. In the past the Italian and French suits were far too high fashion for the Brooks Brothers consumer. Because many European suits are fuller and show roots with the traditional sack suit, the traditional consumer has shown greater interest in buying imports. As a result, Brooks Brothers now offers some items in a more updated look, and it has softened its merchandising approach to attract a broader market.

Perry Ellis began his design career as a design director for John Meyer of Norwich, a womenswear company. He started his own company in 1980 and produced classically contemporary menswear. The clean, simple lines and the high quality fabrics were quickly well-accepted by the public. The company continues to flourish in design and production of both menswear and womenswear despite Ellis' early death.

Andrew Fezza started in the design field creating women's sportswear. Perhaps best known for his exceptional sportswear, he started his business handmaking sweaters. His secondary line, Assets, is an example of diffusion pricing, offering a clothing line at a lower price than his designer line.

Alan Flusser has taken the tradition and elegance of the 1930s and translated those styles into today's proportions. The influence of the British is quickly noted in his apparel. He is known for his attention to detail in tailoring, with a totally pulled-together look including accessories, like suspenders, collar bars, and pocket squares. Flusser was responsible for designing the apparel worn in the movie *Wall*

Street and his total approach to style is evident in Michael Douglas's portrayal of the character Gordon Gekko.

Hartmarx, or *Hart Schaffner and Marx,* is a very large and important corporation in the menswear garment industry. The Hartmarx organization owns and operates menswear stores nationally. They also manufacture men's clothing under a variety of labels such as Hickey-Freeman and Society Brand among others. These brands are found in the Hartmarx stores as well as other fine retail establishments nationally. *Hickey-Freeman* is one of the top-quality and top-selling brands nationally. It is a traditional line with a history of the highest quality. As evidence of the influence and importance of European styling, Hartmarx will produce the Karl Lagerfeld line under the label KL. The couture collection will be manufactured by Hickey-Freeman under the Karl Lagerfeld Couture label.[9]

Alexander Julian is perhaps best known by the public as the colorist of American menswear. His line, Colours, allows the man to express himself through fabrics and colors not seen in traditional menswear. He offers updated traditional apparel with this interesting twist. This consumer wears styles that are appropriate in most business settings, yet show individuality through unusual use of color combinations and textural fabrics. He is one of the few American designers who has had an impact on European clothing designers.

Donna Karan's roots are in womenswear. Originally she designed for Anne Klein, then gained greater popularity with her diffusion line, DKNY, in womenswear. In 1991 she signed an exclusive contract with Barneys for her tailored menswear and sportswear lines. Upscale and expensive, Karan designs for the sophisticated, forward dresser.

Calvin Klein, known perhaps best for sportswear, has produced a high-quality line of clothing since the 1970s. His clothing offers simple, uncluttered styling in classic American lines, fine fabrics, and a high attention to detailing in fit and quality.

Ralph Lauren did not enter the fashion industry by designing womenwear as many of his peers did. Lauren started designing men's ties and was a menswear designer before adding a womenswear line. He is the supreme designer of classic, old-school elegance. His apparel is timeless in style and fabric, and he is a leader in influencing designers of all price points and classifications. More than any other single designer in America today, Lauren exemplifies quality style, and his name has an exceptionally high brand recognition with the public.

Oxxford Clothes, like Hartmarx, is a manufacturing company rather than an individual designer. It is a particularly important organization as it is one of the top United States clothing manufacturers and produces some of the best-made apparel nationally. Oxxford Clothes are found in the highest-quality specialty and department stores. They also offer special-make clothing and made-to-order apparel, whereby the consumer may order slacks, coats, and suits from fabric swatches.

John Weitz was one of the first American designers to open his own boutique in an existing store. Within the New York City flagship Lord and Taylor store, he had his own shop that offered clothing and furnishings with the label, "John Weitz for Lord and Taylor."[10]

International Design Firms

Many consumers still associate European styling with the many earlier imports and American knock-offs of the 1970s and 1980s. That fit was closer to the body and emphasized an exaggerated physique, with a suppressed waist, square shoulder line, and a leg silhouette that was trim through the thigh and wider at the hem. It was a cut that was difficult for many American men to wear. Unless the

[9]Elizabeth Barr, "Karl's Just Dandy," *Daily News Record,* June 3, 1991, p. 6.
[10]Ibid.

man was average to slim, he tended to look overinflated in this close-fitting style. The American male was not used to the high armhole and slim waist of the European garments, and he often felt uncomfortable physically and psychologically in the cut.

That look has been modified appreciably today. The fit is much more "humane"—not so tight on the body. At the upper end of European fashion, it has actually made a 180-degree turn and offers a looser, less constructed look.

England.   The image of the well-dressed Englishman has always been a dapper but conservative one. The irony in this is the contrast presented. The suit may be very well tailored, not extreme, and moderate in padding, suppression, and silhouette. But he may go slightly wild with his furnishings. This same conservative suit may be accompanied by a shirt that has very broad, brightly colored stripes, white collar, and *double cuffs* (across the English Channel, these are known as French cuffs!). His tie may be boldly striped or have a traditional, small pattern, but in very bright colors. This same man likes accessories, and along with the cufflinks, may wear a collar bar, tie pin, and tucked into his coat pocket may be a pocket square. This is not to say that all Britishers sport this look, but it is not considered unusual.

The old school of dress may be more understated, emphasizing fine woolen fabrics and precise tailoring, with less patterns used and subtler colors. Many of the most traditional styles are found in the exclusive shops and custom tailors of the Savile Row area in London. The names of some of these tailor-designer shops are synonymous with quality and excellence in fabrics and fabrication.

Aquascutum offers top-quality ready-to-wear clothes of their own brand. Traditional tailoring is offered in everything from tuxedos to suits to rainwear. Their apparel is also available in some United States locations, and they are probably best known for their outerwear, especially their trench coat.

Burberry's has long provided the well dressed of England and the world with traditional apparel. The organization is perhaps best known for its tailored outerwear. It was Burberry that produced the trenchcoat for the British officers in World War I, and that garment became a classic. The golden, black, and red plaid used as the lining in their coats readily identifies the garments as Burberry make.

Jasper Conran, a young Londoner, started his career designing womenswear. He is one of the more forward menswear designers in England today. Conran mixes traditional styles with unusual colors, fabric patterns, and soft fabrication.

Gieves & Hawkes, a bespoke tailor operation located at 1 Saville Row, offers top-quality, ready-to-wear clothes.

Hackett's offers both ready-to-wear and made-to-order merchandise. The "look" promoted by this operation is that of the classic English gentleman. In comparison with other shops listed here, Hackett's is a new operation. However, its early days were in merchandising fine quality, *used* apparel. They proceeded to produce their own line, which offered the same old-world quality seen in their vintage clothing.

H. Huntsman & Son, an organization that has long been considered one of the very top custom tailors in England as well as one of the most expensive. They use piece goods made exclusively for their shop, and their customers include the world's most wealthy and powerful. Obviously with a record like that, their look is very traditional.

Richard James is another fashion forward designer. Like Conran, he draws from traditional style, but his colors and fabric patterns are far beyond what the traditional Englishman would wear to business. The young, young at heart, and irreverent are most likely to appreciate his style.

Tommy Nutter is a more traditional tailor-designer who uses elegant fabrics and colors, and whose styling is reminiscent of the classic lines of the 1930s.

Italy.   The Italian man has been raised with a greater interest in apparel, and a strong appreciation for the art in fine fabrics, fit, and construction. By far, the Italians are the leaders in international clothing design and manufacture. The rest of the world takes its cues from styling that comes out of the fashion shows in Milan. And the Italians also closely monitor the American market to better understand fit and style modifications necessary for export to the United States.

In general, Italian clothing is highly expressive and at the same time refined in approach. In recent years they have taken the classic lines of the 1930s and 1940s and put today's more sophisticated mark on them. The sack coat, most often associated with British style, has been translated into a softer, more draped silhouette, often with a long, low lapel and lower button stance. There is an ease and elegance about this updated classic that says it is in touch with the past and ahead of the present.

Italy has many, many significant designers today, producing both clothing and sportswear. There is room here for only the most widely distributed and well-known Italian designers of tailored clothing.

Giorgio Armani is undisputedly the foremost menswear designer today. Armani has been the most influential international menswear designer since the 1980s. His clothing is understated in color, tending toward the monochromatic in luxurious fabrics often of a highly textural nature. The cut is draped, with an ease in fit, yet a sense of body and proportion underneath. Extended soft shoulders and a long, very low lapel notch are marks of the Armani coat. Pants are often double and triple pleated with a full, easy leg silhouette. Armani manages to bridge the look of old money with an elegance and sophistication not associated with more traditional "old-school" designers. In addition to clothing, Armani offers furnishings like shirts and ties in finest fabrics, unusual patterns, and sophisticated colorations.

Brioni is at the more conservative end of Italian fashion. The house of Brioni produces the highest-quality, and most expensive, suit available. The quality of the make rivals that of custom made garments and often exceeds them in price. The line is available in specialty stores that offer the very best of European clothing. The suit is very traditional in styling, fitting closer to the body than Armani. Its style is more in sync with the Savile Row bespoke suit but with the refined elegance of the Italian designer.

Valentino is another Italian designer whose styles are available world-wide and who has great influence on other menswear designers. The cut of his clothing is not as outspoken or quickly identifiable as Armani. The fit would be more readily worn by the American man perhaps than the expressive cut of Armani. Yet his fabrics and colors rival Armani in elegance and subtlety. Like Armani, Valentino is well represented in furnishings departments with a fine line of ties and shirtings. He also has his own boutiques in fashionable locations around the world.

Gianni Versace, in contrast to Brioni, is at the least conservative end of Italian styling. This designer is a "colorist." He often defies direction other designers take to color, sometimes sporting extreme and outspoken hues. His styles as well as colors are not for the faint of heart, nor for the mainstream consumer. Some of his style ideas come from historical trends such as the line in which he offered a look inspired by 17th-century leggings. One season he may offer a very baggy pant with a greatly oversized double breasted coat, and the next season his proportions and silhouettes may radically change. His approach is that classic is passé. Versace's apparel is found in the most forward and upscale boutiques and specialty stores.

France.   French clothing design does take a back seat to that of the Italians. The silhouette and cut of French clothing is more understated than the Italian. The coat is not as oversized, and styling is more subdued. Fit falls somewhere between the expressive Italian full cut and the slimmer cut of earlier European clothing.

Styles are disparate at best, with some designers of clothing remaining in the classic genre and others (particularly in sportswear) going beyond fashion forward into the extreme.

It is significant that most of French menswear designers started designing in womenswear haute couture. And most of these designers remain strongly entrenched in the womenswear market as well.

In 1962 *Pierre Cardin* was significant for creating the first "designer" line of menswear[11] after achieving success in the womenswear market. Cardin has long been an innovator in apparel design and merchandising. He has been one of the leaders in garment licensing. In 1983 he was considered the "king of couture licensing, with over 620 licensing agreements. Some 150 products bear his name and are sold in 80 countries."[12] This resulted in his name and logo being seen everywhere including apparel, household furnishings, luggage, leather goods, stationery, and so forth. His name swept from Europe into all other international markets very quickly. In the late 1960s and 1970s Cardin style and fit truly represented European design to the world.

Today, the Cardin silhouette remains in the mainstream of French design, not as oversized as the Italian looks. Cardin apparel and the extensive array of coordinated furnishings are available in department stores throughout the United States.

Nino Cerruti's line is more forward than some of the other French designers, perhaps because of his Italian heritage. The Cerruti organization is a large manufacturing company founded in 1881 (one of its garment labels is "Cerruti 1881") as a textile mill. It also operates mills and produces finished garments in Italy. Like so many other "name" designers, he produces garments at several price points. Fit is precise, and quality is solid.

Christian Dior has been primarily associated with womenswear design. However, the house of Dior does produce mainstream and upscale lines of menswear. As with Cardin, Dior was an important name in the 1970s in bringing European style to the United States. Dior was the first designer to license his name to a manufacturer. In the 1950s he licensed his name to a line of neckties.[13]

Yves St. Laurent is the womenswear counterpart to menswear's Giorgio Armani, though both design for both sexes. St. Laurent, like Cardin and Christian Dior, now are found at several price points and available in many mainstream department stores. Diffusion of price points allows the consumer to locate their merchandise in department stores, specialty stores, and boutiques.

Emanuel Ungaro is a French designer of Italian descent. He offers a slightly more forward style and fit than some of the other French designers. Excellent fabrics and great attention to detail in styling offer high quality and are priced accordingly. The Ungaro line is found in better department stores and specialty stores.

Germany. *Hugo Boss*, true to form for the Germans, offers practical styles with a little bit of fashion. His look is one that can be worn into almost any board room. Boss clothing is for the individual looking for something that is businesslike, with a touch of updated style, in very good taste, and of excellent quality.

[11]G. Bruce Boyer, *Eminently Suitable* (New York: W. W. Norton, 1990), p. 130.

[12]Elaine Stone and Jean Samples, *Fashion Merchandising: An Introduction*, 4th ed. (New York: McGraw-Hill, 1985), p. 279.

[13]Elaine Stone and Jean Samples, *Fashion Merchandising; An Introduction*, 4th ed. (New York: McGraw-Hill, 1985), p. 93.

INDUSTRY TRADE ASSOCIATIONS

There are many garment industry and retail trade associations that offer assistance to businesses, conduct style shows, as well as represent industry interests in legislative and international matters. There are far too many organizations to list here. The groups that are mentioned here represent some of the strongest and most active groups in the United States.

American Apparel Manufacturers Association
2500 Wilson Boulevard
Arlington, VA 22201

American Formalwear Association
401 North Michigan
Chicago, IL 60601

American Textile Manufacturers Institute, Inc.
1801 K Street
Washington, DC 20006

Big and Tall Associates
P.O. Box 76
Glencoe, IL 60022

Clothing Manufacturers Association
1290 Avenue of the Americas
New York, NY 10104

Color Association of the United States
409 West 44th Street
New York, NY 10036

Color Collective Council of America
175 Fifth Avenue
New York, NY 10010

Cotton, Inc.
1370 Avenue of the Americas
New York, NY 10019

Council of Fashion Designers of America
1412 Broadway
New York, NY 10018

International Association of Clothing Designers
240 Madison Avenue
New York, NY 10016

International Fabricare Institute
12251 Tech Road
Silver Spring, MD 20904

Men's Fashion Guild
47 West 34th Street
New York, NY 10001

Men's Fashion Association of America
240 Madison Avenue
New York, NY 10016

Menswear Retailers of America
2011 Eye Street, N. W. Suite 300
Washington, DC 20006

National Association of Men's Sportswear Buyers, Inc.
500 Fifth Avenue
New York, NY 10110

National Outerwear & Sportswear Association
240 Madison Avenue
New York, NY 10016

National Retail Federation
100 W. 31st Street
New York, NY 10001

Neckwear Association of America
151 Lexington Avenue
New York, NY 10016

Wool Bureau, Inc.
360 Lexington Avenue
New York, NY 10017

Young Menswear Association
1328 Broadway
New York, NY 10001

CASE STUDY

In the early 1980s the American consumer was becoming more and more concerned about the economy, and how he was spending his disposable income. This resulted in rapid growth of discount stores across America. Discount stores were widening their product lines, sprucing up the appearance of their stores, opening new locations nationally, and increasing their advertising. In short, the discount store was appreciably increasing its market share. The profit margin on soft goods was greater than on furniture, appliances, or housewares. In the past, discounters were associated solely with close-outs and seconds. They were improving their quality of product buying, however, and offering first-quality merchandise. More and more apparel was being sold by the discounter, and the public was wanting more. Operations like Wal-Mart were growing by leaps and bounds, and were often the only major retail source in small towns across the United States. (Today, there are fewer independent discount retailers, yet the operations that remain are virtual powerhouses, and have enormous purchase power and sales volume. Retail giants like Wal-Mart, K Mart, and Target clearly dominate the current discount scene on a national level. There are also very strong regional discounters like Bradlees located in the Northeast United States, Meijer in Michigan and the Midwest, and Weiner Stores in Texas.)

This was a very important movement at the retail level and presented many challenges for name-brand manufacturers like Haggar. And they were not alone. Other nationally branded manufacturers were feeling the same concerns; how could they tap this lucrative market while maintaining their integrity with their existing lines and customers? As discussed earlier in this chapter, problems develop when a manufacturer offers merchandise under the same name to different retailers at very different price points. This concern becomes much more acute if the manufacturer sells the same label to discount stores as well as department stores. Certainly the department stores would object to their same merchandise being carried in discount stores at lower prices.

In 1983, Haggar Apparel Company conceived a unique idea using licensing to reach this new market for their products and the products of other major national brands. Up to this point the Haggar lines had only been merchandised through department stores and menswear specialty stores.

A solution was found that satisfied the needs of the consumer, offered quality merchandise to the discounter, and at the same time maintained integrity with its original lines offered in department and specialty stores. In a move unique to the garment industry Haggar became the licensor of a complete line of men's apparel. Reed St. James became the "designer" name that would allow some of the country's top-branded apparel manufacturers to join forces and sell to the discount trade. Haggar Apparel Co., as the owner and licensor of the name Reed St. James, signed agreements with name-brand manufacturers who made shirts, ties, underwear, jeans, sweaters, sleepwear, accessories, and leather goods. These items, along with the suit separates and sportswear manufactured through Haggar Apparel, offered the discount store a high-quality, complete, and coordinated apparel line with a designer name. In its infancy, the Reed St. James "family" included organizations like Jockey, Arrow, Jantzen, Wembley, and Levi Strauss. Haggar managed the operation and guided the licensees in coordination of the entire product line. In addition, as licensor, they monitored quality produced by each licensee.

Each manufacturer produced and sold its own line to the approved list of discount stores. Though in most cases the stores purchased from each of the individual licensees separately, each product line reflected the same name, Reed St. James. Hangtags, labels, and in-store promotional materials all reflected a "one company," cohesive image to the consumer. It would appear that all garments had been produced by the same company.

What was truly unique about this concept is that with traditional licensing, the licensee is not typically a highly recognizable, national brand. Most licensees

are, in effect, contractors producing merchandise under a designer name. But in this situation each of the companies involved was already well-known, high-quality national brands with its own niche in the menswear marketplace.

The formulation of this entire line was not a matter of each manufacturer just changing labels on existing garments. Rather, the designs, fabrics, and make were specifically chosen for the discount market. Each manufacturer was to maintain the top-quality level produced in its own branded merchandise, but the styling and product sourcing was different; therefore, the pricing at wholesale and retail was also different. This was not the traditional manner of name-price diffusion, but a totally new concept and one that satisfied many needs in the marketplace.

As with traditional licensing agreements, the licensees pay royalties for use of the Reed St. James name. And they benefit by a venture joining them with other top manufacturers in reaching the sizable and lucrative discount market.

- Why would Haggar want to license other brand-name manufacturers in this venture? Would they be competing for the same retail dollars?
- What advantage would it be for the discount store to purchase a line like this versus buying independently branded merchandise?
- How did this licensing agreement with manufacturers differ from the traditional designer licensing agreement?

TERMS TO KNOW

Define or briefly explain the following:

Knock-off
Diffusion concept
Price point spread
Licensing
Laver's Law
Highly engineered plant
Licensor
Licensee
Celebrity sponsorships
Endorsements
Long run
Ready-to-wear
Stylist
Designer
Patternmaker
Short run
Wear test
Off shore
Private label
Bespoke
Make

CHAPTER 4
MENSWEAR
AT RETAIL

CHANGE FROM TAILOR TO RETAILER

The term *clothier* originally was used to describe a finisher of wool cloth. But by 1790, it had come to mean a dealer in ready-made clothing. The tailor was defined as the one who actually sewed the clothes for men, and this term has retained its usage to this day.[1] The traditional tailor was the first source of purchasing apparel at retail. Tailors took orders for individually cut garments. They had their own sources of piece goods, and the garments were sewn on their premises. The tailors saw the need and acceptance for ready-made garments, and in addition to their "custom" trade, they manufactured garments for sale. Thus the early tailors became later-day retailers. The earliest store that advertised itself as a "clothing" store was in Boston, Massachusetts, in 1813.[2]

DRUMMING UP OF RETAIL BUSINESS

What were the first stores like in the early days of settlement in North America? The fortunate settlers had basically two choices: trading posts and peddlers. Trading was customary early in the nation's history. But as families moved farther away from their neighboring settlers, they were presented with challenges in acquiring their necessary staples.[3]

In the mid-1800s, it was not easy to reach the consumer. Many people lived in outlying areas and seldom visited the nearest town. A shopping trip to town may have been planned well in advance and was a major expedition. To meet the needs of these people, peddlers became the first door-to-door salespeople. *Drummers* would travel from farm house to farm house by wagon. They were almost a general store on wheels. One of the items they usually sold was a very practical, large tin washtub. To let the farmer's wife know they were approaching the property, they would hit the washtub with a ladle, so they were called "drummers" because they sounded like they were playing a drum. This concept was later used in town, when a young employee was told to stand outside the general store, bang on a drum to get attention, and announce merchandise for sale.

We've come a long way from having to "drum up business" in that manner, though creativity, style, and energy are still required to get the attention of the customer and meet their needs. The retail trade has become very sophisticated in segmenting the marketplace by price point and customer. Let's look at how menswear is merchandised today, the different types of retailers, and how they benefit their customer base.

MAJOR CATEGORIES OF MENSWEAR MERCHANDISING

We've already seen how the menswear business is a world apart from the womenswear business. This is again evident as we look at the organization of merchandise into apparel categories. The U.S. Bureau of Census classifies menswear into five categories.

[1]Harry A. Cobrin, *The Men's Clothing Industry* (New York: Fairchild Publications, 1970), p. 19.

[2]Ibid.

[3]William H. Bolen, *Contemporary Retailing* (Englewood Cliffs, NJ: Prentice Hall, 1988), p. 5.

- *Clothing:* Suits, sportcoats, topcoats, overcoats, dress slacks
- *Furnishings:* Shirts, ties, underwear, socks and pajamas
- *Heavy outerwear:* Windbreakers, snowsuits, ski-jackets, heavy sportswear
- *Work clothes:* Uniforms, overalls, workshirts, etc.
- *Other:* Hats and miscellaneous items

Government technically classifies garments in the preceding categories. But most stores group menswear apparel under the categories of *clothing, furnishings,* and *sportswear.*

CLOTHING DEFINITION AND OVERVIEW

Clothing is usually thought to mean any type of garment worn. In the strictest sense of the word, however, this is not true in menswear. Everyone might wear apparel, but only men wear clothing! Technically, *clothing* means mid- to high-end, tailored garments like suits, sportcoats, dress slacks, and tailored outerwear. These are typically the most expensive items in the man's wardrobe. They often require alterations by a tailor, like pant hemming and sleeve adjustments. This is one of the many differences in the language of menswear and womenswear. Throughout this book, the term "clothing" will be used in a technical sense and refer to quality-tailored apparel. Correct use of the term "clothing" signifies more in-depth knowledge of the menswear trade. Though the average consumer will not be aware of the technical interpretation, knowledgeable individuals within the menswear industry will understand and appreciate proper use of the term.

Do not mistake all suits, sportcoats, and slacks to fall in this category though. In the late 1970s some mass menswear manufacturers introduced *suit separates.* This concept, borrowed from womenswear, merchandised coats and slacks of the same fabric on separate racks. The consumer could then match up his own "suit." These garments were made according to highly engineered manufacturing methods. These methods used highly sophisticated automated machinery that cut down on manual labor and resulted in less expensive garments which were styled as traditional clothing.

The benefits were many. A man of unusual proportions could still have a "suit" without all the alterations. The customer could buy just the coat or just the pant, or choose a two-pant suit. The costs of manufacture were low, and therefore retail prices were lower than traditional "clothing."

What was once looked down on by traditional clothing manufacturers, the suit separate has found its way into many more upscale retail operations. In 1991 Brooks Brothers experimented with the concept of suit separates. Their desire was to offer greater high quality options to their customers, both in style variation and fit. They took their suit styles, offered both pleated and plain front pants, but merchandised them in separate displays. They felt strongly that this line, "The Brooks Wardrobe," offered many options for their customers in getting closer fit, especially for those with athletic builds (refer also to chapter 5). It also allowed men to have two pairs of pants with a suit coat.

In most department stores suit separates are merchandised with sportswear rather than clothing. Technically, they are not truly suits. Suits are hung with the pant and coat on the same hanger. Manufacturers refer to this as the *nested suit,* because the pant is nested inside the coat.

In the clothing department, the consumer usually expects more service than in sportswear. The items are more expensive so the customer often has more questions as to quality, make, and fit. More often than not, it may be difficult for the average consumer to discern why one suit costs $150 and another costs $1,500.

It is in situations like this where the knowledge and confidence of the salesperson come into play.

The reason for the difference in price boils down to two factors: quality of fabric and quality of construction. Fabric quality may be seen and understood more quickly by the customer than quality of construction. In the past, the major cost of a garment related to the cost of the fabric and less to the manufacturing costs. With rising labor costs in the United States today, construction often costs more than the piece goods and trim items incorporated in the finished garment. A very well-made and well-designed garment will not only look good, but will fit properly and stand the test of time. It is this last determinant that may not be immediately perceptible. The ability of the garment to stand up to repeated wear has to do with its "hidden" attributes of excellent interlinings, proper pressing in manufacture, appropriate seaming, testing of the garment by the maker, among many other factors. In addition excellent fit is seen once the garment is on. The consumer will not be aware of this by comparing two suits on their hangers. These factors, although they may not be visible, are understood to be an important aspect of quality by the more sophisticated consumer.

Some stores are synonymous with clothing, such as Brooks Brothers and the Hartmarx stores. Their foundation is in clothing, though their sportswear departments are certainly not to be overlooked as important profit centers.

APPAREL DEPARTMENTS

The typical department store will have just one clothing department. There are many exceptions though, with designer clothing departments becoming an important force in menswear. Also, some stores have a *bridge* department that will feature less expensive sportcoats and slacks, along with suit separates and some sportswear. This department is often associated with the man between age 21 and 35. He is out of school and wants a business look, yet his budget may not allow for garments from the clothing department.

With the increased costs of clothing today, the moderate bridge department and sportswear have been given more floor space in many stores. More relaxed attitudes in some industries have allowed men to move into separates rather than formal suits. In turn, this has allowed the man to cut back on more expensive suits and move into sport coat and slacks, or in some cases sportswear.

Constantly changing market conditions affect retail prices and consumer spending habits. Issues like costs of garment manufacture, costs of imports, fluctuating international exchange rates, and increasing costs of operating retail units all affect how the consumer buys and consequently how the retailer apportions his floor space.

In addition to the practical issues mentioned earlier, the retailer must design his space according to the likes and life-style of his customer. The customer will have an immediate instinctive response to the decor of the store. The more comfortable the customer feels in the store, the more likely he will be to make purchases. The store must reflect the taste of the consumer. The more focused the store is on its customer, the more its decor can be suited to that market. A store that has a very broad market base must accommodate a wider range of style in decor. For example, a department store like Macy's offers a very wide range of products, has several pricing levels, and therefore attracts a broad consumer base. Therefore, their interior design must be acceptable to a broad range of people. Conversely, a specialty store that may offer very expensive and sophisticated European apparel may more finely tune their decor to reinforce their image and interest their customers.

Color is one of the first aspects of decor to set the mood of the store. Some stores use warm colors to communicate their style. Wooden paneling, leather chairs, mellow lighting, brass fixtures, and antique furniture help to enhance the image of the store. Often these stores or departments offer classic apparel, as seen in Brooks Brothers. The mood is "old school." At the opposite end of the scale is the very fashion-forward store. Here you are likely to see greater contrast in color, black, white, and silver. There may be more hard surfaces, such as marble and stainless steel. The feeling is colder, and more high tech.

Some stores may want to highlight the merchandise by down playing decor, and taking a minimalist approach. Efforts may be made to mix the new and the old. For example, an original brick wall, which has textural quality and warmth in color, is left uncovered. Yet the fixtures may be high-tech stainless steel. This is a rugged environment and encourages attention to the apparel. The desire here may be to direct the customer to the feeling expressed by the clothes.

The most unusual and extensive use of separate menswear clothing departments may be found in Barneys New York. Several floors of menswear all have different lighting, furniture, and music, creating a unique ambiance to complement the style of clothing sold in that department. This is a perfect example of knowing the customer and designing every aspect of the shopping process to suit his style.

The box on page 44 is a list of some of the brands and designers available in four departments during one season at Barneys. This specialization of departments clearly indicates the catering to individualized taste of the customer.

The International Collections floor of Barneys New York effectively uses high contrast black-and-white decor to set a sophisticated mood. Note use of lighting and unusual ceiling treatment to communicate a forward look.

This furnishings department in Barneys New York says "old world." The use of wood, leather, and area rugs helps to enhance the message of tradition in offerings made here.

English/Traditional

Asher Co., Barry Bricken, Belvest, Brioni Ltd., Burberrys Ltd, Cardinal of Canada, Chester Barrie, Cordovan & Grey, Coppley Noyes & Randall, Country Britches, Gieves & Hawkes, Greif Co., Haspel, Heartland, Hickey-Freeman, Huntsman & Sons, Nick Hilton, Norman Hilton, Oxxford Clothes, Piatelli, Polo by Ralph Lauren

Couture

Allegri, Cerruti 1881, Gianfranco Ferre, Gianni Versace, Giorgio Armani Couture, Giorgio Armani Le Collezioni, Raedelli, V2 by Versace, Vestimenta

Boutique Collections

Correggiari, Enrico Coveri, Hugo Boss, Konen, Mani, Marzotti (Principe), San Remo, Studio 000.1 by Ferre

Contemporary

Armand Basi, Byblos, Comme des Garcons, Dolce & Gabbana, Fabrizio del Carro, Guiliano Fujiwara, Guillermo Capone, Hamnett Jeans, Issey Miyake, Jasper Conran, Jean Paul Gaultier, Junior Gaultier, Kikit, Matsuda, Moschino Jeans, New Republic, Romeo Gigli, Vestium Officina, Yohji Yamamoto

Retail price of a store's clothing is usually reflected in the design and layout of the department. The finer the furniture, the thicker the carpet, and the more spacious and well-appointed the department, the more expensive you might expect the apparel to be. The mix of stock in the clothing department will vary with the season, locale, and clientele. For example, Southern California has a very temperate climate year round, and the locals have a more relaxed and open-minded attitude about business wear. Therefore one is likely to see softer colors and more forward styles than in the Midwest. In the winter, when city streets are filled with slush and grime, conservative Bostonians will relate to more somber, practical colors and heavier-weight fabric to suit their life-style. In northern climes, there will be more obvious changes in stock, following the change of the seasons. Such variations are not quite so dramatic in southern climates.

SPORTSWEAR DEFINITION AND OVERVIEW

Though the emphasis of this text is on tailored clothing, mention must be made of sportswear and its relevance in the man's wardrobe. In the 1960s there was an upsurge in the men's sportswear industry; color and style became much more outspoken. The male found sportswear an alternative way to express himself and offered counterpoint to the mundane clothing of the business week.

Sportswear includes casual pants and shorts, easy-care tops, sweaters, lightweight windbreakers—apparel used for informal or leisure hours. The category can also be broken down into active sportswear and spectator sportswear. *Activewear* is actually worn while participating in sport or exercise. These garments may be made of fabrics allowing for stretch and perspiration absorption, or include special construction for movement in sports, like a stretch waistband for a golf pant. This category has grown tremendously since the 1970s because so many people are exercising, jogging, attending aerobics classes, and so on.

Spectator sportswear offers a great range of styles and fabrics, and can be very avant garde and sophisticated in styling. European influences have made major inroads in sportswear styles, and offer unusual fabrics and patterns. What once was thought of as the "wash-and-wear" category now sports some very expensive "dry-clean-only" garments.

Because of our changing life-styles, new areas of sportswear constantly move in and out of fashion. This category is always in a state of flux because of the whims of the consumer.

The rage of westernwear during the 1970s added a new twist to sportswear. Movies and television have an enormous impact on sportswear, as in the "Miami Vice" look of the 1980s. The result in many stores is an expanded, sprawling mega-department. Wonderful as the options seem, it can confuse the consumer. Many consumers would rather walk out than have to deal with poring over all that is available. This increases the importance of good retail help and strong service to keep the customer happy.

A large store may carry varying levels of sportswear, from the most casual, like sweatsuits, up to the very sophisticated European imports. If the store carries this wide a range, they may break the department down into smaller areas or boutiques.

FURNISHINGS DEFINITION AND OVERVIEW

The furnishings department of menswear would be comparable in womenswear to lingerie, accessories, and notions, with blouses and shirts added. Items in this category include shirts, neckties, pocket squares, handkerchiefs, belts, suspenders, socks, underwear, pajamas, robes, jewelry, umbrellas, scarves, hats, gloves, and so forth.

Tailored clothing including suits, sportcoats, and dress slacks change very subtly in styling from season to season. Sometimes men feel like they wear "uniforms" in terms of standardization of styles. So how can they show their individuality? The furnishings really personalize the man's suit and express his inner self. It is here that he throws away the mold and can have fun with color, texture, and pattern. He can make a statement without going beyond acceptable limits and without spending a fortune. After all, a new shirt, tie, pocket square, and socks are certainly less expensive than a new suit!

These are the necessary complements to tailored apparel, so the furnishings department is usually located near the clothing department for ease of coordination. Stores where furnishings are not adjacent to clothing lose the advantage of easy add-on sales.

Like sportswear, this category has grown in relation to man's increased interest in fashion and self-expression. Where in the past one saw primarily black and dark, solid color socks, there are now many colorful and intricately patterned styles. The practical, yet nondescript somber shades seen in suspenders, or braces, have been replaced by a rash of exotic colors and designs. Some men have become avid collectors of these braces, and they enjoy the amusement of others in seeing them.

Women like the added special touches of colorful pocket squares, collar bars, and elegant reptile belts. All these items have led to increased floor space in the furnishings department. As in womenswear, the accessories are what give a "final touch" or "pulled together look." So goes it in menswear with furnishings.

As in womenswear, however, many consumers like the look, but don't know how, or don't feel confident enough to achieve it themselves. And that's where the fashion professional comes in!

CATEGORIES OF STORES

Department Store

The department store has its roots in the early American general store and is considered to be the backbone of retailing in the United States. As such, it is the type of store most frequented by the general public. It usually maintains a relatively high profile because of its involvement in the community and its special events, which may draw media attention. Many department stores willingly participate in charity events that result in community good will.[4]

A department store is defined by the United States Bureau of the Census[5] as an establishment that normally employs 25 or more people and sells general merchandise in the following categories:

- Furniture, home furnishings, appliances, and radio and TV sets
- General lines of apparel and accessories for the family
- Household linens and dry goods

Most department stores are intent on turning their stock, quickly resulting in great buys that can be found at the end of the month and the end of the season. Customers may be disappointed with the service in some department stores, however. Cutbacks on sales staffs, as well as an increase in part-time employees, have resulted in weakened service and staffs with less product knowledge. The customer looking for exceptional personal attention may prefer to patronize the specialty store.

Some of the top retailers are multistore operations with branches in major United States cities. These stores pride themselves on high-quality merchandise, exceptional service, and attention to the concerns and needs of the customer. Major retail department stores like Macy's, Marshall Field's, Rich's, Foley's, and Dillard's offer great value and service to their customers.

Some of the upscale department stores may offer the customer a personalized shopping service. For example, "Macy's Buy Appointment" allows the man to work one-on-one with an in-store consultant, who assists him in coordinating a wardrobe. These services are most often scheduled by appointment, and the store consultant may develop a devoted client base through exceptional attention to the customer's needs.

Department stores offer the man the following benefits:

Wide variety of styles
Range of prices

[4]Elaine Stone and Jean Samples, *Fashion Merchandising: An Introduction*, 4th ed. (New York: McGraw-Hill, 1985), p. 311.
[5]Ibid.

Good values in private label items (see footnote[6])

Wide range of sizes available

Liberal returns policy

Clothing, furnishings, and sportswear departments

For the most discerning consumer, the department store may not offer all amenities.

The most unusual or forward styles may not be available.

Alterations department may not be as service oriented as the specialty store.

Sales help may not be as experienced or knowledgeable as in specialty stores.

Chain Store

This type of store is defined by the Bureau of Census as a group of centrally owned stores handling similar merchandise and controlled by a central office. The operation may be a chain department store like The Broadway or Bloomingdales. Or it may be a major mass merchandiser like the Gap or Sears. The definition of a chain store by the United States Bureau of Census is a retailer having 11 or more stores. Typically the stores are controlled and stock is merchandised centrally rather than through a parent store. Some examples of upscale chain-specialty stores are Saks Fifth Avenue, Neiman-Marcus, and Lord & Taylor.[7]

The pros and cons of shopping the chain store are very similar to those of the department store indicated previously.

The Specialty Store

The government definition of specialty store stipulates that the store carry limited lines of merchandise, or may specialize in selling one or a very selected type of goods. The consumer, however, has come to interpret the concept of "specialty store" to mean a higher quality of merchandise sold by a more knowledgeable staff.

In shopping the specialty store, the customer can expect a more unique stock mix, more relaxed surroundings, and more attentive service. He may receive the equivalent of personal shopper service with the well-trained, efficient salesperson keeping track of sizes, and style preferences, and contacting him when appropriate merchandise come in. The best specialty stores offer high-quality merchandise and service, often resulting in a loyal, repeat customer for the retailer. Since specialty stores are often smaller than other retailers, they are frequently closer to their customers, offering the attention to detail so lacking in today's marketplace.

The specialty store offers the customer the following benefits:

Unusual styles, sizes, and cuts that may not be found abundantly elsewhere

High-quality merchandise

[6]*Private Label* refers to garments that are made by manufacturers but styled by the retailer. The garments have a store label instead of the manufacturer's label. Often retailers will create several of their own lines with different names. Private-label goods are first-quality merchandise offered at prices often less than those of "brand" names. At the same time they offer increased profit margin to the retailer.

[7]Elaine Stone and Jean Samples, *Fashion Merchandising: An Introduction*, 4th ed. (New York: McGraw-Hill, 1985), p. 317.

Excellent customer service
Liberal returns policy
Pleasant surroundings
Consistency in pricing
Excellent alterations-tailoring department

The consumer should be aware of the following in shopping a specialty store:

Only a few of each size, are offered—sometimes one of a kind.
Very specific classifications of merchandise exist—the store may not carry clothing, sportswear, and furnishings in the same store

Off-Price Store

The off-price store usually buys goods directly from the manufacturer at the end of the manufacturing cycle at reduced prices. Buying at the end of the manufacturer's production run will get them better prices, and the difference is passed on to the consumer. Department stores may have these styles being sold at full retail, but the off-price store can offer them later in the season at greatly reduced prices.

There is usually less overhead in the store itself. In the past, off-price stores were often austere in appearance. Some of the newer off-pricers have "softened" their look, however, in efforts to appeal to a broader range of customers. Selection is limited in these stores. With low overhead and narrower profit margin, service is less than in regular retail stores.

Though off-price stores started as single-store retail operations, the trend toward this type of merchandising is growing. Many have become chains, affording them greater clout with manufacturers. Some of the better-known off price stores include Syms, Loehmann's, Ross Stores, and Men's Wearhouse.

Some of the benefits of shopping the off-price store follow:

Lower retail prices than regular retail stores
First-quality brands
Range of sizes available

The consumer needs to be aware of the following in shopping at the off-price store:

Quality of service varies widely from store to store.
Alterations are rarely available.
Size selection is limited.
Clothing, sportswear, and furnishings may not be found in every store.
Returns policies may be stringent.

Discount Store

The consumer, constantly in search for "better values," brought about an important increase in the number of discount stores in the 1980s. As a result entire malls sprung up in suburbs across the country which catered to the bargain hunter. These malls included discount stores, factory outlets, and some off-price stores. By the end of the1980s the trend slowed down, though many of these malls still exist and draw sizable crowds.

The discount store may be defined as a single-store operation, a chain store, or a subsidiary of a department store, in which merchandise is offered at greatly reduced prices. Overhead is very low, and self-service is the norm. Target, K Mart, and Wal-Mart are examples of discount stores located in cities and towns across the United States. Discount stores may specialize in one type of merchandise like apparel, or they may also offer general merchandise like health and personal care items and hard goods.

Depending on the operation, it may take a hardy soul to seek good merchandise for the price offered. Stock may vary from week to week, and it takes shopping often to find the best buys. It will also take a trained eye as there may be inferior or second quality merchandise as well as first-quality goods. The consumer should not expect many sales because of their already low prices. Returns policies can be quite strict.

Some of the benefits of shopping discount stores include the following:

Lowest prices available
Wide range of product selection

The consumer should also be aware of the following:

Little service or product knowledge by staff
Barebones surroundings
Quality varies—the customer must carefully check merchandise

Factory Outlets

The factory outlet is often associated with the discount store especially with the advent of the discount-factory outlet malls. The type of merchandise usually associated with the outlet, however, is quite different from that of the discount store.

The first factory outlet stores were physically located next to, or in the same building as, the manufacturer. Offering production overruns or "seconds"[8] enabled the manufacturer to move merchandise at a greater profit than selling to a jobber. At the same time, they eliminated the middleman and with little overhead increased their profit margin on this merchandise. Therefore, the only type of goods sold in these stores were items manufactured by that company.

This type of factory store still exists. Merchandise sold in these operations may be offered at 25 to 70 percent below regular retail prices. Many factory stores have expanded and may even include other manufacturer's lines that complement their own stock. This would attract more customers and increase sales for the store.

Benefits of the factory store include the following:

Exceptional prices
Usually a good range of sizes

Concerns to the consumer include the following:

Quality must be carefully evaluated
Stock may include styles that did not sell or garments with quality problems
Barebones surroundings
Tight returns policies

[8]A *second* is a garment with either a mill flaw or a minor manufacturing defect. Any second-quality garment must indicate in some way that it is imperfect. These flaws are usually minor enough so that the garment may be worn. "Thirds," or third-quality garments are usually not salable.

Sample Stores

These operations have excellent prices also, but there can be hidden problems with merchandise. Samples are made to show retail buyers and not necessarily to be worn. There may be shortcuts taken in the manufacture of these garments, and the fit may be imprecise. Conversely, the consumer has the opportunity to find some very unusual styles in these stores, some of which were prototypes and never manufactured in quantity by the maker.

The sample store is most often a single-unit operation buying its goods from manufacturer's representatives or directly from the manufacturer.

Some of the benefits of shopping sample stores include the following:

Excellent prices
Unusual, one-of-a-kind items
Most current styles

Some of the concerns to the consumer include the following:

Must carefully evaluate quality and sizing
Narrow range of sizes
Barebones surroundings
Tight returns policies

Mail-Order Houses

The first mail-order catalog was produced by Montgomery Ward in Chicago in 1872. In 1886, Richard Sears sold jewelry by mail. Sears was a mail-order operation exclusively until 1924, when it became a nationwide giant.

Mail order is an important force in retailing today. Shopping at home is made even easier by the use of credit cards and toll-free 800 numbers. Mail order has become so sophisticated in its target marketing that specialty mail-order businesses flourished. Organizations that specialize in merchandise for the big and tall man make shopping easier, and offer selection to this customer that may not be found elsewhere. There are many catalogs that offer apparel for the sportsman such as L.L. Bean of Maine.

Today, many traditional and upscale retailers also offer merchandise by mail. Some stores offer the same goods in their catalogs as in their stores. Others may have mail-order items that are not available at all at retail. And many mail-order companies have no retail outlets at all. And yet other operations offer their catalog merchandise through "mail-order stores," such as J C Penney. In these units, the catalogs are on display, and sales people take the orders for shipment to the consumer by mail.

For the man, shopping by mail is a very easy and practical way to buy items that are not sized, like ties, suspenders, and jewelry. The more precise the fit, the more difficult it is for anyone to shop by mail and have the same accuracy as in the store. For example, the purchase of tailored clothing is ideally made where a tailor and competent sales assistance are available. Furnishings and sportswear can be purchased quite satisfactorily by mail, however, it is best to order as soon as possible after receiving the catalog to avoid disappointment of depleted stock.

Some of the benefits of mail order include the following:

Ease of shopping
Wide range of styles and sizes available
Wide range of prices available
Most have reasonable returns policies

The home shopper should be aware of the following:

Inability to see and try on item
Length of time to receive item
Alterations are the customer's responsibility
Sometimes items are not available once ordered

Video Shopping

Video shopping improves on mail order by seeing the actual garment worn by a moving person. There are several types of video shopping available for the up to date consumer. Cable television offers the Home Shopping Network where the consumer may sit back on his couch and see items modeled for him. He then would order by calling the toll-free number given on the show. And in some areas, the cable subscriber has a hand-held device that is linked to the television allowing him to place an order electronically. Some retailers have tried selling through video discs. Sears[9] has experimented, offering some catalog merchandise in this medium. More readily available is a product catalog produced by apparel manufacturers. Some catalogs are issued quarterly and can be received by subscription. These catalogs offer the consumer the opportunity to get a greater sense of fit, fabrication, and garment movement, through seeing the garments on models.

No longer is it unusual to see television monitors in retail stores. Manufacturers produce video tapes for stores to use as selling aids. Or the store may run a video fashion show including many designers. Though these monitors are at point of sale, they indicate the increase of acceptance and importance this visual medium has on the consumer today (refer also to chapter 2).

BUYING PRACTICES OF RETAILER

The mid-1980s brought incredible turbulence to the large retailers of the United States. Development of mega-corporations and continual leveraged buyouts wreaked havoc in the retail industry. This has had a very conservative impact in the way organizations buy from vendors today. There is less risk taken, and many stores are cutting back on the number of vendors they carry.[10] The large retailers often have committees, or team buyers, to review and approve suppliers for all their stores. They may allow for some testing of new suppliers in selected stores, but breaking into the mega-buying offices is no easy task for new manufacturers today. This system is referred to as *matrix buying*. The lines chosen as a part of the matrix will be offered in all stores in the buying group. There is a tremendous advantage for any manufacturer that is accepted by the committee. In some operations, however, the determination of what lines will be bought may be made by a few powerful figures at the top of the organization's structure. In these instances the buyers actually become order takers with less of a decision-making role than they might desire.

And what are the criteria used to determine what fortunate suppliers will be chosen? As fewer business risks can be afforded today, the following issues all take on greater significance: brand recognition, quality, production capabilities, reputation of the designer-manufacturer, and ability to ship as scheduled. These

[9]Elaine Stone and Jean Samples, *Fashion Merchandising: An Introduction*, 4th ed. (New York: McGraw-Hill, 1985), p. 317.

[10]Jean Palmieri, "Vendor Matrices: Men's Wear's New Kingmakers," *Daily News Record*, August 5, 1991. p. 18.

are just a few of the criteria used. Long-standing, mutually beneficial relationships are also important, though loyalty can be outranked by aggressive newcomers eagerly waiting in the wings.

Stores are demanding a very high rate of service and quality from their suppliers. They may prefer to work with those suppliers who are on sophisticated *electronic data interchange (EDI)* systems to enhance ease of shipping as well as inventory control.

For brands to be accepted by the buying committees of the large retailers today, they must offer fashion and quality at a good value, the garments must be exciting, and they must not duplicate products already being carried in the store.[11] One of the benefits of this system is increased consistency throughout a large operation.

BAR CODING AND APPAREL INDUSTRY

Bar coding, those vertical lines that appear on every type of price ticket and product label today, has changed the way manufacturers and retailers do business. Though their appearance may at first seem insignificant, they have an enormous impact on everything from inventory maintenance to pricing to reordering merchandise for both the retailer and the wholesaler. You are probably familiar with the term bar code, but there is a much broader base of terminology that encompasses this electronic world.

In the broadest sense, EDI represents the technological and cultural changes that affect every consumer, and a large percentage of retailers and manufacturers today. EDI encompasses the technology of communications as well as the practices by which we do business. This is a cultural change because it means we are doing more business in a "paperless world," a world maintained by computers and highly sophisticated technology.[12]

Basically, a *bar code* is a series of vertical bars of varying widths that carries coded information. A bar code may represent any type of information that a manufacturer wishes to maintain records on. In relation to product pricing, these bar codes are more specifically called *universal product codes (UPC)*. These lines are "read" by a scanner and communicate information to a central data base. A very common example you have probably experienced is the scanning of grocery purchases. A checker passes the UPC bar code that appears on a product label over an optical reader. This reader appears to be a glass plate, yet its hidden electronics communicate data to a computer. Sometimes a hand "wand" is used. The bar code reader sends the UPC to the computer. Almost instantaneously, the computer accesses the UPC information in its data base, retrieves the price, and the price is then displayed on a screen at the point of purchase, or register. This is the same technology being used at retail apparel operations to make purchases. The first "wanding" of a bar code occurred in 1974, and the concept has changed the manufacturing and retailing world forever.[13]

[11]Rachel Spevak, "Passing the Branded Checkup," *Daily News Record*, August 5, 1991. p. 18.

[12]David Hough, "EDI Is Not a Spectator Sport," Sears Communications Company, *EDI World*, March 1991.

[13]Donald R. Katz, "Are Your Groceries Spying on You?" *Esquire Magazine*, March 1990.

"Wanding" of bar codes on garment tickets had a tremendous impact on shortening the response time of manufacturers in filling retailers' reorders.

"The fastest growing area using EDI is the establishment of trading partner relationships between retailers and vendors."[14] It is through such partnerships that retailers and manufacturers both become more efficient and able to offer better service to each other as well as to the ultimate consumer. In the mid-1980s Haggar Apparel Company was an instrumental force in developing system structures to increase productivity and efficiency within its own operation and with its trading partners. In doing so, Haggar became one of the leaders in the use of EDI within the apparel industry.

Most major retailers use EDI to manage their *stock-keeping units (SKUs)*, price merchandise, maintain inventory, and communicate with their vendors. EDI communication has become so very important that many of the major retailers prefer to work with manufacturers who are also on this system. There is a movement by some buying offices to charge a fee back to any vendor who does not operate via EDI. This offers strong incentives to manufacturers to implement the system. Not all retailers are large enough, however, to afford the equipment and services required to transact business via EDI. In such cases, traditional paper orders may be given to the salesperson and manually keyed into the manufacturer's records.

Let's take a look at the intricacies of how EDI moves merchandise and affects so many areas of the retail-wholesale partnership.

The term *Quick Response (QR)* is a concept and process created by United States apparel manufacturers that allows retail replenishment of products at the same rate that the consumer is purchasing the products. The monitoring of sales and inventory is conducted through point-of-purchase "scanning" of the UPC code. This enables the retailer to know his exact stock levels in each item. Based on his predetermined inventory needs in any one item, he can easily calculate what needs to be reordered and when. The immediacy of this system allows the retailer to order by exact size, style, and color, and maintain the stock level desired. This indicates a real ease of stock maintenance at retail. And it means that the retailer need not be out of stock of an item that is available through EDI. This also means

[14]Lance Dailey, "Using EDI in the Retailing Environment," *EDI World*, March 1991.

that the retail buyers may spot consumer trends quickly and make smarter buying decisions much more quickly than in the past. However, the quick response system goes far beyond this initial phase.

Many retailers and manufacturers who participate in this QR process are linked to a network that electronically processes information through the telephone lines. The network receives orders from the retailers and relays the data to the manufacturers. It is in effect a holding tank of data. Use of the networks to transmit information is much more efficient than each retailer and manufacturer handling communication separately.

In turn, once the order is received by the manufacturer and is in the shipping process, the retailer can be notified of the shipment through EDI. The store has immediate, accurate information as to current inventory levels and incoming stock. This means better service and communication with their customers.

To this point we've seen only a few of the benefits for the retailer-manufacturer partnership. Quick Response has an enormous and powerful impact though throughout the apparel industry. For example, garment manufacturers may link in with their piece-goods suppliers to order yardage and to track their orders more effectively. The manufacturer now communicates in a similar manner with the mills so that yardage may be produced at the same rate that the retailer is purchasing garments from the manufacturer. As a result, there is much faster communication at all levels from production of piece goods to sale of the item to the ultimate consumer. The result of this is a "shortened pipeline" wherein response time frames are shortened in every transaction—hence, the term Quick Response!

RETAIL JOBBERS

The retail jobber is a middleman who operates between the manufacturer and the retailer. Many small stores cannot, because of credit, or because of minimum quantities required to purchase from a manufacturer, go to that manufacturer and buy directly. The jobber buys from the manufacturer and offers merchandise for sale to small retailers. The jobber may carry the merchant on credit, which is an added benefit to the small operation. Therefore it serves the purpose of offering the small merchant salable goods, on credit or for cash, and allows them to stay within their budget and buy in quantities they can use. Plus, they receive the garments immediately. The jobber, in essence, is warehousing goods for immediate purchase.

The importance of jobbers to both manufacturers and retailers has changed dramatically from the earliest days of retailing. "The average manufacturer in the 1870s did not have the financial resources that would permit him to extend credit on necessarily long payment terms to the multitude of small stores"[15] across the country. Manufacturers preferred to sell to a few large operations that could buy in large quantities and had the ability to pay bills in a timely manner. Therefore, jobbers were a logical resource for the manufacturer to reach many small retailers nationally. The jobbers who had in-depth knowledge of the retail outlets in their area would purchase from the manufacturer and then resell to the eager retailers. This was a satisfactory arrangement until the jobbers realized their power and became somewhat dictatorial in their dealings with the garment makers.

"He imposed prices that permitted only small profits to the manufacturer," and made threats if delivery terms were not met.[16] The result of this pressure on

---

[15]Harry A. Cobrin, *The Men's Clothing Industry* (New York: Fairchild Publications, 1970), p. 54

[16]Ibid.

the manufacturer was the start of trade advertising to reach the retailers directly and organizations hiring out their own sales representatives into the marketplace. The result of this was decreased economic power of the jobber in relation to the manufacturer. And the jobber has not gained such influential power over garment manufacturers since.

Today, there are two types of jobbers in relation to types of goods bought and how they price their stock. The *regular jobber* purchases goods from the manufacturer at regular cost, just the same as any retailer would. He works on a short markup, meaning that if he purchases an item at $13.75, he'll sell it for $16.75. He only makes $3 on each item he sells in that line. There are also *off-price jobbers* who purchase goods only off price. They may then sell the items at straight wholesale, and their profit is the difference between the off-price and regular costs. Sometimes, they can sell the items to the retailer for less than wholesale. For example, let's say the off-price jobber purchases a garment that regularly whole-sales for $39.75, and they have purchased it for $22. They sell it for $29.75 to their stores, which have now bought it $10 under wholesale. This allows the retailer to offer it on sale without losing the standard profit margin, or he may offer it at regular retail price, which will increase his profit margin.

Jobbers are offering merchandise for sale to retailers in season. Therefore it might be possible for retailers to purchase garments for their store at the same time that the manufacturer is shipping this same merchandise against orders to other retailers. Off-price jobbers are more likely to have merchandise available close to the end of the season. That, of course, is one of the reasons that they have been able to purchase at such low rates.

CASE STUDY

At 5 feet 2 inches Bob Stern understandably had great difficulty in locating apparel that fit properly, and which offered both style and quality. As a result, in 1972 he started the company, Short Sizes Inc. The retail store in Cleveland, Ohio, offered quality and selection for shorter men and drew customers from a very wide area. With the creation of a mail-order catalog in 1984, Mr. Stern was able to target a national market. This was, and still is, a market with great needs.

The big and tall men's market has been addressed through both specialty stores and catalogs. However, the man who is under 5 feet 8 inches has not had the luxury of locating quality, stylish merchandise that offers him precise fit. Though there are almost as many short men as big and tall men, there are fewer retail resources and fewer manufacturers addressing the need. The need may not be perceived as so compelling for the short man. The big or tall man requires garments specifically made in larger sizes. But the short man has had a few "make-do" options. He may have been forced to buy in the boy's department. He could have his shirts and clothing tailored made, though at greater expense than purchasing at retail. Or he may have bought larger-size garments, and had them altered or recut to fit—both an imprecise and expensive endeavor. This is certainly the least effective choice, as recut garments are thrown out of proportion because they are altered so drastically.

The outreach of Short Sizes Inc. now has gone hightech. With the computer's increasingly common usage both at home and in the office, the consumer has access to a broad range of services at the touch of a keyboard. CompuServe®, an electronic, interactive information and service organization reaches homes and offices nationwide. In the case of Short Sizes Inc., subscriber-members may order merchandise or catalogs by computer. This mail-order business now has the capability to reach at least 900,000 CompuServe® subscribers and those numbers significantly advance monthly.

The catalog is offered to prospective customers at a rate of $1 per year and reflects that cost on its cover much in the way of a magazine. As with many catalog companies, interested parties or purchasers remain on the mailing list indefinitely at no charge.

Relationships such as that between CompuServe® and Short Sizes Inc., increases the number of people who become aware of a specialized retail market.

CompuServe®

SHORT SIZES IS PROUD TO ANNOUNCE OUR NEW "SHOP IN A CATALOG"™ ON-LINE WITH COMPUSERVE...

We're very excited about becoming a merchant on The Electronic Mall® with CompuServe this Fall. You can order merchandise or catalogs from us or ask us questions via your Personal Computer at any time of day or night. Also, if you will join our electronic mailing list, we'll let you know about any special values or markdowns that we may be featuring for our customers who are CompuServe members. Our User ID number is 70007,1524 and our GO Code is: GO SS.

If you're not yet a member and would like to join this exciting interactive information service, we've got a FREE Introductory Membership Kit for you just for the asking. Drop us a line or give us a call. Please note that time spent shopping on The Mall is Free. Any questions? We'll be happy to discuss this in greater detail with you. Remember-GO SS!

5241 Introductory Membership Kit   FREE

The challenge for this mail-order organization is to reach the "mail-responsive" shorter man. After all, he *is* presently clothed. He *has* found some source for his apparel, and he *may* not be desperate. But a resource like this can certainly make life easier for the shorter man. One of the unique ways Short Sizes Inc. gains visibility is through public relations and publicity efforts. One of their most innovative approaches was to publish a yearly list of the "10 Best-Dressed Shorter Men in America." That list resulted in great publicity coverage and a substantial increase in their mail-order business. The interest in the original list has spawned another. Now Short Sizes Inc. produces a list of the "10 Worst-Dressed Shorter Men in America"!

Mail-order companies like this offer tremendous value to a highly targeted market that has few other resources. Perhaps the words of a satisfied customer sums it up best: "thanks for all your great efforts in fitting the shorties' of the world!"

- What other creative means can a mail-order company use to increase public awareness of the catalog and strengthen its visibility in a competitive market?
- How does Short Sizes Inc. heighten value and somewhat qualify those who request catalogs? What impact does this have in separating the curious from the serious?
- What other aspects of mass communication or technology can be used to reach a wider marketplace?

TERMS TO KNOW

Define or briefly explain the following:

Clothier
Drummer
Clothing
Furnishings
Activewear
Spectator sportswear
Department store
Chain store
Specialty store
Off-price store
Nested suit
Discount store
Factory outlet
Sample store
Video shopping
EDI
Suit separates
Matrix buying
UPC
Seconds
Quick response
Bar Code
Jobber
SKU

CHAPTER 5

TAILORED CLOTHING: COATS, VESTS, AND PANTS

Let's first investigate the different style features of the coat before launching into the make and fit of the garment. All too often the consumer thinks that a coat is a coat is a coat....that they all look alike. This partly comes from the fact that womenswear changes so erratically from season to season and menswear seems to pale by comparison. Though womenswear changes by revolution, menswear changes by evolution. The transformation is subtle from season to season. Yet it appears, not only in choice of fabric, but in cut, fit, style, proportion. A discerning eye, one which recognizes nuances of fit, quality, and subtle styling changes will readily detect differences in men's coats and suits.

CLOTHING MAKE

An unusual aspect in the manufacture of clothing is the ranking of garments by make. This is not done in men's sportswear, nor in womenswear. To better evaluate and compare garments by different manufacturers, tailored garments are ranked according to the number of hand-sewn operations in that garment. The fewer hand operations there are, the lower the *make* or *grade* number. Garments are categorized in order as follows:

> **X-make.** Completely machine made with no hand operations, least expensive garment available. Some of these fall in sportswear or related separates grouping.
>
> **Make #1.** The next lowest quality of tailored suit with few, if any, hand operations.
>
> **Make #2, 4, 4+, 6.** Other grades in order of quality
>
> **Make #6+.** The very top quality produced. Example of #6+ make would be Oxxford Clothes and Hickey Freeman. These garments require between 120 and 150 separate hand tailoring operations and result in high quality and also high costs.

An X make or #1 make suit might retail as low as $150, while a 6+ make suit can easily pass a retail price of $1,000. This grading system is well known in the manufacturing and design end of the business. However, many retailers and merchandisers are unaware of its existence. Those who are aware of it usually have experience in the manufacturing end of the menswear industry.

DROP

An important element in the cut of a man's suit is the *drop*. The drop is the *difference in inches* between measurement of the coat chest and the pant waist. For example a man who has a 40 inch chest and a 34 inch waist has a 6" drop. The term drop is used when referring to suits, where the coat and pant are sold as a unit.

The drop has a big impact on both the cut and the fit of a suit coat. When a coat has a greater drop, there is a bigger difference between the chest and the waist. This results in a more tapered silhouette of the coat from the chest to the waist. If the coat has a smaller drop, or fewer inches in difference, the waist is closer in measurement to the chest and the silhouette is straighter. Men who have less than a 6" drop are full through the waist and may require a *stout* or *portly* cut (see "Sizing").

6 inch drop is the most common proportion among adult men and may be referred to as the *full cut, or regular,* model. The waist of the coat can often be altered down to a 7 inch drop for the trimmer man who has a smaller waist. Depending on

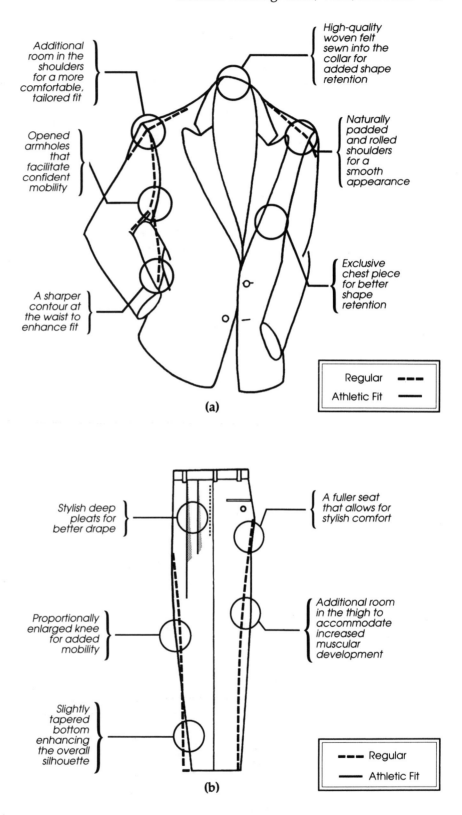

Additional room in the shoulders for a more comfortable, tailored fit

High-quality woven felt sewn into the collar for added shape retention

Opened armholes that facilitate confident mobility

Naturally padded and rolled shoulders for a smooth appearance

A sharper contour at the waist to enhance fit

Exclusive chest piece for better shape retention

Regular ----
Athletic Fit ——

(a)

Stylish deep pleats for better drape

A fuller seat that allows for stylish comfort

Proportionally enlarged knee for added mobility

Additional room in the thigh to accommodate increased muscular development

Slightly tapered bottom enhancing the overall silhouette

---- Regular
—— Athletic Fit

(b)

Organizations like Farah, Inc., have produced their own lines, in this case, John Henry, to satisfy the very special needs of the athletic build. Promotional materials like these help to educate both the retailer and the consumer to the differences in cuts.

width of seam allowances and the way the garment is constructed, it may be altered slightly to fit a fuller build.

7 inch drop is considered the *young man's silhouette*, though with men of all age groups working out today, the term could be a misnomer. This silhouette is becoming more popular and manufacturers are producing more offerings to retailers as a result.

8 inch drop is the most difficult to find. This is often called the *athletic cut* because it has a full chest and a small waist. In addition, this cut is designed so that the leg of the pant is typically fuller for the more developed thigh. The armhole may be lower due to muscle development in the upper arm area. The upper back is usually broader and the chest frequently fuller for the man who works out and has more developed muscles.

Though this is the hardest silhouette to find at retail, more and more customers have this need due to the increased interest in fitness. Many athletes and weight lifters require this drop or larger. Sometimes a 7 inch drop garment may be altered. It will be easier to fit this customer in separates, than in suits. For extreme cases, garments may have to be custom made. More manufacturers are seeing the needs for this customer and more selection should be available at retail in the future.

Athletic cut sportcoats are being manufactured today by companies which recognize this customer's need due to his physique. The "Athletic" customer may have a drop of up to 10", presenting very serious difficulty in locating suits at retail. This customer may be most easily fitted in the moderately priced suit separates (Chapter 4). Since there is no suit pant, the term "drop" does not relate to the sportcoat; however, the proportion of the garment may still be an Athletic cut.

A suit is always sized by the actual chest measurement. A man who measures 42 inches in the chest would wear a size 42 coat or suit. To determine the corresponding waist size for the suit pant, you must know the drop for that particular suit model. Of course, checking the ticket on the pant waistband would conversely inform you of that suit drop. Or, if you were very familiar with that manufacturer's models, you might know the drop, and could determine the waist size.

Most manufacturers produce garments in more than 1 drop in order to reach a wide market. Of course, their range in fit depends on the profile of their average customer. A company or designer which markets to the younger man may offer a 7 inch and an 8 inch drop, but may not produce a 6 inch drop. Many companies produce different lines under various names to address the varying fit and style needs of different consumer markets.

SUIT COAT VERSUS SPORTCOAT

What is the difference between these two terms? The *suit coat* has a matching pair of pants and the sportcoat is sold by itself, of course! But there are greater differences than that. The suit coat also typically is styled more conservatively than the sportcoat. The buttons used are usually subtle, matching the suit in color, the conservative pockets are usually of the besom variety (see "Pockets"). The fabric is also of a weight appropriate for both coat and pant.

On the other hand, the *sportcoat* has much broader style possibilities. Buttons may contrast in color and can be made out of metal or leather, which would be inappropriate for a suit. The pockets may be very stylish patch or patch with flap. It may have other style features like elbow patches, throat latches, belted back, etc. In addition, there is a lot more latitude in choice of fabric, from very heavy woolens, suedes, and velvet to the more traditional gabardines and worsteds.

The *blazer* is a very specific type of sportcoat. The traditional blazer is navy blue with metal buttons, patch pockets, and could be single- or double-breasted.

Today, the term *blazer* has loosened and may include almost any color of the rainbow, so long as it is a solid color. The buttons may be metal, leather, bone, or plastic.

COAT STYLE

Cut

The *cut* of the coat relates to the proportion and silhouette of the garment. There are five cuts of men's coats. These cuts apply to both suit and sportcoats.

Drape. The "drape" is the full, easy cut initially associated with clothing of the 1930s, popularized by the Duke of Windsor. It had additional ease, or fullness, in the chest and shoulder blade area in the back. There was a softness to the coat with a slightly extended shoulder and less padding overall.

In the late 1980s this fuller, softer cut reappeared in European houses and was sometimes referred to as "The Slouch Suit." The cut was quickly emulated by some of the more high-fashion American houses. In the early 1990s it became clear that the style was starting to reach the masses. Traditional manufacturers began to include in their lines a fuller, more forward model to avoid losing market share to other makers. These manufacturers did not eliminate their traditional lines but added to their offerings. Conservative retailers added a fresh new look to their stock with the revamped 1930s look.

The silhouette has worked its way into much of the mid- to high-end menswear clothing in the United States and Europe. It has a broader, more ample look through the upper body, and the shoulder line may be longer and softer. In some cases the sleeves are worn longer than in the more traditional garments, and double-breasted styles are more common. These styles have an ease about them yet at the same time make a strong and confident statement. The suit pants may sport deeper pleats and a fuller leg.

The styling of a European garment may be a bit too forward for very conservative types, so both profession and personality type must be taken into consideration when looking at this cut for a consumer.

Trim European Cut. From 1970 to the mid-1980s, the most traditional European coat was cut for the man who was both style and body conscious. He was very concerned about how the coat looked and how it felt. The mainstream *Trim European, or continental*, garment usually has a 7-inch drop. It is traditionally cut fairly closely to the body and is best suited for the slimmer man. The armhole is cut higher, and the shoulder area is usually padded a little more than the American or British cuts. The *skirt, or sweep*, which is the circumference around the bottom of the coat, is slim, adding to the trim look. This cut of European garment was extremely popular in the 1970s and early 1980s. When it first came into fashion, it was very forward. In the mid-1980s it was considered less extreme in its close fit and waist suppression. In the most conservative professions like banking and law, it made too much of a fashion statement.

The garments most often associated with Europe range from this traditional continental look to the more forward drape look mentioned earlier.

American Cut. This coat is cut for the man who is more concerned about comfort. He is the average build and therefore there are more men who buy this cut than any other. The coat usually has a 6-inch drop and a low armhole for comfort. The shoulders will have soft-medium padding, often referred to as a *soft, natural, or Ivy League* shoulder. The skirt of the coat is also fuller than the traditional

European cut, adding to the straighter lines of the silhouette. The cut is favored by those in the most traditional professions and the most conservative personality types.

A subcategory of this cut is the *Ivy League* cut, which is certainly American in its heritage and is often associated with the apparel of the old-school Northeast of the 1950s to 1960s. This is an important look to understand as it periodically returns. It is associated with a fairly narrow lapel, conservatively slim body, and trim silhouette in the pant.

Modified American Cut. Sometimes referred to as the *modified European* cut, it falls in between American and traditional European in styling and silhouette. This cut came into being in the 1970s when many American men wanted the fashionable look of the trim European cut but the more comfortable fit of the American cut. European and American designers, seeing another market evolving, made adjustments and added this new cut to their existing lines. The trend continues today with Italian designers closely monitoring the American market and making adjustments constantly to meet the interests and buying habits of the American consumer.

The drop may be either 6 inches or 7 inches with some style features of the European coats. It has a more expressive shoulder line than the American cut with the fuller armhole of the American cut. The waistline has a more suppressed appearance, and the coat skirt is a little slimmer than the American cut.

British Cut. This is the most traditional of all cuts. It originated from the *sack* coat, which had straight lines, virtually no shaping, and only slight padding. Interestingly, designers in the late 1980s brought about a resurgence of the sack coat in the fashion-forward end of the business, often in sportswear. These garments had very straight lines, three button fronts, very soft shoulders, and minimal interlining.

Today's British cut is still very soft in terms of interlining and shoulder padding. The ease of the drape cut may be evidenced in the chest and upper-back area. The shoulder is softer and with more of a downward angle than the American. The coat, however, may have slightly more suppression in the waist than the American cut with the same full skirt of the American cut. It usually has a 6-inch drop but a 7-inch drop is sometimes seen in this cut.

Savile Row in London is the area renowned for top-quality, custom-tailored menswear. The English suit styled and cut in one of the high-end shops on Savile Row has exquisite workmanship, fine British fabrics, and superb fit. Many manufacturers both British and American will play on the name Savile Row to ally themselves with the best in men's clothing. A term often used in relation to English tailored garments is *bespoke*. The bespoke suit is the English equivalent of the custom-tailored suit (Figures 5–1 to 5–5).

Design Features

Design features do not affect the fit of the garment but determine the unique look of the garment. The pocket, front design, vent styling, lapel shape, and so on, all make up design features of a coat.

Coat Front. A coat may be designed as either single- or double-breasted. The *single-breasted* style suit fits many body types favorably, and therefore is the most commonly seen model. The opening of the coat is centered on the body front, and it is distinguished by a curved cutaway at the bottom edge. The *cutaway* gets its name because the fabric has literally been cut away to form the curved edge. This style may have one, two, or three buttons on the front.

Figure 5–1. Drape cut.

Figure 5–2. Trim European cut.

Figure 5–3. American cut.

Figure 5–4. Modified American cut.

Figure 5–5. British cut.

The *one-button front* is a fashion-forward style seen most often in European garments. The *button stance*, or button position, is lower on the coat front than the two-button model, and results in a long lapel and a sleek look (Figure 5–6).

The *two-button front* is the most common style of single-breasted coat. It is designed so that only the top button is to be buttoned. Depending on the amount of cutaway, buttoning the lower button could throw the coat out of balance at the shoulders (Figure 5–7).

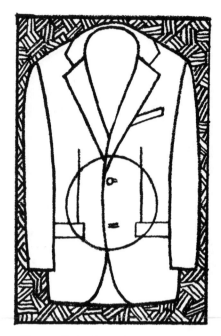

Figure 5–6. One-button, single-breasted style.

Figure 5–7. Two-button, single-breasted style.

The *three-button front* is the most conservative of the three and seen in very traditional suits, less often in sportcoats. Sometimes it is designed for the top and second button to be buttoned, producing a very short lapel line. Other times, the designer intends for only the center button to be buttoned. This garment has a conservative look. It may be interpreted as a "retrospective" look in fashion-forward styles (Figure 5–8).

The *double-breasted* front is distinguished by an off-center opening and double rows of buttons. It does not have a cutaway and, instead, has a horizontal line across the hemline of the coat front. This styling is best placed on the man who

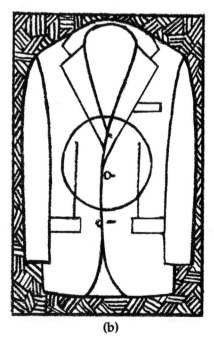

(a)

(b)

Figure 5–8 (a, b). Two variations on the three-button, single-breasted style.

is average to tall in height and average to slim in girth. It has a tendency to add the illusion of weight because of the horizontal hem and the extra buttons. This coat only looks neat when it is buttoned. Unbuttoned, the front swings out away from the body and looks haphazard. In addition, the extra layers across the front make it a warmer garment and the warm-natured man may find it difficult to wear comfortably.

Though double-breasted models never go completely out of style, their popularity gains renewed strength periodically. In the early1990s double-breasted suits and sportcoats made up to 25 percent and higher of suit stock in some retail stores. That is an exceptionally high percentage considering that double-breasted models traditionally occupy about 5 percent of a store's mix.[1] As with any styling, they will be seen at the highest end of fashion initially and work their way down to the mass market. It is more typically the man in age from 25 to 40 who purchases this style.

Lower quality shows up a little more quickly in the double-breasted model than in the single-breasted style. The peaked lapel, most often seen on the double-breasted coat, requires precise garment cutting, sewing, and pressing. The button placement on the fronts must be accurate for proper closure and front overlap at the hem. And the large front panels can result in a poor fit, if the garment is not cut, sewn, and pressed well.

There are many combinations of front closings in the double-breasted model. These will be referred to with the actual number of buttons on the front versus the number of functioning buttonholes. For example, you may see a term like "DB 4/1," which means the coat is double-breasted, has four buttons on the front, and one of the front buttons has a functioning buttonhole. The following illustrations show some of the more common configurations of double-breasted coats.

The *two-button front* has one functioning buttonhole (DB 2/1). The button stance is low, producing a long sleek lapel. This is quite slimming because of the long, diagonal line (Figure 5–9).

Figure 5–9. Two-button, double-breasted style.

[1]John Simone, "Tailored Clothing, '89," *Stores Magazine*, February 1989.

The *four-button front* may have one or two functioning buttonholes (DB 4/1 or DB 4/2). The DB 4/1 style is made with the top buttons set farther back from the opening. This also has a fairly low button stance. The DB 4/2 has the buttons positioned so that they form a square on the coat front. In this configuration, both opening edge buttons are functional as in the illustration. Some men will button both buttons, though it is not often seen. The most common choice is use of the top functioning buttonhole. Buttoning only the lower button produces a very long lapel line and looks awkward (Figure 5–10).

The *six-button front* may have one or two functioning buttonholes (DB 6/1 or DB 6/2), with the top buttons set farther back from the opening edge. As in the DB 4/2 coat, with this style, the wearer has a choice of button closure. Past fashion has seen the popularity of three functioning buttonholes (DB 6/3). Though this has not been in favor recently because it appears somewhat victorian, it may return to favor in the future (Figure 5–11).

Lapel Style.   A major factor in the look of a coat is the styling of the lapel. The three lapel styles in traditional menswear are *notched, peaked, and shawl.* The *gorge seam* joining the collar to the lapel affects the look and shape of the lapel. The longer and lower the gorge seam is, the more forward the styling tends to be. A low gorge is often seen in European clothing; a high gorge is often associated with more conservative clothing like American and British cuts.

The *notched lapel* is the most common of the three styles. Though the angle of the notch can vary, it is most commonly a little smaller than a right angle. Illustrated is the notch with a low gorge versus one with a high gorge (Figure 5–12).

The *peaked lapel* is a more stylish feature and seen most frequently in double-breasted styles and formal wear. Because of the long lapel edge formed by the peak, it tends to be slimming for the wearer. It may also be made with a high or a low gorge. This is a more difficult style to produce, and in lower-end garments, quality and shape must be closely checked (Figure 5–13).

The *shawl* collar is most often seen in formal wear such as tuxedos and dinner jackets. It is an elegant style and has no gorge seam (Figure 5–14).

Figure 5–10. Four-button (two to button), double-breasted style.

Figure 5–11. Six-button (two to button), double-breasted style.

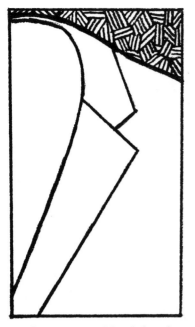

Figure 5–12. Notch lapel.

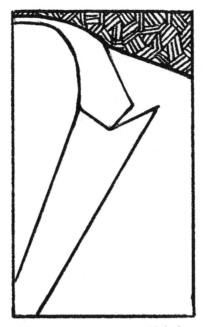

Figure 5–13. Peaked label.

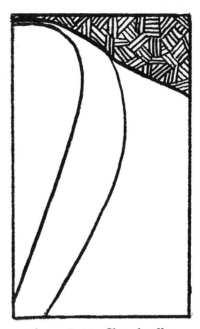

Figure 5–14. Shawl collar.

Edge Finishes. The front opening edges of a coat are to be finished in a similar manner to the pocket edges. For example, if the lapel and front edges are topstitched, the pockets or flaps should be topstitched also.

Topstitching is seen in suits and sportcoats. The stitching is usually about 1/4 inch away from the front opening edge and along the edges of the pockets or flaps. The stitch is produced by machine and is the most common form of edge finish (Figure 5–15).

Bluff edge is a clean edge with no stitching whatsoever. It is seen often in suits and can be found in some sportcoats. Though most often associated with besom pocket variations, patch pockets variations can be made. Application takes a high degree of skill, however, and are expensive to produce. This is a little dressier than the topstitched style (Figure 5–16).

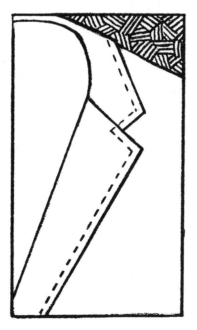

Figure 5–15. Topstitching.

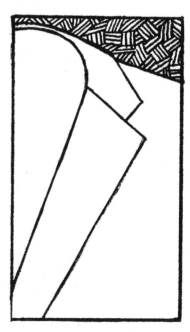

Figure 5–16. Bluff edge.

Pick stitch historically was done by hand and required high skill levels to produce effectively. Therefore it was only used on the finest garments. Today there are machines that duplicate the look at a fraction of the cost. But the association with more expensive coats remains. There is an old-world, elegant quality to this edge finish, and it is seen in high-fashion suit coats and sportcoats (Figure 5–17).

Darted Front. Most coats today have vertical darts to help shape the garment. There is one dart on each front panel. Older, very conservative style coats may eliminate the darts producing a silhouette with straighter lines. This used to be referred to as a *sack coat* (See also British cut) though that term is seldom used today. Garments designed specifically for the heavier man may not require the shaping of these darts (Figure 5–18).

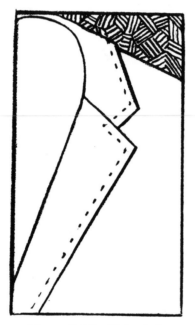

Figure 5–17. Pick stitch.

Figure 5–18. Darted front.

Pocket Styles. There are two basic pocket styles in tailored clothing: *besom* and *patch*. But both styles have many variations. When the garment is purchased, often the pockets are basted closed. This is for the manufacturer to press the garment more easily and to avoid having the consumer stretch the fabric in try-ons and after purchase. To help maintain the shape of the garment the man is advised to leave the pockets closed and use only the inside coat pockets.

The *besom pocket* looks like a very large bound buttonhole. It may also be referred to as a *slash, inset, or double-welt* pocket. This style is simple and elegant, often found in European garments. A very common variation has the besom with an inset flap. The besom and its variations are most common in suits, though they can be found in sportcoats (Figure 5–19).

In the besom with *inset flap*, the top part of the besom is visible over the flap. This style may be worn with the flap in or out (Figure 5–20).

Sometimes the besom with flap style will be made with an additional small pocket positioned above the besom on the right front. This top pocket styling is referred to as a *ticket pocket*. The flaps are aligned with the front edges parallel to the right front opening edge (Figure 5–21).

The besom with slanted flap is called a *hacking pocket*. This is often associated with formal horseback riding jackets and is seen frequently in the British styling (Figure 5–22).

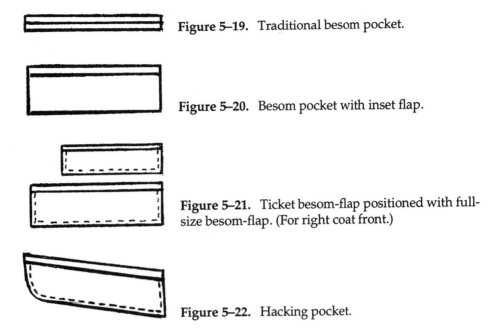

Figure 5–19. Traditional besom pocket.

Figure 5–20. Besom pocket with inset flap.

Figure 5–21. Ticket besom-flap positioned with full-size besom-flap. (For right coat front.)

Figure 5–22. Hacking pocket.

The *patch pocket* is a more informal style than the besom variations. Styling in patch pockets is only limited by the imagination of the designer. The patch may be open at the top or be covered by a flap. Application of a flap makes it slightly more conservative than an open pocket. Whatever the patch pocket variation, it is commonly thought less formal than the besom styles and therefore is more appropriate for sportcoats than suits. Illustrated are the four most common variations of the patch pocket (Figure 5–23).

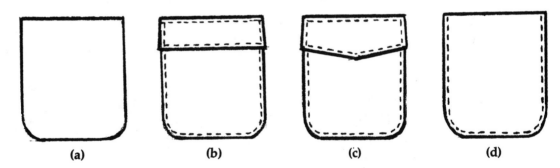

(a)   **(b)**   **(c)**   **(d)**

Figure 5–23. Four patch-pocket variations: (a) open patch pocket—bluff edge (difficult pocket to manufacture and often associated with more expensive garments); (b) topstitched patch pocket with flap; (c) topstitched patch pocket with pointed flap; (d) open patch pocket with topstitching.

The *breast pocket* is always positioned on the left coat front because most people are right-handed. The traditional style of breast pocket is called a *breast welt*. It is on a slight downward angle in relation to the fabric grain (Figure 5–24).

In sportcoats, the welt may be replaced by a *breast patch pocket* (Figure 5–25).

Shoulder Treatments. There are four shoulder treatments created by the cut of the garment and the padding used (refer to discussion on coat cuts for additional information; Figure 5–26).

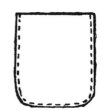

Figure 5–25. Topstitched breast patch pocket.

Figure 5–24. Breast welt.

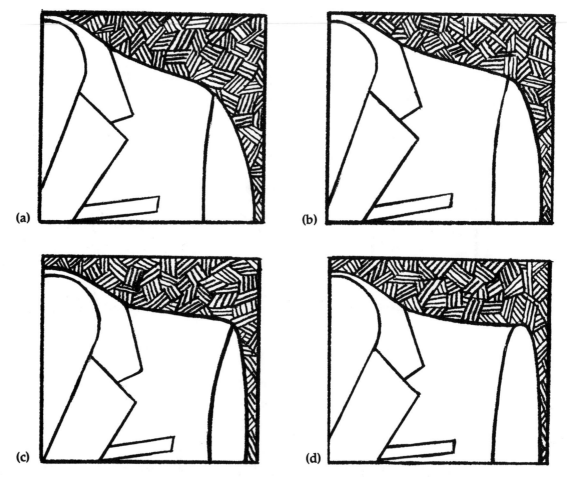

Figure 5–26. Four shoulder-treatment illustrations: (a) natural shoulder; (b) padded shoulder; (c) square shoulder; (d) rope shoulder.

The *natural or soft shoulder* is rounded and considered the most conservative style, frequently seen in British and American cuts, and often associated with the traditional *Ivy League* look. This shoulder style is not effective for the man who has very sloped shoulders, as it only emphasizes that. In the reappearance of the sack coat influence in forward styling of the late 1980s and in very forward, oversized European garments, this shoulder styling may also be used.

The *padded* shoulder has medium amount of buildup and is common in the modified American and modified European models. It has more shape than the natural shoulder.

The *square* shoulder is built up more than the regular padded shoulder and adds the illusion of height to the man. It is often associated with the slim European styles.

The *rope* shoulder has the appearance of raised rope at the top of the shoulder and is the most expressive of all shoulder styles. It actually builds on the square shoulder and is associated with highly styled garments.

Sleeve Vents. Why are there vents on the sleeves of a tailored coat? Some say that physicians used to keep their coats on in surgery, and the opened vents facilitated rolling up their sleeves. Others say, perhaps in jest, that Napoleon had the buttons put on his men's coats to prevent them from wiping their noses on their sleeves! Whatever the reason, the tradition of the sleeve vent remains.

Though most of today's coats do not have working buttonholes, two, three, or four buttons usually are placed alongside the vents. In the past the number of buttons used to correlate to the quality and expense of the garment—the more buttons, the finer the coat. This is not so today, however. Automated button-sewing machines and inexpensive plastic buttons have allowed manufacturers to put up to four buttons on almost any garment (Figure 5–27).

The *working sleeve vent* has real working buttonholes. It is the original-style sleeve vent and allows the wearer to unbutton the sleeve and roll it up. This is very expensive to make and is usually seen on custom- or tailor-made suits.

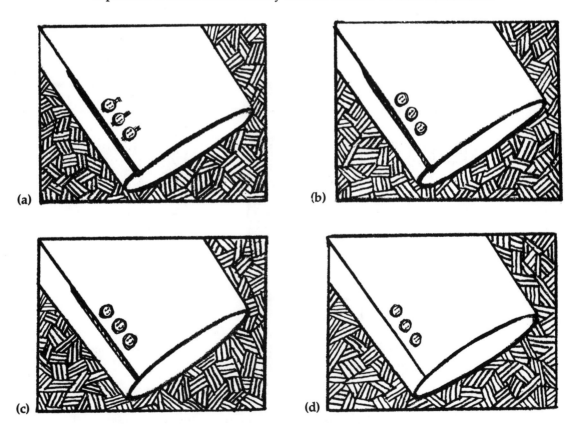

Figure 5–27. Four sleeve-vent–treatment illustrations: (a) working sleeve vent (fake buttonhole vent looks like this, but buttonholes are not cut open); (b) open sleeve vent; (c) mock sleeve vent; (d) no sleeve vent.

The *fake buttonhole vent* initially looks like the working sleeve vent. There are buttonholes sewn on the sleeve, and the buttons are sewn on top of the buttonholes. The holes are not cut through, however. They are there for the look only and are not functional. Removal of the buttonhole stitching would allow a tailor to alter the sleeve as there is no material cut by an actual buttonhole slit.

The *open sleeve vent* splits the sleeve at the bottom only and simulates the look of a working sleeve vent, but it does not have working buttonholes. Sometimes a manufacturer will put imitation buttonholes on the sleeve to give the look of a real buttonhole. If this sleeve must be altered the threads of the "hole" can be removed with no problem. This type of open sleeve vent is found on most coats.

The *mock sleeve vent* has a folded flap of fabric that simulates a vent, but there is no split at the bottom of the sleeve. This is a very inexpensive way of getting some of the look of an actual vent. It is usually found on less expensive garments.

Some coats have *no vent*, but the designer has placed buttons along the seam of the sleeve at the bottom. This may be found on very inexpensive or casual coats.

Back Vents. History also plays a major part in the existence of back vents in mens coats. The vent opening in the back of the garment allowed for greater freedom of movement and comfort. Though we no longer have the physical requirements for vents, the tradition remains, and back vents are very common in menswear.

The *center vent* (or *single vent*) originated for horseback riding. The coat spreads open at the seat and allows the wearer easy movement. This style is the most common vent treatment today (Figure 5–28).

The *side vents* (or *double vents*) allowed the wearer to ride horseback comfortably, but also allowed for the wearing of swords on either right or left sides. This style is found in all cuts, but very popular in British and European models even more than American ones (Figure 5–29).

The *ventless* (or *no vent*) model is a more updated look. It is best worn by a slim man and is common in European garments (Figure 5–30).

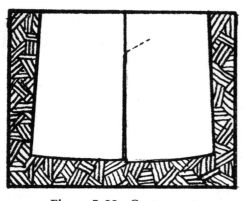

Figure 5–28. Center vent.

Figure 5–29. Side vents.

Figure 5–30. Ventless back.

Miscellaneous Style Treatments. In most cases, the more styling details the coat has the less conservative is the garment. These details tend to date the garment when the style becomes very fashionable. Very little is innovative, and most can be traced back to very early styles that had practical purposes. Figure 5–31 shows a few of the styling treatments you may see in sportcoats.

Coat Linings. Coats may be *fully lined, three-quarter lined, half-lined,* or *unconstructed*. The *fully lined* garment is often thought of as a sign of the most expensive make. This is true, the very finest coats have luxurious full linings. But ironically, this can also be a sign of the least expensive! It is sometimes less expensive to cover up X-make construction, for example, with an inexpensive lining fabric than to half-line the coat and have shoddy workmanship easily visible. In either case, there is a center pleat that runs the full length of the back to allow for ease of movement.

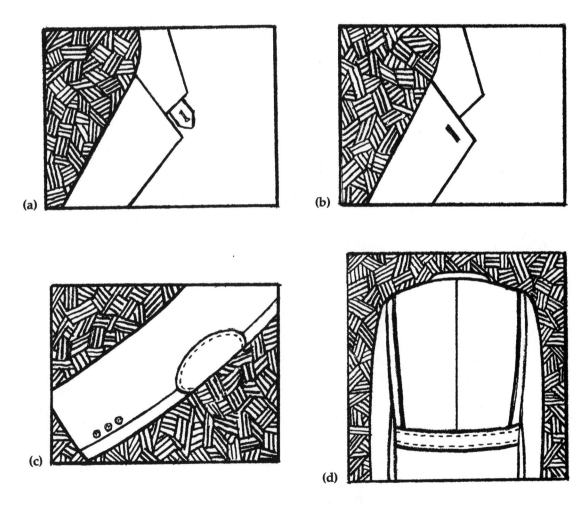

Figure 5–31. (a) *Throat latch or wind tab*: Its original purpose was to close the top of the lapels for protection from the elements. (b) *Boutonniere*: Its original purpose was the same as the throat latch. Today it is often the position for a lapel flower as an accessory for dress occasions. (c) *Elbow patch*: Its original purpose was to keep the elbows of the coat from wearing out or to cover a worn area of fabric. This was in common usage before central heating when men wore their coats while working at a desk. (d) *Belted with biswing back*: This back was originally designed for ease of arm movement. It is frequently seen on hunting jackets and casual wear for sport, as in safari-style coats.

Figure 5–31 (*continued*) (e) *Norfolk jacket*: This style was popularized by the duke of Windsor and was one of the earliest sportcoats worn in the United States. It is often associated with hunting jackets in tweed or woolen fabrics, and may sport a biswing back. (f) *Gun patch*: This style is found on many hunting jackets. It is positioned on the right shoulder to take the recoil of a rifle. The most authentic style of gun patch is one made of leather. Because most people are right-handed, a coat that has a single gun patch on the left shoulder has probably been custom-made for the wearer. (g) *Western style with arrowheads*: This front has two gun patches with the patches and flaps sporting curved lines typical of western styling. Most often the back of the coat also has a similarly curved back yoke. The triangles at the top of the darts are called arrowheads.

The *three-quarter lined* garment has the fronts lined to a point just short of the side seam. Then a *yoke liner* with a center pleat falls almost to the waist in the back. If the coat has vents, the vent has a small lining attached to it also. Some less expensive coats have the lining attached to the side seam and are referred to as *half-lined*.

A *french facing* is usually found in an *unconstructed* coat. These are associated more with sportswear or may be found in some lightweight summer coats. The facing of the coat (extension of the lapel on the inside) is widened. It is made of the same fabric as the coat. It may extend all the way to the side seam or cut diagonally across the coat on the inside. The sleeves may be lined so the coat can be slipped on and off easily. Also, the manufacturer may opt to include a yoke liner on the back panel. The french facing is the least common way of finishing the inside of a coat.

COAT SIZING AND THE MAN'S BUILD

Clothing Size Scales

The average suit and coat-size scale runs from size 38 to 46. Sizes 36 and 48 to 52 are "fringe" sizes, and are carried by some stores. In the big or tall category, sizes 48 to 52 are more readily available.

The most common clothing size scale is offered in even-numbered sizes, such as 36, 38, 40, and so on. Although most manufacturers make sizes 39, 41, and 43, not all stores carry them.

Suits are then sized by lengths: shorts, regulars, and longs. Most stores display their clothing by length, with the shorts, regulars, and longs being separated for easy customer access. Some men require extra shorts or extra longs. The extra long will be most readily available through specialty stores for tall men. There are more specialty stores for tall men than short men.

Coat/ Suit Size Scale
(Chest Measurement and Garment Size)

Coat Size	38	39	40	41	42	43	44	46
Short 5'3"-5'7"	*		*		*		*	
Reg. 5'8"- 6'0"	*	*	*	*	*	*	*	*
Long 6'1"- 6'3"			*	*	*	*	*	*

* Size Typically Available in These Lengths

Special Sizes. The gentleman who falls in the extra large range will best be suited in a specialty store devoted to the *big and tall* man. This market is often referred to in the garment industry as *B & T*. Manufacturers who specialize in producing these sizes even have their own trade show entitled B.A.T.M.A.N. which stands for Big and Tall Men's Apparel Needs. The male consumer who wears a size over 54 will have a very difficult time locating apparel at retail and may have to resort to special make (see chapter 11). Also special orders may be placed through some stores to satisfy the needs of these customers.

Higher-end clothing manufacturers are now offering options for the big and tall man. Some of these include Perry Ellis, Hart Schaffner & Marx, Hickey-Freeman, British company, and Gieves & Hawkes.

Portly and *stout* men have proportionately larger waists than the average man. The stout build tends to be a little taller than the portly physique. The portly man may have a smaller chest circumference than waist circumference. The portly and stout man will also have a more difficult time finding clothing at retail. Very often, these men will be forced to have garments custom-made to fit their needs because of poor selection of ready to wear.

Determination of Customer's Size

First you must determine whether the man wears a short, regular, or long. The illustrated chart can be used to determine the proper length. These lengths are found in virtually all stores. If his height falls in the extra short or extra long category, he can expect both more difficulty in finding selection, and he can also expect to find higher prices. The extra longs are a bit easier to find than the extra shorts. There are many more specialty stores today for tall and big men. The very short man may have to special order merchandise, order by mail from specialty houses, or consider custom clothes.

After height comes the body circumference, which determines the numerical size. Measurement for determination of size should be done with everything removed from shirt pockets. Standing behind the customer, ask him to raise his arms while you position the tape measure around the largest part of both the chest and the shoulder blades. The measurement is taken when the customer has lowered his arms and is breathing naturally. Be careful that the tape is not too tight, or you will have an inaccurate measure. If the measurement falls between sizes, it is best to move up to the larger size, unless he is interested in a coat that is by design very oversized. For example, if your tape measure reads 40 3/4 inches, he would wear a size 41 coat. Measuring is an imprecise science and becomes more accurate with practice.

It is important to note that though measurement of the customer for size is done with everything removed from shirt pockets, fitting by the tailor should be done with all normally carried items *in* the pockets. The reasoning here is that the man is probably going to carry these items in his shirt pocket (and pant pockets) most of the time, and the coat must fit well with whatever he will personally carry.

Coat Measurement Definitions and Locations. These measurements and terms are commonly used by tailors and designers. If you are working with a tailor, he or she may use these terms with ease, and a general understanding of the words will facilitate communication. The terms are used less often by sales associates unless for purposes of comparing one garment to another. In that situation, they become most valuable. Let's say, for example, you knew that a coat from stock fit your customer well except for the sweep, which was too small. You could find replacements that had similar fit except for larger sweep, just by comparative measuring.

Take special care in measuring so that all like measurements are taken in a similar manner, that way you are "comparing apples to apples," or you may come up with conclusions that are inaccurate.

1. *Point to point*: With coat laid flat, measure across the back from shoulder seam point to shoulder seam point. This is a very important measurement in comparing the proportions of either suit or sport coats. Manufacturers and retailers may refer to a sample size 40 coat, which has a 19-inch point to point as traditional, whereas a 20 1/2-inch point to point would be more oversized and expressive. This measurement is significant because it does reflect general trends of coat fit, and it fluctuates as do the lapel width, leg silhouette, and tie width.
2. *Center back*: Measure along the entire center back lengthwise seam from neckhole at the collar seam to the hem of the coat. This will give you the total coat length measurement.
3. *Across back*: Lay the coat flat with the back facing you. At midpoints of armhole, measure across the back of the coat. This is a critical measurement as it affects the comfort of the coat when arms are raised or brought forward.
4. *Skirt or sweep*: With the coat buttoned and laid flat, measure across the width of the coat at the hemline. This is best done with the coat facing you. This is a very difficult measurement to take accurately. It is advised to measure several times to ensure as great an accuracy as possible. This is easier to determine on a double-breasted coat because of the square front opening.
5. *Half waist*: With the coat opened and the left front laid flat, measure horizontally across the coat front from the waist buttonhole to the center back seam. Make sure your tape measure is kept at a right angle to the center back seam.

PROPER COAT FIT

When a man is considering purchase of a suit, he should try on the coat before the pant. The coat is more difficult to alter than the pant and therefore can be the qualifier as to whether the suit is a possibility for him.

Check the garment in the following order, first standing behind the customer as he looks in the mirror, then standing in front of the customer as you check the front of the garment.

1. *Neck*: The coat should hug the neck at the collar. It should neither stick out away from the shirt collar, nor should there be excessive fullness horizontally below the coat collar. Both of these conditions can be altered by a good tailor, but alterations charges will be incurred.

2. *Shoulder*: The shoulder line should lay flat and smooth with no ripples or pulls. The sleeves should not pull at the top of the shoulder (too small) nor should they extend far beyond the natural curve of the shoulder. This cannot be altered successfully without tremendous expense, and should not be considered except under the most extreme of cases and with an expert tailor.

3. *Back*: The back should lay flat and smooth, with no ripples lengthwise or crosswise. A little fullness may be desired by the customer for comfort. The fullness should lay along the side seam just below the armhole. There is usually seam allowance in the center back seam for alterations. The coat may be made a little larger here, or it can be taken in if too full. Comfort is a factor, so you must ask the customer how the coat feels.

4. *Length*: The coat should be long enough to just cover the rear end. Another area to check is the bottom of the coat in relation to the hands. The coat should fall just inside the cupped hand of the relaxed arm. If the fingertips can still touch the coat hem, the length is appropriate.

5. *Vent*: As you look at the back, check how the vent falls. Of course, the coat must be buttoned to see if the vent(s) hang cleanly. Whether center or side vent, they should not open when the coat is buttoned.* If so, sometimes alterations on the side seams or the back seam may alleviate the situation. If the sweep is too full, the vents will tend to cross over themselves. This can be easily adjusted by the tailor.

6. *Lapel*: With the coat buttoned,* and everything the man usually carries in his inside pockets, check the lay of the lapel. With the normal items in the pockets, the lapel should lay flat against the chest. If the client is full in the chest, or *pigeon chested*, there is going to be a problem of the lapel "breaking" out and away from the body. There's not much that can be done in most cases on this. It is better that the man leaves his coat opened and not attempt to wear a double-breasted style. If the man has very discriminating taste, purchases the top-quality clothing, and the store has an excellent tailor, some alterations can be made. It takes a very patient and talented tailor to achieve successful results, however, and alteration costs can add greatly to the cost of the garment.

7. *Armhole*: In most cases, you cannot tell visually about the fit of the armhole—you must ask the customer how it feels. This is a very subjective thing. If the armhole is too high for him, it will feel tight, and he will never truly be happy with the garment. Try another style, fit, or manufacturer.

8. *Waist suppression*: Do not pull the coat out at the front to check its fullness. If it drapes cleanly and it doesn't look big as it hangs naturally, then it fits correctly at the waist, regardless of the fullness. However, if excessive folds

*In any fitting, a single-breasted coat should always have the waist button buttoned. The bottom button should be unbuttoned. The garment is designed so that the bottom button is not to be buttoned even though there is a buttonhole there. Buttoning it will result in a coat out of balance on the body. The greater the cutaway on the front, the greater the imbalance would be. On a double-breasted garment, because the front is square, the buttons may be buttoned with no impairment in fit, although most commonly the middle button is used (see coat styles in chapter 5).

appear at the front then it may need to be altered. This should be checked with the coat buttoned. If it is too tight and there are horizontal pulls, it could be released somewhat in the side seams, depending on the coat style.

9. *Sleeves*: The bottom of the coat sleeve should be the same distance from the tip of the thumb in relation to both hands. With the man wearing the correct length shirt sleeve, which will just cover the large wrist bone, the coat sleeve should be 1/4 inch to 1/2 inch *shorter* than the shirt sleeve.

With french cuffs, more *linen* (term frequently used by tailors in reference to the amount of shirtsleeve showing) will show naturally because the shirt cuff falls lower on the wrist. Coat sleeve alterations are the most common alteration; they can be easily shortened or lengthened. Many American men tend to wear their coat sleeves too long, with no linen showing.

RECOGNITION OF COAT QUALITY

In addition to all the fit points discussed previously, quality of the garment must be checked. It is entirely possible that two coats of the same color, style, and size, and made by the same manufacturer, hanging next to each other on a rack, may have different levels of quality. It is not too difficult, after closely inspecting any garment, to find some defect. Today, with so many manufacturers contracting and subcontracting production, it is not uncommon to find the exact same style with differences in make.

Here are some of the major quality areas to check in tailored coats.

1. Shoulders should be smooth with no ripples or uneven seams.
2. The gorge seams should form smooth straight lines.
3. Buttons should be sewn on with waxed thread and the shank, or neck, wrapped with thread to avoid pinching the coat front when buttoned.
4. Buttons should close easily through cleanly cut and neatly sewn button-holes.
5. The coat front should "break" or roll at the lapel just above the top button on a two-button front or above the top button on the most conservative three-button front.
6. The collar should cover the undercollar material along the back.
7. The pockets should be positioned squarely on the coat front and balanced on each side.
8. Sleeves should be set in the armhole with no puckering.
9. Linings should be pressed smooth.
10. Plaids should match in pocket areas, as well as on lengthwise seams, center back, center front, and collar to center back seam. Vertical stripes should match in pocket areas and collar to the center back.
11. Pressing should not have left any marks or lining imprints on the coat.

VEST

The man's vest is really a very practical garment. It keeps the man warm because it fits close to the body. In most cases it is adjustable through a belt in the back. Yet it allows free movement of the arms when the coat is removed.

Historically a vest kept the coachman warm as he drove horse and carriage. It also allowed the clerk in a cold drafty office to remain warm, without being hampered by a jacket. Likewise, today, when the man removes his suit coat, a vest allows him to maintain a certain degree of formality—he still appears "dressed." Vests were the norm up until World War II, when the shortage of piece goods put this garment in a decline. Today the style goes in and out of fashion, yet will always be considered classic.

When a suit is vested it is termed a *three-piece suit*. Frequently the designer of a three-piece suit will allow a little extra room in the coat for the wearing of the vest.

Styling

The vest may be designed with a five- or a six-button front. Traditionally the bottom button is left unbuttoned. Some vests are actually designed with the bottom button and hole set back from the front edges so that they cannot be closed. As so much of our menswear clothing tradition, this comes from England, where a member of English royalty unwittingly forgot to button the vest completely. This "look" remains with us today. In addition, leaving the bottom button unbuttoned allows the man greater comfort when he sits.

Some vests have darted fronts, which both add to the style and assist in achieving a close body fit through the abdomen and chest.

The back of the vest is made of the same lining as the coat, whereas the front is the same as the coat shell fabric. Styling may include two or four welt pockets on the front. Sometimes two small patch pockets may be applied. These are found usually on less formal fabrics, however, and the corresponding coat would also have patch pockets (Figure 5–32).

(a)	**(b)**	**(c)**

Figure 5–32. Three vest styles: (a) five-button plain front vest with two welt pockets; (b) five-button darted vest with two patch pockets; (c) six-button (five to button) darted vest with four welts.

Proper Vest Fit

If the man is buying a vest as a part of a three-piece suit, he should be sure to try the coat on top of the vest to ensure proper comfort.

The vest should fit like a second skin and therefore should have a definite waistline. This can be achieved through shaping in the center back seam, side seams, and darts in the front. The custom-made vest may not need a belt in the back as it will be shaped specifically for that customer. Lesser-quality garments will forsake the darted front and the center back seam, relying on the belt for fit. This results in a garment that may have excessive fullness in the back on the slim man, however.

1. The front diagonal edges should lay flat against the man's chest. If the man is very full chested, sometimes referred to as *pigeon chested*, he will have the

same problem fitting the vest as fitting the coat. It will have a tendency to buckle out away from the chest. In an off-the-rack garment, there is little that can be done to remedy this, and he is better off staying away from that style, which only emphasizes the chest.

2. The neckline should lay flat on the front and back. This is easily altered to fit cleanly.

3. The vest should cover the waistband of the pant. If the man chooses to wear a belt, he must be sure that the belt and buckle do not show. The top of the vest should show above the top button of the buttoned coat. A shirt that peeks out below the vest looks sloppy.

Sizing

Vests are sized according to the chest measurement and the torso length just as the coat is. Whatever size coat the gentleman wears, he will require the same size vest. In a three-piece suit, the vest will be nested on the same hanger as the coat and pant.

Quality

The vest is a very easy garment to make in comparison with a coat or pant. The consumer should expect excellent quality from a vest. Here are some other quality areas to check.

1. Small, close stitches, free from puckers, which can stand up to a very close fit.
2. Back vest belt buckle that is easy for the consumer to adjust and will not loosen itself.
3. Pockets that lay flat and are balanced on each front.
4. Points at the bottom vest front that lay flat and do not curl upward.
5. Lining smooth with no pressed-in marks on vest front.

PANTS

Next to the coat, the pant is the most complicated and expensive clothing garment to produce. Though men's tailored pants may all seem to look the same, there are many subtle variations. Silhouette, hem style, pocket style, front finish, and waistband all join to give each pant a special look.

Like coats, many of the design features today have been seen in menswear for years. Though they may no longer serve a functional purpose, they remain as a part of traditional style.

Definitions: Pants, Slacks, And Trousers

The old fashioned term for pant is *trouser*. The term is certainly used today, but may infer a fuller cut and a traditionally styled garment. The typical trouser has pleats, a full-leg silhouette, a high *rise* (distance from the crotch to the waist), a *watch pocket* (for a watch on a chain) and cuffs. Though it has beltloops, it is often worn with suspenders.

Slacks is a comparatively new term. It originated after World War II and usually was used in reference to separate pants, the kind one would wear in leisure or "slack" time. This could be interpreted in the broadest sense to include casual styles. To be more specific, many people refer to *dress slacks* to mean those styles appropriate to wear with sportcoats. Today, the term is used widely to mean any type of pant except the leisure jean style.

When referring to the suit, the term *pant* is most often used, although neither slacks nor trousers is incorrect.

Pant Design Features

The style of the pant is based on the waistband, front, hem finish, leg silhouette, and pockets.

Waistband. There are two basic types of waistbands: beltloop and beltless. The norm is for suits to be sold with a beltloop-style pant. Beltless pants are far more commonly sold as separate slacks. The customer could have the beltloops removed from the suit pant in many cases if he so desired, though it is unusual to do so.

The *beltloop* style is the most common as well as traditional waistband treatment. The number of loops is determined by the size of the garment. The larger the waist size, the more loops there should be. The more casual the pant, the greater likelihood that there will be topstitching on the loops. In dress slacks or suit pants, there is usually a loose beltloop placed in a side pocket. Because so many pants are altered in the center back seat seam, the loop is not sewn on and is to be positioned in the center back after any alterations (Figure 5–33).

The *beltless* style allows for more style variation. This style reached great popularity in the 1970s when the European version was often referred to as the *continental* waist. Today, in its most basic form, the pant has a plain waistband and may have an extension on the front of it (Figure 5–34).

A variation of the beltless pant is made with an elastic, *stretch waistband.* This is sold under many proprietary names like "Sansabelt" by Jaymar-Ruby and "Expandomatic" by Haggar Apparel. These are very comfortable pants and particularly enjoyed by men with larger waists. Some men will refer to this style as a

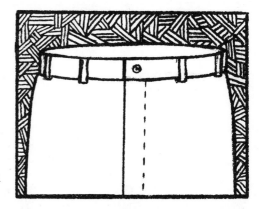

Figure 5–33. Beltloop pant with a plain front.

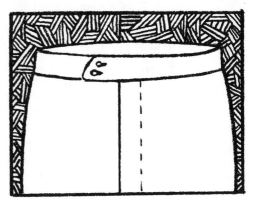

Figure 5–34. Beltless (continental) pant with extension waistband.

golf, or tourney, pant. Because of the freedom of movement it affords, it is often worn for golf. Its styling and fabric typically allow it to cross from dress wear, or street wear, into more formal sportswear.

Another variation of the beltless model is the *adjustable waistband*, which may have metal clamps on fabric strips on the sides of the pant. This allows the wearer to make the waistband tighter or looser. Sometimes this is combined with the stretch waistband (Figure 5–35).

Though there are many other variations on the beltless style, they are mostly associated with sportswear and do not fall in the clothing category.

Figure 5–35. Beltless pant with adjustable waistband.

Pant Front. There are two basic styles of pant front: *pleated* and *plain front.* It is critical that the customer be consulted as to whether he will wear pleated pants or not. This is a very personal matter, and some men feel quite strongly about it.

Pleated pants are very traditional. They are preferred by many older, conservative men. And yet at the same time, they have gained preference by the younger set and are seen in some very fashion-forward makes. The more fashion-conscious man may choose to wear pleats and snappy suspenders as a fashion statement—another testimony to the adage "what's old is new again."

Suit pants are made in both pleated and plain front styles. Pleats gained a strong following in the 1980s and into the 1990s. A high percentage of manufactured suits are produced with pleated pants. Be sure to check the pant style before having a client try a suit on; handing the consumer a suit style he will dislike as soon as he gets in the fitting room can be a real problem.

The most common style of pleated pant may have one or two pleats on each front panel. The pleats may turn toward the front or toward the side. Those that have the fold pointing toward sideseam are the more slimming, as they form a flat panel on the body front (Figure 5–36).

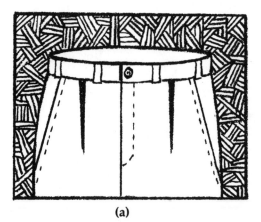
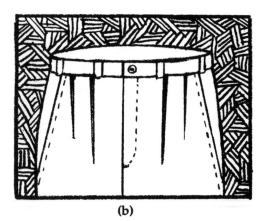

(a)   (b)

Figure 5–36. Two pleated pant fronts: (a) single-pleat front; (b) double-pleat front.

The number of pleats and the depth of the pleat will have a big impact on the silhouette of the pant leg. A double-pleated front with deep pleats requires more fabric and will produce a fuller leg. The extra room is comfortable, but some men do not like the look of the wide leg. Some very high-fashion styles may have three pleats on each front panel of the pant.

The plain front pant results in a slimmer leg silhouette than the pleated pant (Figure 5–37).

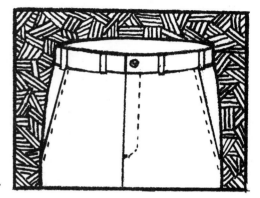

Figure 5–37. Plain front.

Pant Hem Finish. Most dress slacks and all suit pants are merchandised at retail *unfinished*. This means that the bottom of the pant leg is unhemmed and can be adjusted to any length. However, some *finished* pants are available at retail. They are usually of the less expensive variety and may be found in sportswear or the bridge department. The customer also has a choice as to the type of hem finish he wants. In determining the finish and length, the tailor will also want to know if the customer wants a *break* in the pant leg.

The front of the pant leg at the hem should always touch the top of the shoe. If it just skims the top of the shoe, but does not rest on it, it has a *clean crease*. This produces a clean, unbroken crease line. The man may prefer a *break* in the crease, however. In this case, the pant is long in the front, and it rests on the top of the shoe. This results in a slight drape or breaking in the front of the crease line.

There are pros and cons to each choice. The benefit of the clean crease is its crisp neatness. The pant that has a break will look longer when the man walks and sits, as there is more fabric. It also is a way of getting the cuffed pant longer, without requiring a slanted hemline (Figure 5–38).

Another factor in finishing the pant leg is the angle of the bottom. A pant that has a slanted hemline, slightly longer at the back, produces a longer leg line. This angle is called a *cant*. The angle is much more difficult to make on a cuffed pant because of the additional fabric folds. On a hemmed pant the cant may be up to 3/4 inch longer in the back than on the front.

There are two basic finishes: *hemmed and cuffed*. Choice is based on personal preference but can be influenced by the man's build.

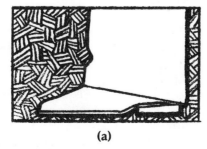
(a)

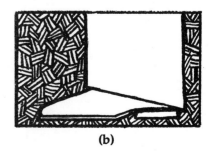
(b)

Figure 5–38. (a) Break in creaseline on hemmed pant; (b) clean crease on hemmed pant.

The cuffed style, referred to in Great Britain as *turnups,* started for a very practical reason. Men walking through the damp British moors rolled up their pants to avoid getting them wet, and this evolved into the accepted style. So their historical reference is associated with sportswear of the country gentlemen, but today they are seen in suit pants as well as slacks. They can be perceived as fashionable or conservative.

An added benefit to the cuff is its weight. Because of the extra fabric used to make the cuff, it is heavier at the hem. This tends to keep the pant hanging clean and aids in retaining the creaseline. Because cuffs form a horizontal line on the leg, they tend to make the leg look a little shorter. They are best avoided for the short or very heavy man. For the average to tall man, cuffs are an interesting option.

By nature of the way the cuff is folded, it produces a horizontal line perpendicular to the side seam. It is extremely difficult to sew a cuff resulting in a cant at the bottom of the pant. Therefore, the length of the cuffed pant tends to be shorter than the hemmed pant unless the man has a break in the crease. Figure 5–39 shows the difference the break makes in the length and angle of the cuffed pant.

The hemmed bottom is preferred by more men than the cuffed pant. It is well suited to all builds and especially effective in a long length for the shorter man because of its unbroken line at the bottom. The tailor can more easily cant a hemmed pant versus a cuffed pant.

(a) **(b)**

Figure 5–39. (a) Clean crease on cuffed pant; (b) break on cuffed pant.

Pant Silhouette. There are three basic silhouettes of men's pants: the *straight* leg, *flared* leg, and *tapered* leg. The tapered leg, the most conservative of the three, was popular in the 1950s and 1960s. The flared leg was very fashionable in the late 1960s and the 1970s. And the 1980s mainstream fashion found the straight leg in favor. This style remains popular into the 1990s. We will probably see a swing back to the tapered leg and ultimately to the flare again, however.

In looking at the shape of the pant leg, the straight-leg style may be wide or narrow, the flared leg may be a dramatic flare, and the tapered leg may be pegged at the hem. It is the *shape* of the silhouette that determines the style, not necessarily the *size* of that shape (Figure 5–40).

Pant Pocket Styles

Pants in the tailored clothing category do not have patch pockets. Patch pockets are considered too casual for suit pant or dress slacks. The side pockets become less formal and more stylish as they angle away from the side seams. There are four sideseam pocket styles.

The *on-seam* pocket is in a direct line with the sideseam. This style pocket is often found in suits and on more formal dress pants. It is the most conservative style pant pocket (Figure 5–41).

The *quarter-top* pocket slants slightly away from the side seam. It gets its name because it originally was designed to slant one-quarter of the way across a front pant panel. This pocket is also found on suits and dress slacks, but is not as conservative as the on-seam pocket (Figure 5–42).

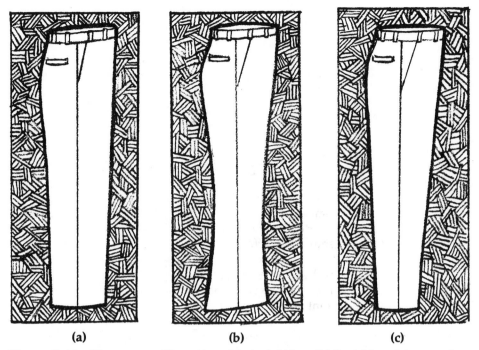

Figure 5–40. Three pant silhouettes: (a) straight leg; (b) flared leg; (c) pegged leg.

Figure 5–41. On-seam pocket.

Figure 5–42. Quarter-top pocket.

The *half-top* pocket is less conservative than the two side-pocket styles. It can be seen in some dress slacks and also sportswear (Figure 5–43).

The *western* pocket style is the least conservative of the four styles. It is typically associated with informal slacks (Figure 5–44).

Pant back pockets are variations on the besom welt. Most pants have two back pockets. However, some European style pants that fit close to the body will have just one pocket, usually on the right side.

The *besom* pocket is made in the same way as on the coat. Variations may have flaps, though flaps on dress slacks usually make them less formal (Figure 5–45).

Some pants have a *watch pocket* on them. This small pocket is on the right front along the waistband. It was originally designed for the sole purpose of holding the man's pocket watch. The watch was often attached by a chain, or *watch fob*, to the man's vest. The pocket is considered more decorative than functional when it has a buttoned flap over it. However, some men do use it for change, keys, or theater tickets (Figure 5–46).

Figure 5–43. Half-top pocket.

Figure 5–44. Western pocket.

(a)

(b)

Figure 5–45. Two back-pocket drawings: (a) back-pocket besoms; (b) back-pocket besom with buttoned flap.

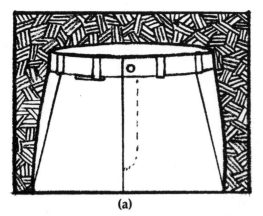 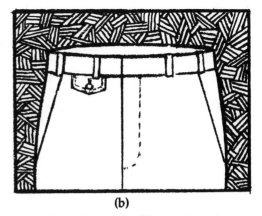

(a)   (b)

Figure 5–46. Two watch-pocket drawings: (a) watch pocket; (b) watch pocket with buttoned flap.

PANT SIZING AND THE MAN'S BUILD

Pant Size Scales

Manufacturers produce dress slacks in waist sizes with unfinished bottoms. Some also offer the pants prehemmed or precuffed by inseam length. In either case, the sizes produced typically run from waist size 30 to 46. Sizes 28 to 30 and 46 to 48 are considered fringe sizes, not produced in great quantity, and more difficult to locate at retail.

As in coats, the most popular sizes are the even-numbered sizes, like 32, 34, 36, and so on. The smaller waist sizes, like 29, 31, 33, are often more available in odd sizes than the larger waist sizes. Each manufacturer determines its own scale of sizes offered based on the needs of its customers.

Unfinished bottoms are frequently found in the better fabrics and makes. This also allows the retailer to inventory fewer items and adjust hems as necessary. The bottom of the pant usually has a raw, pinked, or zig-zagged edge.

In the finished variety, the retailer must carry more stock to offer both waist and inseam. Some retailers will purchase long lengths and alter as necessary. Finished bottom slacks have two numbers on the ticket. Size 32 × 31 represents a 32-inch waist and a 31-inch inseam. The first number is always the waist size.

Inseams generally run from 28 inches to 34 inches. Some manufacturers make 36-inch finished bottoms, but there are few available. This length would be for a very tall man, or one with disproportionately long legs. He would find this length most easily in a specialty store. With the finished bottom, the manufacturer determines the cant. The customer may have alterations done on the hem, however, to achieve any desired shorter length or to have the cant decreased.

Determination of Customer's Size

The only circumference size required is the man's waist measurement in most cases. This should be taken with the tape measure on the natural waistline over the shirt but *under* the pant waistband. In most cases, length of the pant will be altered to fit.

If, however, the interest is in a finished bottom pant, then the inseam length must be known. The inseam length is determined by measuring from the point where the inseam meets the seatseam at the crotch, along the inseam, to the finished length at the customer's shoe. The distance from the waist to the crotch is called the *rise, or stride*. The rise must be in proportion to the man's height and build. There are three rise lengths: *regular rise, long rise, and short rise*. If the man is tall and he wears a long coat, he will probably require a long rise pant, a short man will need a short rise, and the average-height man will wear a regular rise. As in coats, some extra short and extra long rise are available but difficult to find.

Of course, there are always exceptions. An average-height man may be short waisted and have a long rise. In this case the fit of the pant is made more difficult in a suit. Because he would normally buy a regular length in a suit, the pant rise may not be long enough. He would be easier to fit in separate slacks and a sportcoat. Other alternatives are to have clothing custom made or some garments from off the rack can be altered sufficiently to work for him.

Sometimes the term *rise* is used to describe how high up the waistband sits on the body or how low on the hips it sits. For example, a very conservative, traditional pant may be styled so that the waistband sits high on the body, termed a "high rise." Sometimes a very fashion-forward style pant may offer a high rise also. A trim, European pant may be styled so that it sits low on the hips, or it has a "low rise."

BEFORE   **AFTER**

Proper fit has an enormuos impact on appearance.

Pant measurement definitions and locations. Though these measurements and terms are commonly used by tailors and designers, they are important for the fashion professional to know and use correctly. They can be important in working with a tailor and in comparing the fit of one garment to another. These measurements are made on the garment from stock, not on the customer.

1. *Waist*: With the pant zipped closed, measure from side to side on the *inside* of the waistband and double the reading for the actual measurement. This should be the same as the customer's waist size.

2. *Seat*: With the pant flat, measure 3 inches up from the crotch point then measure across from side to side.

3. *Knee*: Fold the leg in half, bringing the bottom of the pant leg to the crotch point. Measure across at the folded point. This will also show if the pant is flared or tapered.

4. *Inseam*: As a finished garment measurement, this is done only on a hemmed or a cuffed pant. Measure along the inseam from the hem to the crotch point.

5. *Outseam*: As a finished garment measurement, this is done only on a hemmed or cuffed pant. Measure from the pant hem along the sideseam to the bottom of the waistband.

6. *Rise*: This is the difference between the outseam and the inseam. Measure the outseam and the inseam. Subtract the inseam from the outseam measurement, and you have the rise. This is sometimes referred to as the stride.

PROPER PANT FIT

1. *Rise:* The rise has a big impact on the way the pants look and feel when standing, and even more when sitting. It may be obvious if the rise is too long. It will look too long in relation to the man's height, and the pant will look baggy in the seat. If the client doesn't mention the rise, you must ask him if the rise feels right, or is too high (tight) or too low (loose) on him. European-influenced garments, or young men's garments, may have a lower rise, sometimes called a short rise. In this styling the pant sits lower on the hips, similar to the way many jeans fit. Most conservative men will not like this fit. It cannot be easily altered, and it is best to consider another cut garment.

2. *Seat*: There is a seat seam allowance in most pants that will allow for some alteration in this area. The well-fitting pant should have a seat that is free of pulls, strain, or excess fabric, indicating it is too large. Alteration of the seat often is made in conjunction with alteration of the waist.

3. *Waist*: If the waist is too small, it will be obvious. If the waist is too large, it may not be as readily apparent. If the customer comments that the pants are too big, slip your finger in the waistband at the back and see how much excess there is. If it is more than 1 1/2 inches total, alterations could throw off the balance of the garment. A *recut* may be done, but this is expensive and involves virtually taking the pant apart. Sometimes this must be considered on a suit pant when working with a client who has an 8-inch drop or more.

4. *Fly*: When the pants fit properly in the waist and seat, the fly should have no strain on it. If there is a fly "pull" and horizontal lines appear across the front of the garment, it could be due to the pant being tight in the seat. It is important to check the fly area. A pull can be due to manufacturing problems and may be impossible to fix. This condition will only worsen with wear.

5. *Pockets*: Side pockets should lay flat when the man is standing. Pockets that gape open may be an indication of a pant being too tight. But it can also be an indication of poor make. The condition will only worsen with wear. Pockets that fall directly on the sideseam tend to lay flatter than those that are cut on an angle away from the sideseam. Some high-fashion pants have angled besom pockets cut into the front panels. These pockets tent to lay flat. *Note*: If the man carries a lot of keys and change in his pockets, he will ruin the pants. The pants will show wear in that area, and the pockets will tend to bag open.

6. *Silhouette*: This is a subjective factor and relates to the current style, the man's personality type, and his preferences.

7. *Length*: The man has the choice of cuffs or plain hems. The correct pant length touches the shoe in the front with either a break or a clean crease. The back of the pant bottom should extend at least to the midpoint of the shoe *counter*. The counter is the firm leather back of the shoe, where the vertical seam is. The pant may be as long as reaching the heel of the shoe. It should not drag on the floor, however. Having a break in the crease along with a healthy cant will allow the pant to be longer in the back. It is also wise to consider that residual shrinkage of up to 1/4 inch may occur in dry cleaning, so a longer pant is often of benefit. As previously discussed, the cuffed pant tends to be shorter because of the difficulty in achieving a cant. A break in the crease, however, will allow the pant to be longer (Figure 5–47).

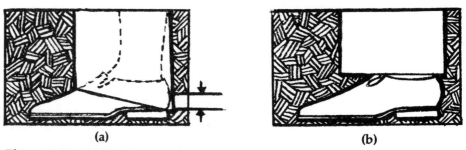

(a)   (b)

Figure 5–47. (a) The length of the pant should be between the midpoint of the shoe back (counter) and the point where the heel meets the leather counter. (b) The pant hem that is too short will make the leg look shorter.

RECOGNITION OF PANT QUALITY

The following points are important factors in pant quality:

1. There should be a smooth closure at the waistband, with no pulls or fullness.
2. When closed, the fly should lay flat, with no pulls or puckering.
3. Pockets should be reinforced with sewn tacks at the top and the bottom to handle stress points.
4. Inseams and outseams should be pressed open (unless topstitched), and lay flat with no puckering.
5. The fly should be lined on the inside.
6. There should be a button fly tab or a French fly extension on the inside of the pant to keep the fly laying flat and pressure off the zipper (Figure 5–48).
7. If lining is used on the inside pant front, it should extend below the knee level to prevent bagging.

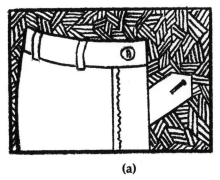 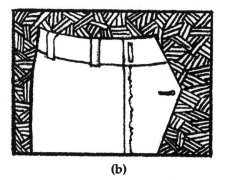

Figure 5–48. (a) Button fly tab; (b) French fly extension.

8. Pocketing should be of quality fabric, not show through the shell fabric, and pressed flat.
9. The seat seam should have an extra wide seam allowance on the inside to allow for alterations, and the seam edges should be finished neatly.
10. Stiff banding should be used inside the waistband to avoid waist rollover when worn.
11. Back pockets should be reinforced at the stress points with sewn tacks.

CASE STUDY

Bob Handler was in need of a couple of new suits. He had worked with the same salesman in his favorite specialty store for several years. But the salesman had retired, and Bob was introduced to Jack Segal, who had replaced him. Jack knew nothing about Bob and had only moments to determine the sales approach to take with him.

Bob was 44 years old, tall, slim, and dressed in a sophisticated, European, double-breasted suit. His tie was an unusual, abstract pattern, and he wore a pocket square in the coat pocket.

Jack asked him questions to determine his needs. Bob explained in detail his concerns about his appearance, the type of look he liked, his color preferences, and brand names he preferred.

With detailed information like that, Jack was able to pinpoint quickly some suits that would appeal to this customer. He made special efforts to ensure that the tailor made every adjustment the customer had mentioned. As Bob was preparing to leave, Jack got his telephone number and address and said he'd call when the suit was ready to be picked up.

When Bob returned to pick up the suit, Jack called the tailor, and, together, they evaluated the alterations made. Jack asked if Bob foresaw any specific wardrobe needs in the near future. Jack said he'd be happy to watch incoming stock and call Bob when something special he might like would come in.

Jack had taken special pains with this customer to ensure repeat business. He did not want to be perceived as just another salesman. His approach was that Bob *would* be a client, not just a one-time customer. That attitude would help to cement a long-term working relationship.

- What were the aspects of Jack's techniques that showed he really cared about the fit of the suit for Bob?
- Even if Bob had not given such a detailed explanation of his likes, how would Jack have been able to discern a direction to take him in wardrobe selection?

TERMS TO KNOW

Define or briefly explain the following:

Grade number	Boutonniere
X-make	Bi-swing back
6+ make	Norfolk straps
Blazer	Gun patch
Drop	Arrowheads
Athletic cut	French facing
Sportcoat	Portly
Drape cut	Stout
Sack coat	Point to point
Savile Row	Sweep
DB/4/1	Linen
Gorge seam	Beltless
Notch lapel	Tourney waist
Peaked lapel	Adjustable waistband
Shawl lapel	Pant break
Bluff edge	Clean crease
Topstitching	Rise
Pick stitch	Cant
Besom	Counter
Ivy League shoulder	Turnups
Rope shoulder	French fly
Working vent	Watch pocket
Wind tab	

CHAPTER 6

TAILORED

OUTERWEAR

The term *outerwear* in the consumer's viewpoint means any garment made of cloth that is to be worn over streetwear as a form of protection from the elements. This would include anything from a down jacket to a woolen car coat. In the menswear industry an overcoat, topcoat, or a raincoat would *not* be considered outerwear, however. Those three types of garments would be considered tailored clothing. The public uses the term outerwear much more loosely. For our study, we will look only at *overcoats, topcoats, and raincoats*. To bridge the consumer's concept of outerwear with the clothing industry's definition, we shall refer to this grouping of clothing as "tailored outerwear."

Most outerwear today is made outside of the United States. The outerwear that is still being manufactured in the United States is made of wool or poplin-type piece goods. These are typically American-manufactured materials. At least 75 percent of outerwear sold in the United States today is manufactured abroad, with the greatest share coming out of the Orient—Korea, China, Taiwan, Philippines, and India, to name just a few.

Tailored outerwear that is found in the clothing department includes overcoats and topcoats. Today the terms might be used interchangeably, but there is a definite difference between these garments. The knowledgeable fashion consultant uses the terms as originally intended. It is also important, when working with a customer, to be sure you know what *he* means when he uses either of the terms. Both are made somewhat like the suit coat, in the interlining, lining, and some seam construction that is used.

The *overcoat* is a heavyweight, long coat for cold winter weather. This garment is a necessity in northern climates or areas that have severe winter weather. The coat is oversized, to be worn over a suit coat. There are many different styles in both single- and double-breasted models. Of course, the double-breasted model will be even warmer than the single-breasted because of the extra layers on the front.

There are fewer overcoats sold today than in the past. They are expensive to make. Heavier and more expensive fabric is used. Add to that the increase in popularity of the all-weather coat, and it is clear why there has been a decrease in production of the overcoat.

The *topcoat* is a lighter-weight version of the overcoat. It is used in areas of milder winters. It also may be used in northern climates for crisp spring and fall evenings. Because lighter-weight fabrics are used in this coat, it may fit closer to the body and allow for finer detailing. It still has enough oversize to accommodate a suit coat underneath. Styling is similar to the overcoat, though fewer topcoat weights are made double-breasted.

In the past, if you used the term *rainwear*, it was understood that you were looking for a raincoat. Not so today. Rainwear can mean the standard raincoat as well as the all-weather coat. The *raincoat* is oversized like the topcoat and the overcoat. But it is much lighter weight and can be worn all year round. Some raincoats are made with special linings and interlinings that allow the garment to be washed in the home washing machine. Raincoats are treated with water repellant, which must be recoated after dry cleaning or washing.

As we have seen with so many other garments, the raincoat has its origins in Great Britain, where inclement weather made it a standard in every man's wardrobe. One of the major rainwear manufacturers in the United States is London Fog—the name is testimony to the necessity of the garment in England!

One of the most classic styles of raincoat is the *trench coat*, sometimes fondly referred to as the "spy coat." The coat gets its name from the coats the army officers wore in World War II. It is a very practical garment with belted waist and sleeves, which keep the wind and rain out. It has extra flaps on the front and back upper body to help keep the wearer dry, as well as oversized lapels, which close with a throat latch to afford extra protection from the elements (Figure 6–1).

The item of rainwear that has become the new favorite is the *all-weather coat*. This garment evolved from the raincoat. Its styling and construction may appear

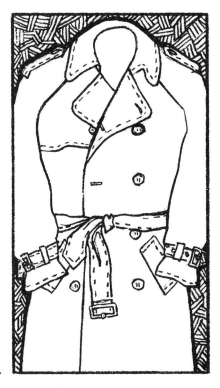

Figure 6–1. Trench coat.

to be just the same on the outside as a regular raincoat, or even a trench coat, but its inside construction is quite different. It is made to be worn all year like its "father," the traditional raincoat. But it can weather winter storms much more effectively because of its warm lining. The lining most often zips out. This lining may be wool, a highly napped synthetic fabric, or may be quilted for warmth. Sometimes it is designed with a double collar and includes a woolen collar buttoned to the inside of the neckhole. This is not only very functional in providing additional warmth, but it is also a decorative style feature. It can be removed in mild weather.

OUTERWEAR DESIGN FEATURES

Coat Fronts

The coat front may be designed as single-breasted or double-breasted. Of course, with its extra layering on the front, double-breasted offers greater warmth and protection. In outerwear, all buttons are made to be buttoned as opposed to suits or sportcoats, where the buttons may be a part of the style. Another common style closure is the *fly front*. The buttons are covered by a flap, and it produces a very clean look to the coat font. It is also functional in keeping the coat buttonholes draft free (Figure 6–2).

Figure 6–2. The fly front has a lengthwise flap that covers the buttons.

Shoulder and Armhold Treatments

The shoulder of the outerwear coat must be large enough to accommodate the shoulder of a suit coat. At the same time it must be comfortable and allow for adequate arm movement. Some armhole treatments have a more tailored look, like a suit coat. Others appear more relaxed and less formal. Often, it is this less formal armhole that allows for the greatest degree of arm and shoulder movement. This is an important feature when assisting a customer in purchase of the garment. The man who does not like the feel of a constricted, or close fitting, garment may prefer a raglan or split-raglan sleeve.

The three most common *armhole treatments* are the *set-in sleeve, the raglan sleeve, and the split-raglan sleeve.* The manner of sewing the sleeve to the body of the coat at the armhole may also be referred to as the *sleeve treatment* even though it relates to just the top of the sleeve.

The *set-in sleeve* is so called because the separate sleeve is sewn first. It forms a cylinder, which is then "set in" to the round armhole. It is the most difficult of the sleeve treatments to sew and if not done well can result in a puckered armhole. It has a tailored appearance and is constructed in the same manner as the suit coat sleeve. This sleeve is found often in topcoats and overcoats, and less in rainwear. Note that the front and the back look the same (Figure 6–3).

The *raglan sleeve* is constructed quite differently from the set-in sleeve. It is a much more comfortable armhole and allows for ease of movement. Note the similarity, for example, to the construction of a baseball-shirt armhole. This often has a seam running lengthwise down the top of the sleeve, though it is not necessary to its construction. The seams may be topstitched or not. It is found often in rainwear as well as overcoats. Note that the front and back look the same (Figure 6–4).

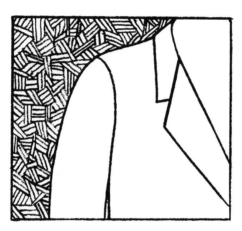

Figure 6–3. Set-in sleeve.

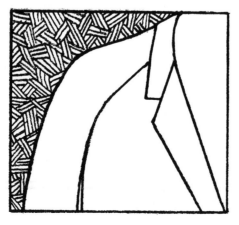

Figure 6–4. Raglan sleeve.

The *split-raglan sleeve* looks like a set-in sleeve on the front and a raglan sleeve on the back. Because of this it appears to be tailored like the set-in sleeve from the front view, but it has the comfort feature of the raglan on the back. This style sleeve has a seam running lengthwise down the top of the sleeve. The seams may be topstitched or not. It is found in all types of outerwear (Figure 6–5).

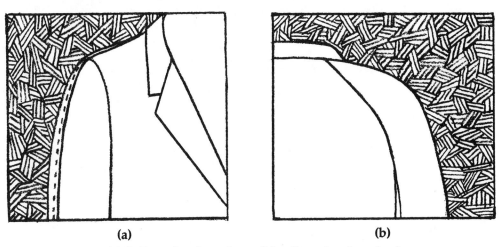

(a)   **(b)**

Figure 6–5. (a) Split raglan from front; (b) split raglan from back.

Pocket Treatments

Of course, the only limit to pocket design is the imagination. There are some standard styles, however, which are common enough to be expected in traditional men's outerwear.

The *welt* pocket is very common. Its construction is very similar to the breast welt on the suit coat, though it is larger and usually positioned on an angle for easy access. Sometimes the manufacturer may put an additional slash on the inside opening of the pocket. This allows the man to put his hand all the way through the coat into his pant pocket without unbuttoning his coat. It is a feature that is very practical for men in cold weather.

Many tailored overcoats and topcoats have a *breast welt*. It is virtually the same construction as on a suit coat (Figure 6–6).

The *patch* pocket is also quite common and may be topped by a flap. Its construction is basically the same as on a sportcoat front.

Figure 6–6. Breast welt with lower welt pocket.

The *besom* pocket may be used in outerwear also. It is larger than the besom on a suit coat. The besom may be positioned on a slant, or it may be horizontal on the coat front.

A variation of the besom is the besom with flap. It is usually positioned horizontally on the coat front. The besom may have a double welt so that the flap may be tucked into the pocket; when this is done, it appears like the treatment shown in Figure 6–7.

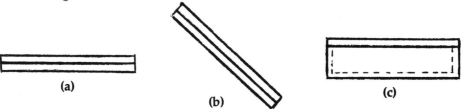

(a)

(b)

(c)

Figure 6–7. (a) Straight besom; (b) angled besom for bottom pocket use; (c) straight besom with flap.

Miscellaneous Design Features

A designer may choose to add other design features to the coat. These are some of the more common choices.

Epaulets originated from the military. They look similar to officer's shoulder boards. The epaulet may button to the coat on the shoulder at the armhole or toward the neck. The button used to be functional in that it would hold the straps of guns, canteens, and so forth, on the man's shoulder. Today, the epaulet may be attached permanently to the coat without a functioning buttonhole, and it may be pointed toward the neck or toward the armhole (Figure 6–8).

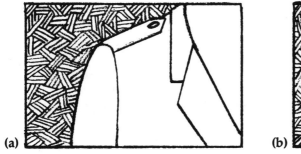

(a)

(b)

Figure 6–8. (a, b) Epaulets.

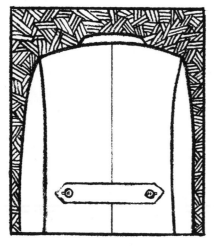

Figure 6–9. Belted back.

The *belted back* also comes from the military coat. It usually has a button at each end of the strap, though it can be sewn directly into the side seam (Figure 6–9).

Cuffed or belted sleeves add some style as well as function. Though the cuff was originally intended so that the sleeve could easily be made longer, it no longer serves that purpose. The extra weight of the cuff helps it stay down. The belt or strap can tighten the sleeve (Figure 6–10).

The coat may be fully lined or half-lined with a back yoke liner, as in suit or sportcoat. Other style features are the boutonniere, wind tab, and bi-swing back as seen in sportcoats.

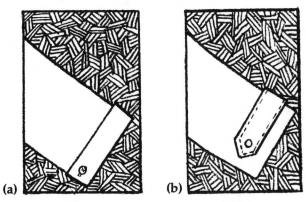

Figure 6–10. (a) Cuffed sleeve; (b) belted sleeve.

TRADITIONAL COAT STYLES

Many traditional coat styles have been translated to womenswear, as well as being classic men's topcoats and overcoats. These include the *British warmer, reefer, polo coat, chesterfield, and Balmacaan* (Figures 6–11 to 6–15).

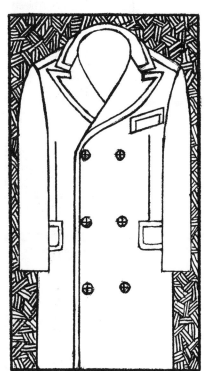

Figure 6–11. The British warmer is a very traditional coat. It can be made in an overcoat or topcoat weight. It is usually styled as a double-breasted model with set-in sleeves.

Figure 16–12   Figure 16–13

Figure 6–12. The reefer is a single-breasted version of the British warmer. It fits, however, closer to the body and has a slimmer silhouette. The reefer is the style most commonly thought of in relation to the term topcoat.

Figure 6–13. The polo coat looks similar to the British warmer. Historically it has been made of camel hair. Today it is most traditional in a camel color though it is available in a variety of colors. It is distinguished by a belted back, patch pockets, and a six-button (two to button) front.

SIZING OF OUTERWEAR

Outerwear is sold in the same sizes as suits and coats. Some consumers think that they need to purchase larger sizes in outerwear to accommodate streetwear worn underneath. On the contrary, outerwear is oversized to allow for the extra room needed to wear over streetwear.

PROPER TAILORED OUTERWEAR FIT

In addition to the factors on the suit coat, also watch for the following:

1. The coat should allow freedom of movement, even when worn over a suit or sportcoat.
2. The coat should extend well below the knee. A coat that is too short will make the man appear boxy and shorter.

Figure 16–14

Figure 16–15

Figure 6–14. The chesterfield coat is single-breasted. In its most traditional form, it is a solid-color gray with a black-velvet collar. This is a dressier coat and may be in topcoat or overcoat weight.

Figure 6–15. The Balmacaan is usually a heavier coat and therefore is thought of as an overcoat. It gets its name from an estate in Scotland and is sometimes called a "bal" for short. The bal coat is looser and fuller than the other styles with raglan sleeves and a rounder, standing collar.

3. The sleeves should be longer than the suitcoat and shirt sleeves.
4. The collar should stand higher in the back than the suit coat collar, and it should hug the neck.
5. If the coat has a very long center back vent for ease of walking, the customer will be most comfortable if that vent has a button and buttonhole to keep it draft free in cold weather.

RECOGNITION OF TAILORED OUTERWEAR QUALITY

In addition to all the same quality features of the suit or sportcoat watch for the following areas:

1. Quality lining fabric that will last for the length of the shell fabric.
2. Buttons that have been secured with extra-strength thread.
3. Buttonholes that are neatly sewn with strong thread and cleanly cut.

4. Replacement buttons sewn to the inside of the coat or provided with the garment.
5. Pockets that are reinforced at stress points.
6. Single rear vent that allows for leg movement but does not allow draft.

CASE STUDY

Russell Simpson lives in Virginia. He works as a salesman and travels the East Coast to work with his accounts. In September Russell decides to purchase a coat in preparation for winter. He has always liked the stylish features of the trench coat and feels his budget would allow for this purchase. The coat he buys will need to service him for work, some social situations, and for all types of inclement weather.

- As a salesperson in a retail store, what might you suggest to Russell?
- What fiber content would be the most appropriate for his coat choice?
- If Russell had a bigger budget for his wardrobe, and he wanted to have two coats, what would you suggest for styles and fabrics?

TERMS TO KNOW

Define or briefly explain the following:

Overcoat
All weather coat
Topcoat
Trench coat
Fly front
Set in sleeve
Raglan
Split raglan
Breast welt
Epaulets
Belted back
British warmer
Reefer
Polo coat
Chesterfield
Balmacaan

CHAPTER 7
FURNISHINGS

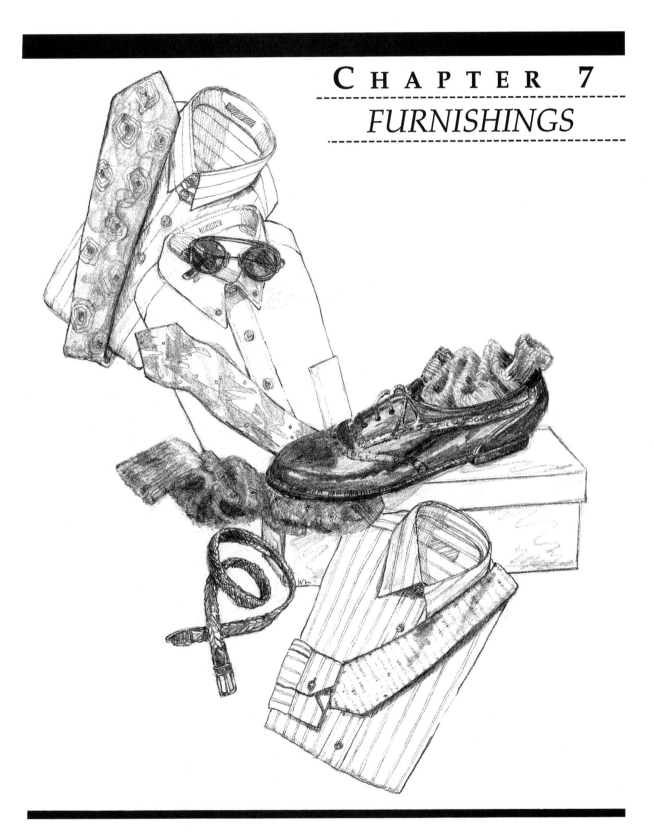

The furnishings department is where the "personality" items are found in menswear. The man's choice of suit or sportcoat and slacks are like words telling others who he is. But it's the furnishings that are the adjectives, defining him more clearly and letting us know more about him.

This is also the department where many men feel very unsure of themselves and are relieved to have a professional's assistance. There's a parallel here with the woman who feels uncomfortable about what kind of accessories to use. So she either uses none or stays on the safe side with an old standby.

We've investigated clothing, and now our customer has bought his suit. His next major concern will be the shirt—one that will work with the suit, looks good on him, and will be easy to care for.

Wearing of the shirt actually began as far back as A.D. 400. In its infancy, it was worn as an undergarment, providing protection from the rough, scratchy outer apparel. It certainly was not intended to be a decorative item, just serviceable and protective. It was much later that the shirt came to be looked on as a way of expressing the man's individuality. And its message became even clearer as it came to be a determinant of a man's position in society. The term "blue-collar worker" communicated that this man did not wear the white shirt preferred by an office worker, or management. He was one of the rank-and-file "workers." The length of the sleeve also denoted rank—the long sleeve communicating a person who worked at a desk. The manual laborer was more likely to wear a short sleeved shirt, which was practical for him; the long sleeve style could get in his way, become torn in equipment, and most certainly would become dirtier than the short-sleeve model.

Early shirts were made individually, by hand. Then came the industrial revolution. Shirt manufacturers began to mass produce the garment, and they simplified the make. For instance, at that time there was only one sleeve length for the long sleeve shirt—long! Men wore sleeve garters to keep the cuffs in place. White was the standard color, and collar sizes were 14, 15, or 16. So stocking was simple for the retailer. Shopping was easy for the consumer—there was no choice.

Today, because of the new fabrics offered, the many colorations available, and the sizing structure, men often find the row upon row of shirt displays confusing. Shirts take up major floor space in the furnishings department. The man may not buy five suits a year, but chances are good that he will either purchase or receive as a gift at least five shirts. When he enters this area of the store he is presented with many options.

Let's look at the dress shirt first, in our investigation of furnishings.

DRESS SHIRT VERSUS SPORT SHIRT

There are two major categories of shirts: dress shirts and sport shirts. The *dress shirt* is more clearly defined than the sport shirt: It has no more than one pocket and has no additional decorative details on it. Anything else decorative added to the body of the shirt like epaulets, flaps on the pockets, or trim items would put that garment in the category of *sport shirt*.

There are style variations that do apply to both categories, however. Collar styles, front closures, and plain pocket shapes may be interchangeable in both categories. For example, the button-down collar is used in the design of both dress shirts and sport shirts. The French cuff style, though, is relegated to the dress-shirt category.

There have been very few new style variations in shirts since the 1930s. In fact, the fashionable 1930s produced most of the stylish shirt models seen today. The Duke of Windsor was an important trendsetter of that time. He initiated styles that were very high fashion then and are still worn today.

One of the few new shirt style innovations can be attributed to Perry Ellis. Shirt styles produced by that company are easily recognized by one large forward pleat at the top of each sleeve where it is sewn in to the armhole at the shoulder. This has become a "signature" of that line and produces a fuller sleeve.

Today, for leisure, the man may wear jeans or casual slacks with a sportcoat to the movies or dinner. There is a choice of either dress shirt or sport shirt in that situation. It is the blending of casual pant with more formal coat that offers the alternative. When it comes to traditional business situations, however, there are fewer options.

Collar Styles

The most critical aspect of any shirt is the style, make, and fit of the collar. This is the part of the shirt that is seen the most, particularly on the dress shirt, because the rest of the shirt is so often covered with a coat.

The two most popular collar styles by far in the United States are the *straight point collar* and the *button-down collar*. Because of the crisp look of the straight point collar it looks appropriate with any cut of coat or suit. The button down, because of its soft roll, looks less formal and more appropriate with less dressy suits. The button down works well with British and American cuts, but coordinates poorly with sophisticated European garments. Here are the most common collar styles in men's shirtings (Figure 7–1).

Straight Point Collar. The straight point collar is dressier than the button-down collar. It uses *stays*, metal or plastic strips, inserted into the collar points to keep their shape and retain a crisp appearance. Traditionally the stays were removable for laundering purposes, but many manufacturers now produce collars with a high-quality collar interlining that incorporates a nonremovable stay. The *point spread*, or distance between the collar points, varies, and choice should be made based on the face shape of the man. The man who has a round or square-shaped face will look best in the more slimming straight point with a narrow point spread. The oval face shape may choose any point spread, perhaps with a preference for the medium spread.

English Spread Collar. The English spread collar goes a step beyond the straight point collar in terms of a wider point spread. It looks best on the man who has an oval or narrow face. This collar style is very common on British shirts, or styles of British influence. This style was made popular in the 1930s by the Duke of Kent, the brother of the Duke of Windsor. It is available more readily at retail than the Windsor collar.

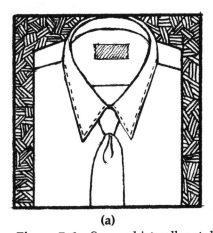 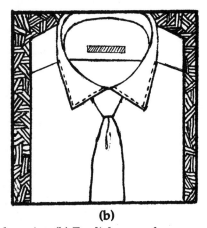

(a)   (b)

Figure 7–1. Seven shirt-collar styles (a) straight point; (b) English spread.

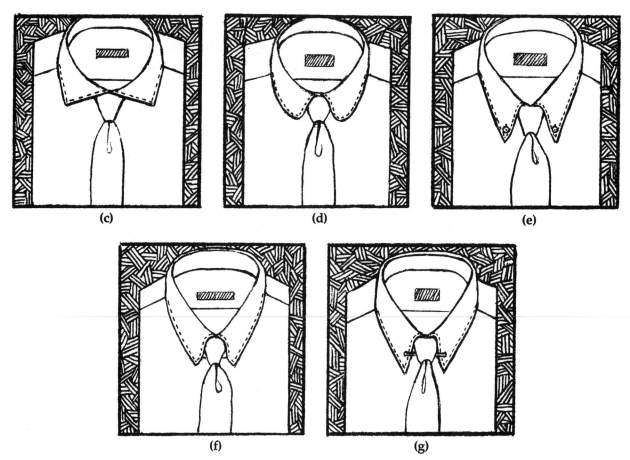

Figure 7–1 (*continued*) (c) Windsor; (d) rounded; (e) button down; (f) tab; (g) pinned.

Windsor Collar. The Windsor collar was brought into vogue by the Duke of Windsor in the 1930s. It was popularized to accommodate the large Windsor knot. It is a very stylish collar and tends to be in favor at some times and out at others. It is very fashionable when British styles are popular. Because of the wide point spread in this style, it looks best on the man with an oval to narrow face shape.

Rounded Collar. This style originated in England and was made popular by the students at the Eton school. It is associated with the Ivy League look and looks best coordinated with traditional-styled suit. The man with the full or round face will only accentuate that shape by wearing this collar style. This style is effective for the man who has a long, narrow face shape. It may also be worn pinned, which gives it a dressier look. Many round collars are sold with eyelet holes for use with collar pins.

Button-Down Collar. The history of this collar has an impact on its interpretation in daily dress. Polo players in England put buttons on their collars to keep them from flapping as they rode horseback. Therefore, it is associated with less formal attire than the preceding collars. It does not use stays and produces a soft roll over the tie. The style was introduced to the U.S. by Brooks Brothers and is associated with an Ivy League look. The button-down collar is a style that moves easily from business to casual wear. It looks less appropriate with European styling.

Tab Collar. This collar is held firmly in place by small fabric tabs on the underneath side of the collar. It keeps the tie neatly in place and serves much the same purpose as a pin on a pinned collar. This style was made popular by the Duke of Windsor in the 1930s and was very popular in the 1950s. The tab collar that hugs the neck serves to emphasize and "show off" the tie, in much the same way as the pinned collar does. The man with an oval or narrow face may wear this effectively. The man with a full or round face, however, may appear pinched in this tight, fitted look. Some men find this collar style uncomfortable because of its close fit.

Pinned Collar.   This is actually a variation of the straight point collar. The pin on a pinned collar may be purchased separately, and be clamped on any straight point or rounded collar that the point spread allows. It gives the appearance of a pin, yet does not pierce the cloth. The true pinned collar has a small eyelet hole in each collar point. A real pin with decorative ends (usually balls or knots) goes through the holes and screws together. This keeps the collar points in place and holds the tie firmly. The look was first made popular in the 1920s and the accessory may also be referred to as a *collar bar*. This is a very stylish look and thought of as a dressier collar. It can be worn with any cut of coat—British, American, or European.

Collar Lengths

The shape and length of the collar points change with the fashion of the day. The size of the collar should always be in proportion to the size of the lapels and the width tie the man is wearing (refer to chapter 10 on proportion). There is some variation available at retail, however, at any one time.

In general, the man should wear a collar size and shape that complements his own size. In other words, a very large, tall man will look awkward in a very small collar with short points. Conversely, a man of slight stature and small face will look overwhelmed by a large collar and long points.

Proportion and balance are the keys here, and the man does have some choice at retail. He may also opt to have his shirts custom-made. He can then carefully choose the collar style and size desired. Today, the cost of custom shirts has dropped tremendously, and the shirt may be custom-made to his specific measurements or made to order using the manufacturer's stock patterns, but with the customer's choice of fabric and collar styles.

Sleeves: The Long and the Short of It

The *long-sleeve* model shirt is the only appropriate style to be worn for business. It is much more formal than the short-sleeve shirt, and is the only appropriate business choice with suits and sportcoats. Even in climates that are very warm in the summer, the long-sleeve shirt is the correct choice. In a more informal setting, a long-sleeve shirt with the sleeves rolled up still looks more businesslike than the short sleeve shirt.

The *short sleeve* is seen often in sport shirts. Though manufactured in dress shirt styling, it is best avoided for formal business situations.

Long-Sleeve Cuff Treatments

There are two types of sleeve cuffs: the *French cuff* and the *barrel cuff*. The barrel cuff is by far the most common of the two, and the French cuff is by far the dressier and more elegant of the two (Figure 7–2).

Barrel cuff.   This cuff style may be offered in a one- or two-button model. The one-button model is most often offered on shirts of exact sleeve length, for example a 32-inch sleeve. The two-button cuff is often found when a split size is manufactured, for example, for sleeve length sizes of 32 inches or 33 inches. This allows the man to adjust the cuff to fit and stay in place regardless of his actual

 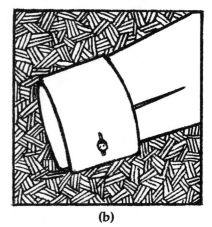

(a)   (b)

Figure 7–2. Two cuff treatments (a) barrel cuff; (b) French cuff.

sleeve length. Of the two, the higher-quality shirts use the exact sleeve length and therefore have a one-button closure.

French cuff. This is a very elegant and more formal cuff treatment. It is a very wide cuff that folds back over itself. There are four buttonholes in the cuff. When the cuff is folded and the holes aligned, decorative cufflinks are used as the closure mechanism. Many men use their cufflinks as a manner of self-expression, and they can become a signature look for the elegant dresser. Because it uses more fabric, it is more expensive to manufacture. Far fewer French cuff shirts are made today than in the past, and the man can also expect to pay more for them. The British refer to this style as "double cuffs." The style is more common in English-, French-, and Italian-made shirtings. Because the sleeve is not a style to be worn rolled up, it is usually associated with upper management and communicates an air of sophistication.

The sleeve fullness that is sewn into the cuff presents a challenge to the designer. The designer may opt to narrow the sleeve at the cuff as much as possible to sew the sleeve into the cuff without any fullness. This reduces fabric and manufacturing costs so less fullness is found on less expensive garments.

On better shirts, the designer does not skimp on fabric at the cuff. How is this extra fullness handled then? The designer may gather the fullness evenly all around the cuff, often found in English shirts, or the fullness may be flat pleated into the cuff (see Figure 7–2), more often associated with American and French shirts (Figure 7–3). Either way, this is often an indicator of the quality level of shirtings.

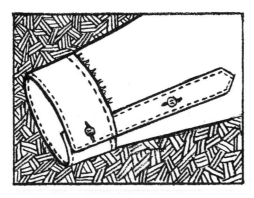

Figure 7–3. Fully gathered sleeve fullness into barrel cuff.

Shirt-Sleeve Vents

The opening associated with the cuff is the *sleeve vent*. The vent treatment may be manufactured several ways and is often an indication of the quality of the garment. The less construction in this area, usually the less expensive is the garment.

The better shirtings use a *sleeve placket*. This is a separate piece of fabric sewn at the opening edge. It reinforces the sleeve opening and often has a button hole on it. The longer the placket, the more the need for a button and hole. Because there is greater cost in that application, less expensive shirts may apply a placket, but make it shorter and thereby avoid putting a buttonhole on it.

The old English term for this placket is *gauntlet*. This term will be used by people specializing in English merchandise or by those who have been in the menswear business for a long time. Today it may sound rather stuffy and is a term understood by few. See Figure 7–3 for an example of a buttoned gauntlet.

Opening Edges: Shirt Closures

The opening edge of the shirt may be made in two ways. The edges may be folded under in a *plain front* edge, or a *front placket* may be used. The making of a placket uses more fabric and is a more complicated manufacturing process. Fine shirts of both styles may be found at retail, however. One benefit of the placket is it tends to reinforce the buttonholes more than the plain front edge (Figure 7–4).

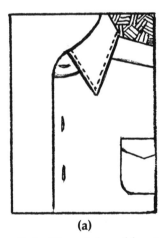
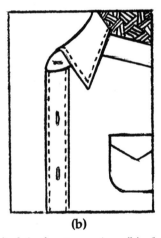

| (a) | (b) |

Figure 7–4. Two styles of front openings (a) plain front opening; (b) placket front opening.

Shirt Back Styling

The style of the shirt on the back is greatly dependent on the cut of the shirt and whether it is to fit close to the body or not. The most traditional full-cut styling may have a *center back box pleat* at the horizontal seam of the *yoke*. This produces additional fullness and is seen often in the very traditional button-down collar, Ivy League look. Along with the pleat may be a small loop. This was originally designed for hanging up the shirt and is called a *locker loop*. Today it is a purely decorative touch.

The better-made shirts may use a *split yoke*, which has a seam down the center. This allows for more shaping in the back and shoulder area and consequently better fit.

The designer may opt to make the pleat an *inverted box pleat*, but the amount of fullness is just the same. Sometimes a small pleat is positioned on the shirt back at each end of the yoke. These pleats also provide some additional fullness for forward arm movement through the shoulder blades.

The *yoke with plain back* is more commonly found in shirts that fit close to the body. There is no pleat at the center of the back, which reduces the amount of fullness. In addition, if the styling is fitted, you will find darts on each side of the center back seam.

In fact, if the man purchases a shirt that has a plain back, the shirt may have darts added easily. This will produce a closer fit. This cannot be done, however, on a shirt that has a center pleat (Figure 7–5).

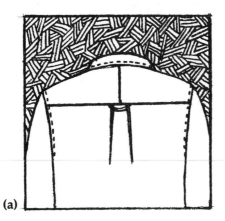

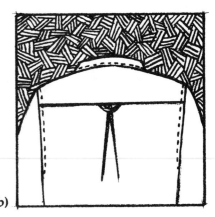

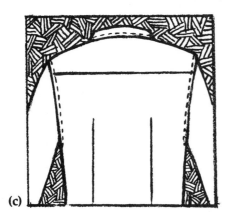

Figure 7–5. Three shirt backs: (a) split yoke with locker loop; (b) yoke with inverted pleat and locker loop; (c) yoke with darted back.

Shirt Colors

The most common solid color sold at retail is still white. It is always correct in any circumstance. It is also the preferred choice for evening wear, as it lights up the face and provides pleasant contrast for any suit or tie. A crisp, white shirt is a real asset to sending a serious, more formal business message.

The next color most preferred by men is blue. This color is friendly, sincere, and flattering to many. In the button-down style it takes on a casual air and translates into sportswear very easily. Blue is less formal than white in a business shirt.

Pink and lavender are more sophisticated colorations. Someone with a good eye for color can create very subtle coordination here with suits and ties. Many women respond to these shades on men; however, there are men who intensely dislike pink and lavender shirts on other men. In the most conservative professions, the man should take care and observe carefully those around him and determine the accepted shirt colors in his field.

Yellow and ecru are other solid color shades available at retail. These colors are not as easily worn by all men. Those with golden skin or sandy-reddish hair will wear these colors best. There is less formality in the yellow family than in blue or white. It coordinates well with brown, and red-brown shades. Ecru, or shades of off-white, can offer some of the contrast of white, yet be just a little friendlier.

In patterned shirts, the stripes have favor in the business arena. The narrower the stripe, the greater formality in the shirt. When the man wears a stripe that has a very wide-colored band, it draws attention to this garment and can easily clash if a fancy is chosen in tie or suit. Great care must be taken here to avoid having one's businesswear "scream" at others! This wide stripe is not unusual to find in some British-make shirtings, especially those with white collars and double cuffs.

Tone-on-tone coloration means that the shirt is one solid color with a pattern, often a stripe, in the very same color in the fabric. This is frequently seen in "white-on-white" shirts. This fabric styling is seen at all price-point levels from the most expensive to the least expensive. It gains favor at certain times and fades out at others. It is to be worn as a solid color, and can be coordinated with fancy ties and suits.

Checks and plaids usually remain in the sportswear arena and are less acceptable in formal business situations.

Shirt Fabrics

The most favored of all shirtings is the *broadcloth* fabric. It is a flat weave with a smooth finish and is found most often in the straight-point collar style. The second most common fabric is the *oxford cloth*, which is frequently associated with the button-down collar style. A variation of oxford cloth is the *pinpoint oxford*, which is made with a finer yarn and has a smoother finish. This fabric is made in both collar styles.

Fabrics may be 100 percent cotton or blends of cotton and polyester. The benefit of the all-cotton shirt is its absorbency, smooth hand, and coolness in the warm weather. The man who is warm natured will find this the most comfortable fiber content. It will wrinkle easily, however, and only looks best when it is professionally laundered and pressed. Some of the very best shirtings are made of Egyptian cotton, Pima cotton, and Sea Island (Georgia) cotton—all of which are long staple cotton yarns that produce a very soft, silky, smooth hand and feel luxurious to the touch. Their elegance is also reflected in the price of shirts of these fabrics!

When polyester is included in the fiber makeup, it helps the shirt to shed wrinkles more readily. The higher the percentage of polyester, the more wrinkle resistant the shirt will be. Conversely, the inclusion of this man-made fiber will reduce the life of the shirt and make it a little warmer to wear. Do not mistake this shirt to be wrinkle free after home laundering. Most of these shirts will be aided in appearance greatly by a touch-up by iron.

SHIRT SIZING AND THE MAN'S BUILD

Men's shirts are sized by two measurements: neck and sleeve length. The most common neck sizes are in the 15-inch to 16-inch range. The standard scale most stores carry runs 14 1/2" to 17 1/2", offered in 1/2-inch increments.

The standard sleeve length scale runs from 32" to 36". So a long-sleeve shirt may be sized 15 1/2" × 32", for example. The neck size is always first, followed by the sleeve length.

Some manufacturers will offer a *split-sized sleeve* length. In this case, the ticket will read 15 1/2" × 32/33". This shirt can be worn by a man with either a

32-inch sleeve or 33-inch sleeve. The sleeve has two buttons on the cuff that will allow the man to tighten the cuff and keep the sleeve in place if it is a little too long. Manufacturers who produce shirts sized like this offer a benefit to the retailer. The retailer can stock fewer shirts and satisfy the needs of more consumers. It requires a lot more stock to offer exact sleeve lengths. Of course, the fit is not quite as precise. But if the man's sleeve length is actually 32 1/2", he has an advantage in this make. The better quality shirts are made in exact sleeve lengths to offer the best fit.

If there is any question in what size to buy, it is always better to get the neck or sleeve size larger than too small. A too-small neck size is miserably uncomfortable and a too-long sleeve can always be shortened.

Men who have shirt neck sizes larger or smaller than the standard scales will most easily be serviced at custom shirt makers. The cost of custom shirts has dropped appreciably, and some shops offer them at rates close to ready to wear.

Short-sleeve dress shirts are sized by neck measurement only.

Shirts that are to be worn for sport may initially appear to be a dress shirt; however, styling as stated previously may be quite different. Of course, the fabric alone may make it a sport shirt. But a dead giveaway is its sizing. Many sport shirts are sized as small, medium, large, and extra large, and dress shirts are not. This is how the sizing relates to measurements for most manufacturers:

	Small (inches)	Medium (inches)	Large (inches)	Extra Large (inches)
Neck	13 1/2–14 1/2	15–15 1/2	16–16 1/2	17–17 1/2

Shirt Cuts

As in suits, there are several different cuts in men's shirts. The proper cut is determined by the physique of the man as well as his personal preferences for fit. There are three basic cuts: full cut, tapered, and fitted.

The *full-cut* shirt, sometimes referred to as *box cut, or regular cut*, has almost straight-cut sideseams. There may be a very slight suppression in the waist area. It is the most popular cut and is worn by all builds. Only the slimmest man may find it too full in the waist. This is considered to be the most traditional shirt cut.

The *tapered* shirt angles down from under the armhole to decrease fullness in the waistline. It has the look of the full cut without all the fullness. This shirt cut is favored by those who prefer a traditional European cut suit as well as by many trim men who wear traditional clothing.

The *fitted* shirt not only is cut angled like the tapered shirt, but it usually has two darts in the back. This makes it quite suppressed in the waist and can only be worn by the slimmest man. It also may be worn by those preferring European-cut apparel yet at the opposite extreme is often seen in Western wear clothing. This cut is not typically favored by the very conservative or the most traditional man.

Customer Size

Because there are only two measurements involved in purchase of ready-made shirts, size determination is relatively easy.

The neck band measurement is made by measuring the circumference of the neck just below the Adam's apple. Because collars are sized in 1/2-inch increments, you should always move up to the larger size if the actual body measurement is between sizes.

The sleeve measurement is a little trickier. The sleeve is measured from the *cervical point*, the dominant spinal column bone at the base of the neck, to the shoulder point at the top of the arm. With the arm bent at the elbow and perpendicular to the body, the tape measure is brought around the point of the elbow to the large wrist bone. Measuring with the arm bent allows for a comfortable sleeve length when working at a desk or when driving. Again, it is always better to go with the longer sleeve length if the measurement is between sizes.

Special-Make Shirts

Special-make shirts have become a booming business. A man may have shirts custom-made, or made to order or made to measure (refer to chapter 11). In any case, the consumer chooses his color and fabric from swatches. He also chooses his collar and cuff style. The options differ when it comes to fit. In the *made-to-order* shirt, the style options chosen are applied to stock body patterns offered by the manufacturer. The customer may choose from whatever fits are offered by that company, but he has achieved his individual look through color, fabric, collar, and cuff style. With the *made-to-measure* shirt, the customer's body measurements are taken: neck, sleeve, waist, and others depending on the manufacturer. Those measurements are then used to adjust stock patterns for better customer fit. This customer receives garments with a more finely tuned fit as well as an individualized look through color, fabric, and color and cuff style.

Most stores offering special make shirts require a three to four-shirt minimum order at any one time. An example of a store specializing in manufacture of such shirts is the Custom Shop. It has retail stores located in every major city nationally, and its size has allowed the average man to be able to purchase high-quality shirts at virtually the same prices as many of the mass manufactured shirts found in many fine specialty and department stores.

Shirts may also be *custom-made* through a tailor. This option may be needed for someone who has extremely unusual fit requirements, or for the man who desires a unique style, unavailable through more common channels. These garments would be then manufactured in the shop under the direct supervision of the tailor. The customer may prepare to pay quite a bit more for the tailor-made custom shirt, however, over the other options mentioned earlier.

SHIRT MERCHANDISING AND DISPLAY

Stores often devote a goodly amount of floor space to shirts. There are many sizes to carry; multiply that by the number of colors, collar styles, short versus long sleeves, and fancy patterns, and you see the display and merchandising dilemma posed to many retailers.

Most shirts are marked clearly with size and cut so that the customer may locate merchandise fairly easily. But the more stock there is, the more confused is the customer. It is also very easy for the customer to quickly choose the wrong shirt and get home to discover a 100 percent cotton, when he wanted permanent press; a tapered shirt, when he needed a box cut; or barrel cuffs, when he wanted a French-cuff model. Therefore, the customer is often aided greatly with feedback and technical assistance from the fashion professional.

PROPER SHIRT FIT

1. The well-fitting collar should allow for one finger to be inserted without stress on the neck. Anything looser than that is too loose!
2. The tops of the collar at the neckhole, center front, should meet, with no

gaping space over the top button. This will produce a clean finished look when the necktie is knotted correctly.

3. The body of the shirt should be loose enough to avoid any strain at the buttons on the opening edge. The placket edge should form a straight line vertically on the body.

4. The tails should be long enough to remain tucked in. The very tall or short man may need to purchase his shirts through a specialty store or through a custom shop.

5. The sleeve length should reach the wrist bone as the arm falls relaxed by the side. The sleeve vent should remain closed, possibly through the use of a buttoned placket if the opening is long.

RECOGNITION OF SHIRT QUALITY

1. The collar is a key quality point. It should be sewn with close, small stitches and form clean, uniform-size points. There should be an interlining with collar stays, unless evaluating a button-down style. The best collars have a fused top collar that will keep its shape through many launderings. Loose interlinings will more easily become misshapen. There should be adequate overlap of the collar in the center back so that the neckhole seam doesn't show when worn.

2. The placket or front edge should be reinforced with either an extra layer of shell fabric or an interlining. Buttons must be securely sewn, with no dangling threads. Buttonholes should be cut cleanly to avoid pulls when unbuttoning the shirt. Better shirts include extra buttons often sewn on to the shirt tail hem. The finest shirts have mother-of-pearl buttons, which can be identified by a mottled color on the underneath side.

3. An important quality area to check is the armhole. Better shirts are sewn with a reinforced armhole. A term seen both in packaging and on garment labels is *single-needle tailoring*. This refers to a method of manufacture that produces a higher-quality make. It is recognized by a single row of top-stitching about 1/2 inch to 5/8 inch away from the armhole seam. This seaming costs more to manufacture and results in a stronger, pucker-free armhole.

4. A generous-buttoning sleeve placket is a mark of the best traditional shirt. The less attention to detailing in this area will usually indicate skimping on construction costs.

5. Better shirts have a *shirt tail hem*. This is a deeply curved hemline that reduces bulk when tucked in. It allows enough fabric to avoid any pullout and a possible show-through problem. Less expensive shirts will be made with a shorter, straight-bottom hem. That construction is easier to make and uses less fabric. There is also a greater likelihood of the hemline bunching and leaving marks through the pant.

ACCESSORIES

There are trends in accessories, just as there are overall trends in men's and women's apparel. Sometimes accessories become more important in relation to the entire wardrobe. For example, as clothing becomes more and more expensive, men look closely at each suit purchase as a major investment. The man may decide that rather than buy a new suit for the next season, he will spruce up his present wardrobe by addition of new shirts, ties, suspenders, pocket squares, belts, and so on. These items can make his existing wardrobe appear fresh and renewed with far less expense. And during prolonged belt-tightening periods, accessories are promoted more, greater creativity is seen in offerings, and men are more receptive to being adventurous with these items. It is during these periods that one will see a plethora of exotic or highly expressive ties. As the tie boom diminishes, another accessory may take its place like snappy suspenders or a profusion of pocket squares. Women have practiced accessory updating of wardrobe for years, and the concept is coming into its own for men. This is evidenced by recent numbers of new accessory, furnishings, or specialty stores for the man. If the clothes the man wears are the words that speak about him, then the accessories are the adjectives that describe him more completely. Here we will investigate the more common elements of accessories for tailored clothing.

Ties

No other single item the man wears says so much so quickly as his tie. The most somber, dignified man may wear an outrageous Santa tie during the holidays. The world-famous trial lawyer may sport a brightly patterned red pair of suspenders under his stately Oxxford suit. At the end of the day, the business executive may change his serious blue-striped tie to a sophisticated European lavender floral design—he could add a patterned pocket square and thereby change his total appearance to the world.

The two most common styles of ties today for men are the *necktie* and the *bowtie*. The necktie is by far the tie of choice for most men. There is an added advantage of wearing a necktie as it creates a vertical line down the body, which tends to make the man look taller and slimmer.

The *bowtie* is worn more for formal occasions than for traditional business. Often, the man who wears bowties may be perceived as somewhat idiosyncratic. He may not be understood by others, and some may distrust him because of his insistence on being so very different. We often associate the bowtie with certain professions, like the dotty college professor, the patrician lawyer, the introverted librarian, and so on. Incorrect as the interpretation may be, perpetuation of the stereotype reinforces the public's perception of the idiosyncratic nature of the accessory. Repeated use of bowties may become a "signature" look of the wearer, a very personal style purposefully adopted by an individual. Care should be taken by the man of liberal use of bowties if neckties are the common style in his profession. In any case, the bowtie looks best when combined with the button-down collar. Of course, it is an essential in formal wear (see chapter 8).

An *ascot* is a form of neckwear that dresses up the man's daywear. Its roots are decidedly British, and the look may not be readily related to in the United States. The ascot is a large soft tie that has a double wrap knot; one end folds over and is often held in place with a stick pin on the front. The ends are then tucked inside the open shirt collar. Because the tie is not tight around the neck, it may slide out of place. It is advisable to lightly pin it at the center back of the collar to prevent it from "traveling." Use of the ascot produces a "dressy casual" look for day and is worn with sophisticated sportswear. The stereotype often promoted on television and in old movies is the ascot worn with the at-home smoking jacket in the early evening.

The *necktie* was originally worn by the men who rode atop horse drawn coaches. The lead coachman handled four horse reins, and the ties the coachmen wore were referred to as *four-in-hand* ties.[1] Though the term is still accurate today it is most often associated with the long, cylindrical knot that was tied then and is still used.

[1]John Duka, "A History in the Making," Fashion/Dallas, *Dallas Morning News*, October 19, 1983.

Neckties are most commonly available in two lengths: regular and long. Those found most readily at retail are the regulars. The man has some flexibility in creating the finished length of the tie by way of where he knots it. Long lengths are available for the very tall man and are most easily found in specialty stores for big and tall men, or the major department store. There are some short tie lengths manufactured, but this is a highly specialized market and will be found at stores that cater to the man 5 feet 5 inches and under. Unfortunately, this man may have to rely on the limited and less sophisticated selection available in the young men's or boy's department.

The fabric of the tie is cut on the bias, that allows it to conform easily to the shape of the neck. This bias cut results in the angled lines seen in striped ties. Neckties are made with an interlining, that gives it body and keeps it from stretching out of shape. If you look inside a tie, you will often be able to see this wool lining, that most commonly has bias stripe lines on it.

In the late 1960s there was one primary resource for tie interlining. An organization produced several weights of interlining and differentiated them by lines woven into the fabric. The heavier the fabric, the more lines were woven in. A leading men's magazine wrote an article at that time about tie quality and construction. In the article the writer mentioned that the most expensive and "best" ties were constructed with a heavy interlining that could be identified by five gold stripes if the consumer peeked under the tie lining. This led to some misunderstandings that remain today in relation to the purpose of the interlining stripes and their relation to the quality of ties in general.

To dispell the myth, "the number of stripes on the lining indicates the weight of the lining, not the quality of the tie."[2] If a tie manufacturer is producing a tie of a very heavy shell fabric, they would not want to use the heaviest interlining, or the knot the man regularly ties would be much larger than usual. Most companies adjust the interlining to the weight and hand of the shell fabric so that the resulting knots will be of uniform size and will not present problems for the man when he knots his tie. Therefore, a very expensive, heavyweight fabric may require a much lighter weight interlining with only one or two stripes, whereas a very lightweight fabric may need greater heft in the interlining to produce an acceptable knot.

It is critical that the tie be in proportion with both the shirt collar and the lapel width of the coat. The man should also use a knot that is appropriate for his face shape. Width of men's ties is measured across the bottom of the tie at the widest point. The width varies according to the proportions of the day. Ties in the early 1990s ranged from 3 ⅞ inches up to as wide as 4 ¼ inches. Leon Morrison of the specialty store Tie-Coon in Dallas, Texas, puts it this way, "Width is not so much a factor today as pattern and fabric. Though a 3 ⅞ inches tie may look slim to some, there is more concern that the shape of the tie be correct to produce a slim knot." The tie with a narrow throat at the top that tapers nicely is more likely to result in the slim knot proportionate to the style of the day. It is the size of the throat, the taper of the tie, and the type of interlining used that will affect the size of the knot, regardless of the type of knot made.

The tie is often a fragile piece, and care should be taken in keeping it clean and maintaining its shape. Because it is cut on the bias, it can easily become misshapen. After each use, the tie should be unknotted in reverse, rather than pulled apart. The less stretching it receives, the longer it will last. It should *never* remain knotted overnight like a noose. A tie that remains knotted for extended periods may become permanently misshapen because of the bias cut. Instead, it should be stored either as a rolled coil or hung on a tie rack.

Cleaning is a special problem. Because of the agitation and friction involved, ties do not fare too well in the dry-cleaning process. So the man should take special pains to avoid getting his ties spotted. Some men will wear a tie until it needs

[2]Robert Talbott Company, Carmel Valley, California.

to be cleaned, then throw it away and buy a new one to replace it. Of course, the amount spent on the tie will have a large part in determining the course taken! Today, there is a stain repellent product on the market made specifically for silk ties. It is sprayed on the tie before wear, and will repel soil and spots.

The ties that knot the best and produce the finest quality look are of 100 percent silk. Ties have a high markup and therefore are an important profit item for retailers. Prices vary widely. Silk ties may be found today in some discount stores for as low as $8. High end imported ties may soar in price to $80!

The man is better off avoiding polyester ties. They don't knot well, and the fabrics do not look as good. Because silk ties can be found costing as little as polyester, the man should not sacrifice a quality look for a few pennies saved.

Patterns, Colors, and the Tie's Message. The "safe" and most acceptable tie patterns are the ones worn by the mainstream. A *foulard* fabric has a small repeating pattern that is nonrepresentational. The stripes and the foulards are the most often worn and easily understood of all patterns. Put them in the standard red, white, and blue combinations, and you will have a tie that could be found in almost every man's closet.

Repp or regimental are the most traditional of all stripe styles. These have strong pure colors with very distinct stripe lines, no fading of colors one into the other. Historically the regimental stripes represented the regiment of a particular militia in England. So they have very traditional roots. The repp is actually a type of fabric that has a heavy rib and makes the stripe line appear even bolder. Repp is sometimes spelled "rep" and comes from the word "rib."

The *club* tie also has its roots in the traditions of England. It is sometimes referred to as a *school* tie. It historically was printed with a crest that represented affiliation with a particular school or men's club. Today, the club tie includes any repeated representational pattern like golf clubs, tennis rackets, and so on. As in the past, this type of tie gives clues to the owner's interests or affiliations.

Paisley ties have made a big comeback. They are a classic pattern of a curved tear-drop shape. The English design was an imitation of an Indian design. It was first produced in Paisley, England, and took the town's name. Paisleys may be made in very traditional patterns or combined with stripes as well as made larger and more nonobjective in form as in sophisticated European ties.

Dots and plaids take on different meanings depending on size and color. A white pin dot, which is the smallest size, can be very elegant and formal in a dark background. However, as the dot grows into a large polka dot, it sends different messages. Make that dot white on a red background, and one associates it with a clown. It can work for a man with a strong sense of humor, but real care must be taken here because of the association.

Plaids are traditional when of conservative size and color. Like the dot, when they become large and strong in color, they tend to scream out and make too much of a statement, overwhelming the suit and the wearer!

Knitted ties are associated more with sport and informal business attire than with formal suitings. Of course, they may be worn with solid-color shirts, but also work well with checks, tattersalls, and plaids. Particular care should be taken in storing woolen knits over the summer, as they are very attractive to moths! Knitted ties are friendly and relaxed—they are inappropriate for many professional situations.

Florals gained in popularity at the end of the 1980s and into the1990s. What had previously been thought of as a feminine pattern is being sported in the board room as well as in political circles from Boston, Massachusetts, to Bismarck, North Dakota. The man wearing these patterns must be very sure of himself as there is still a segment of the male population that looks askance at the idea of wearing such patterns.

Conversationals include patterns such as theme ties, art ties, and those of fashion-forward design. Theme ties were popularized in the early 1990s. The theme tie takes a concept, like beer cans or antique cars, and with bright color and almost comic style repeats the design overall. The designer Nicole Miller produced the first highly popular theme ties and was quickly "knocked off" by other manufacturers. Fashion-forward and art ties include many European, nonrepresentational designs. As with the floral patterns, more men are accepting the concept of self-expression through these colorful and visually textural patterns.

Necktie Knots. There are three basic necktie knots: *Windsor, half Windsor, and four in hand.* The Windsor knot is a large triangular knot that works well in a widespread collar like the Windsor collar. Of course, this knot also got its name from the Duke of Windsor. With the average-thickness tie, the Windsor knot is very large, too large for today's styles. If the tie is very lightweight and thin, however, this knot may work. Otherwise, the man may look like he has a grapefruit under his chin!

The half Windsor knot is also triangular but not as large as the full Windsor. It is made with one less knot wrap than the full Windsor. It is quite popular today and can be worn with all collar styles except perhaps those with a very close point spread. If the tie is thick, it may produce a knot too large for a pinned, or tab collar, unless the throat of the tie is narrow and the interlining is thin.

The four-in-hand knot is very popular today also. It is the most traditional of all knots. It gets its name from the necktie style worn by English coachmen. The carriages they drove were led by four horses. Because the drivers held the reins of four horses, this form of transportation was called "four in hand." The necktie styles and knots worn by these coachmen bear that same name. It produces a long, cylindrical knot that works well with many collar styles. If worn with a very widespread shirt collar, it may produce a trendy look, so the rest of the man's outfit should send the same message; otherwise he may look out of sync.

The well-knotted necktie has a slight dimple in the center at the bottom of the knot. This dimple makes it look a little dressier and "shows off" the tie a bit. Better not to have a dimple in the tie if it is off center—it will look haphazard!

With the necktie knotted correctly, the point at the bottom of the tie should come at least to the top of the pant waistband, preferably to the center of the belt buckle. Today, many men like to wear their ties even longer. This increases the illusion of height because of the extended vertical line. Better that the tie be a little too long than too short. A too short tie will make his mid section look bigger, and he will also look shorter.

Pocket Squares

Pocket squares add a touch of color and style to the coat front. Originally the pocket square was a handkerchief, which was put to functional use. It has evolved into a fashion statement. Though many men like the look of a pocket square, they may not feel at ease with the idea because they are unsure about coordination or how to wear it.

The most conservative man may choose a plain white cotton or linen pocket square folded square across the top—sometimes referred to as a *Truman fold*. This is reminiscent of the1940s and the 1950s, but has become popular again. It is actually a power look and says "no nonsense."

A man may take that same white linen, however, and fold it with the points up. This adds more of a fashion look to the coat. The crispness of the linen (cotton) and the stark contrast of the white says "sharp and authoritative, but with an air of elegance."

Once the man switches to silk and adds color, the message changes. The man is showing a greater interest in style and fashion. It is a look that is well appreciated by women but may be misunderstood in some professional circles. Some men will interpret this to mean the wearer is more interested in how he looks

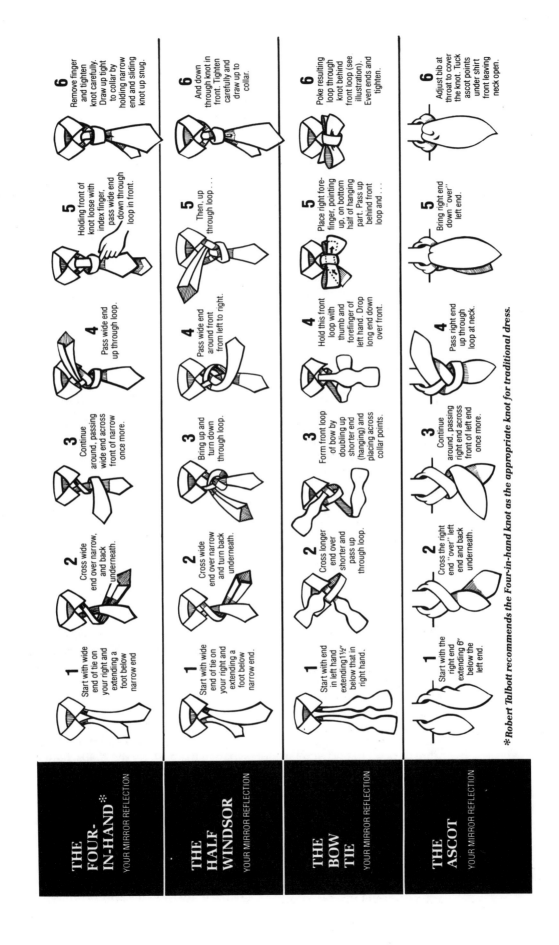

THE FOUR-IN-HAND*
YOUR MIRROR REFLECTION

1 Start with wide end of tie on your right and extending a foot below narrow end

2 Cross wide end over narrow, and back underneath.

3 Continue around, passing wide end across front of narrow end once more.

4 Pass wide end up through loop.

5 Holding front of knot loose with index finger, pass wide end down through loop in front.

6 Remove finger and tighten knot carefully. Draw up tight to collar by holding narrow end and sliding knot up snug.

THE HALF WINDSOR
YOUR MIRROR REFLECTION

1 Start with wide end of tie on your right and extending a foot below narrow end.

2 Cross wide end over narrow and turn back underneath.

3 Bring up and turn down through loop.

4 Pass wide end around front from left to right.

5 Then, up through loop . . . .

6 And down through knot in front. Tighten carefully and draw up to collar.

THE BOW TIE
YOUR MIRROR REFLECTION

1 Start with end in left hand extending 1½" below that in right hand.

2 Cross longer end over shorter and pass up through loop.

3 Form front loop of bow by doubling up shorter end (hanging) and placing across collar points.

4 Hold this front loop with thumb and forefinger of left hand. Drop long end down over front.

5 Place right forefinger, pointing up, on bottom half of hanging part. Pass up behind front loop and . . .

6 Poke resulting loop through knot behind front loop (see illustration). Even ends and tighten.

THE ASCOT
YOUR MIRROR REFLECTION

1 Start with the right end extending 6" below the left end.

2 Cross the right end "over" left end and back underneath.

3 Continue around, passing right end across front of left end once more.

4 Pass right end up through loop at neck.

5 Bring right end down "over" left end.

6 Adjust bib at throat to cover the knot. Tuck ascot points under shirt leaving neck open.

Robert Talbott recommends the Four-in-hand knot as the appropriate knot for traditional dress.

121

than in his work. Bankers, lawyers, and physicians should take care during their professional hours.

Because of the softness of the silken fabrics, the man may choose to wear the square with the points up, or with the points pushed in the pocket and soft fullness above the pocket opening. In any case, the pocket square should not drape out over the pocket—it looks foppish and is truly distracting. Once the square is set properly in the pocket, the wearer should not have to be fussing with it (Figure 7–6).

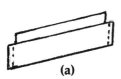 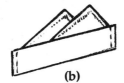  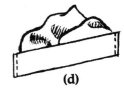

(a)   (b)   (c)   (d)

Figure 7–6. Four styles of pocket-square treatments: (a) Truman fold is very conservative and works best in a crisp white cotton or linen; (b) points up usually requires a crisp fabric, like linen, to keep the points from falling over; (c) soft fold has the points stuffed inside the pocket and works best with a soft silk; (d) combination fold has the square folded in half with the points up in the back and a soft fold in the front.

In terms of coordination, the pocket square should pick up at least one color from the man's tie. Of course, a solid-color pocket square will always be appropriate. But how about fancies? *Avoid at all costs* the tie and pocket square sets that are made out of the same fabric. They look too contrived and look like something a mother would buy her son for his first suit. Instead, it is much more elegant to use a fancy of another pattern. Whoa, you say—that clashes! Think of it instead as sophisticated blending of textures and colors. Remember, when the square is in the pocket you only get the *essence* of a pattern, and you don't *see* the whole pocket square. Paisleys and dots work with just about everything so long as there are some common colors in the square and the tie.

When assisting the man on pocket squares, put the square in the pocket of a coat. Then take a folded shirt, lay a knotted tie in the collar, and set this inside the coat. The man needs to see the total look and that the patterns do work together. It will not look as odd to him as seeing the pocket square laying on the counter next to the tie, with the patterns screaming at each other!

Socks

Socks were first worn as lightweight shoes by comic actors on the Greek and Roman stage. They ultimately evolved through fashion history to be worn by the general public to provide warmth and protection.[3]

Men's socks are also often referred to as *hosiery* by the knowledgeable retailer and consumer. From the 1930s to the 1950s there was great interest in patterned hose for men. Patterns included traditional argyles, birdseye, plaids, stripes, and so on. An unusual embroidered pattern called "clocking" entails a linear motif that runs up the side of the sock. *Clocks* are still worn today, though more difficult to find at retail stores than in the past. By the 1940s, patterned socks accounted for up to 60 percent of the hosiery market. With the advent of automated machinery came stretch socks of the "one-size-fits-all" ilk. This cut down appreciably on variation of style and pattern. Instead men wore somber solid colors, and the foot lost some of its style.

Today, stylish feet are making a comeback. Far more patterns are available, from the United States, Britain, France, and Italy. Men are rediscovering the fun of a shock of color and pattern peeking out from below a pant leg.

[3]Paula Dietz, "The Sock," *Esquire Magazine*, Autumn 1985.

There are different schools of thought as to the coordination of socks with clothing. One school says the sock should match and blend with the color at the pant hem. Another school says that the sock should match and blend with the shoe. However, the school of high style says that the hose should pick up a color that the man is wearing above the waist. That's where you see the unusual colors and patterns coordinated to work with the tie, shirt, or sportcoat color.

The first aspect of a sock to be concerned with typically is the length, and then the fiber content. Socks are generally available in three lengths: *ankle,* sometimes referred to as *regular* length, *midcalf,* and *over the calf length.* The only truly appropriate length for business is the over the calf length sock. It is distracting and unpleasant to see a shock of hairy skin protruding out from a crossed leg. Save the shorter socks for weekend or evening.

Many men are very particular about the fiber content of the sock. The most favored fiber for socks is cotton; it is cool and comfortable all year round. The next most favored fabric is the blend of cotton and man-made fiber. The 100 percent nylon sock may be too warm for many men to wear all year round. The 100 percent wool sock is preferred by some men, and the wool may be made with a fine enough yarn to be worn all year round. Because some people's feet sweat profusely, the all-cotton or all-wool sock may be preferred as they "wick" up the perspiration. Blends of fibers are also offered, and there is a special benefit in use of a natural and man-made fiber blend. The heel and toe reinforcement will last longer when a blend is used versus the all-natural fiber type.

The sophisticated male dresser pays attention to the quality of his hosiery. Some continental dressers will only wear hose of fine cotton lisle or silk. This is splendid when he is also wearing a beautifully tailored suit. The thicker the material of the sock is, the less elegant it looks. A thick, wooly sock, regardless of color, looks clumsy with a finely tailored suit. It would look odd with woolen slacks, and a casual sweater or a tweed sportcoat. Remember, total coordination is the key—from head to toe.

Belts

The belt a man chooses says a lot about him. Quality is a big factor here. Because the belt will last a very long time, it is worth investing in a good one that will speak well for him long after he bought it. Cheaper-quality belts will fray along the edges, crack, and show buckle lines much quicker than a good leather belt.

The best-quality business belts have simple buckles, in thin goldtone. The buckle should not make a huge fashion statement unto itself; it can look gaudy. Let the fine leather speak for itself. Some belts are designed so that the tail end of the belt slips under the buckle and is hidden under the belt. This is a real advantage for a man of fluctuating weight, as you don't see the tail end. But realize that they also often have very glitzy buckles! Avoid any buckles that have logos on them; they are not responded to well today.

Reptile, snake, eel skin, and alligator are elegant looks and can beautifully add style to an outfit. Of course real alligator is very expensive. Some snake and reptile belts are quite reasonably priced. Check to see if the skins are pieced around the belt; those will be less expensive than a one-piece skin. Realize, though, that reptile belts with rough scales will wear off easily. Eel skin is very thin and delicate and can scar easily. Do not expect belts like these to last as long as leather. Conversely, most men will not be wearing this type of belt as often, so that may not be a problem.

And what color to wear when? The man should match his leathers. In other words, if he is wearing a black shoe, he should choose a black belt; a brown shoe calls for a brown belt. He may substitute one of the skins mentioned earlier for a cowhide leather, but it must be in the same color family as the shoe.

Every man needs at least one good black and one good brown leather belt. Beyond that, he can choose other colors, based on shoes in his wardrobe, or choose other skins he likes.

Braces

Braces, more commonly known as suspenders in this country, originated for purely functional reasons—to hold up the pants! They are worn in place of a belt—*not* in addition to a belt. Over the years they also became a style feature of menswear and allowed the man great freedom of expression in color and pattern.

From a functional viewpoint, suspenders are more comfortable than belts. They allow the man to wear his pants a little looser and therefore to be more at ease in the waist. In addition, for the very large man, or the man with a belly, they keep the pant at the waistline. Otherwise, the pant can slip below the waist and accent the midsection.

For the man wearing pleated pants, the suspenders help to keep the pleat cleanly creased as the weight of the pant pulls at the brace attachment, which is normally close to the pleats.

The straps of most suspenders are 1 ¼ inches to 1 ½ inches wide. Better suspenders are made of silk or rayon, often in a repp or satin weave. Elastic suspenders are not on the same level of sophistication, though of late they have gained popularity.

The only acceptable suspender for the professional man is the type made with leather or woven fabric *paddles*. The leather strips at the end of each strap have the buttonholes at the ends and attach to buttons on the inside of the pants. Fabric paddles are created by looped fabric, resulting in a "hole" to accommodate the buttons. Clip-on suspenders are inappropriate except perhaps for the teenager for fun. Avoid paddles made of imitation leather; they not only look cheap, but they will crack and not last like leather will. Suspenders are adjustable in strap length. Each front strap sports a metal clamp, which allows adjustment of length (Figure 7–7).

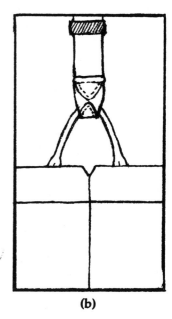

(a)   (b)

Figure 7–7. (a) Front of suspender with adjustable metal clamp and paddles buttoned inside of pant; (b) back of suspender showing elastic portion at bottom of "Y" and paddles buttoned inside pant.

Because this is usually a traditional look, many suspenders just do not lend themselves as well to European clothes. The exception here is with the trend setter's forward, oversized suit from Italy.

Shoes

A whole book could be, and has been, written just on the psychology of shoe styles and history associated with each style. We will make an overview here of most common business styles and how they should be coordinated. Realize that style variations are endless, left only to the imagination of the designer.

Of all items the man wears, there is no other item that produces such strong feelings and self-understanding as the shoe. After all, the man walks around in these all day having a huge impact on the way he moves and feels, as well as on his energy level.

What is of prime importance in determining shoe style is that it is appropriate to the style of the suit purchased as well as to the man's personality and build. Nothing looks more ridiculous as a big man in a dainty European slip-on or a man of slight stature wearing heavy gun boats of wing-tip style.

The Italians and the English make very high-quality shoes and often have very different messages. The typical *Italian shoe* has a thin sole, a low vamp (slip-on) and fine, light details. It works well with a more continental, sophisticated, sleek wardrobe.

The *English shoe* carries a heavier look, with a more pronounced welt around the shoe. The sole is also heavier. This look works well with American and British cuts, which balance better with the weight of this shoe style.

Of course, the only material to consider for shoe construction is real leather, not imitation leather. Real leathers breathe and adjust to foot shape. Man-made materials are hot because they don't allow the foot to breathe, and they will not mold to the foot. Anyone who has ever worn this type shoe has learned that the difficult way.

Good shoes are all leather. The shoe is lined with leather, and the heel and sole are also made of leather. Shoes must indicate on them the material content. Be sure to check for this! As in the segment on belts, other beautiful skins are available in shoes. But imagine if they are delicate in belts, what a beating shoes can take. One scrape on an eel skin shoe, and it's marred forever.

As in belts, every man needs at least one pair of black shoes and one pair of brown shoes. From there he can branch out to oxblood red, cordovan, and perhaps gray or blue for the extensive wardrobe.

The *plain oxford* is just exactly as its name pronounces—void of decoration. Therefore, it makes less of a statement and can be worn with many different styles. In a very fine leather, it can appear quite dressy.

The *cap-toe oxford* may be either made with a plain seam line or with circular cutouts at the seam. This is a basic in any well-dressed man's wardrobe and will take him almost anywhere. It will look better with suits than with sportcoat and slacks because of its formality.

The *wing-tip* shoe gets its name because of the winglike shape on the toe of the shoe. In the British make, it is very heavy and, to some, old-fashioned. It is considered stuffy looking in some circles, though the European models soften it a bit. There are many traditional dressers, however, who won't wear anything else (Figure 7–8).

Tie shoes have been traditionally the choice for the business professional. The message is no nonsense—a must for the most conservative arenas. There are changes in the wind, however. More men have enjoyed wearing slip-ons for informal business, with sportcoats and slacks. And now, the slip-on is creeping into coordination with the suit. Of course, the style of the slip-on is very important. It must be a fairly formal-style slip-on, not a loafer. And the quality of the shoe must

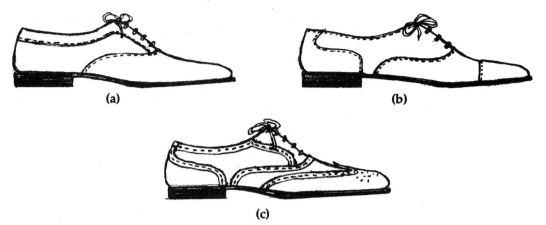

Figure 7–8. Tie shoe styles: (a) plain oxford; (b) cap-toe oxford; (c) wing-tip.

be impeccable to get away with it with suits. In many conservative professions among the "old guard," and in certain parts of the country, like Boston and Washington, the tie shoe is de rigueur, but this is changing.

The *dress slip-on* may be styled with roots in the cap-toe oxford, or it may have some wing-tip features. This styling lends itself more easily than some slip-ons to being worn with a suit.

The *tassel loafer* is somewhat akin to the golf shoe with its tassels. Therefore, it may well be too informal for many suits. The suit would have to be a more casual color or fabric to pull off wearing this style.

The *penny loafer* gets its name because the custom has been to insert a "lucky" penny in the slot on the vamp of the shoe. This style is much too casual for suits, though it may be worn with informal slacks and sportcoats.

The *monk strap* style usually has little decoration, other than its namesake strap across the vamp. For some men, this is a good cross between a tie shoe and a slip-on. Because the strap is adjustable, it can be tightened to stay on the foot with a narrow heel (Figure 7– 9).

Figure 7–9. Slip-on styles: (a) dress slip-on; (b) tassel loafer; (c) penny loafer; (d) monk strap.

Because good shoes are very expensive today, the man needs to take special care so they will last. To begin with, he should not wear the same pair of shoes two days in a row. The shoes retain moisture after wear and need to be allowed to dry out naturally. By far the best way to do this is to put *wooden* shoe trees in them and let them air dry. *Never* use plastic shoe trees; the plastic forces the moisture back into the shoe, whereas the wood helps to absorb it. Though shoe trees may initially seem expensive ($10 to $20 a pair), they pay for themselves many times over because they help the shoes last longer. The man should have as many sets of shoe trees as he has good leather shoes. In an emergency, if the man is caught in the rain, he can stuff newspapers in the shoes to get out much of the water, then later insert the shoe trees.

Shoes should be polished often. This lubricates the skin and keeps it supple, and avoids cracking. Besides being protective, the shoe looks better with a good shine on it!

As soon as the heel starts running down on the sides or in the back, the heels should be replaced. Continuing to wear shoes with bad heels will make the shoe wear unevenly and can throw the foot off balance. Shoes with worn-out heels are often perceived very negatively by others as an indication of not taking care of details. This perception may reflect on the way the man handles his business affairs.

CASE STUDY

Sarah Corberger was a new sales associate in the furnishings department. She understood quality of accessories and had an eye for being able to coordinate them well.

One of her first customers had brought a suit from home and wanted to update it with some new furnishings. Sarah noted the subtle colorations of the suit, and chose a selection of shirtings and coordinated some ties to go with it. She spread the shirts across the coat front and laid the ties alongside the coat. The shirts were pastel solids; the ties were foulards and stripes. Then she picked some colorful paisley pocket squares that tied together the shirt, tie, and suit colors. She laid down the pocket squares beside the ties.

Her customer, who had no feel for color or pattern coordination was overwhelmed. He only saw a mass of color and conflicting patterns, and he questioned her judgment. In consideration for her effort he bought one shirt and left the store.

Sarah observed another sales associate working with a customer. She noticed that the items were carefully coordinated for the customer. The shirt was positioned inside the coat front, a tie was knotted and slipped into the shirt collar, and the pocket square was inserted into the pocket. A complete look was shown. The large, colorful pattern of the pocket square was diluted when it was put in the pocket, and only the blending of tie and pocket square patterns was noticed.

The sales associate then proceeded to put together several different combinations in the same manner. The satisfied customer left with three shirts, four ties, and two pocket squares.

- Why did the second approach work better than Sarah's?
- Why was the first customer confused by the display?
- What type of customer would this sales approach work well with?
- Why will the second sales associate probably develop a strong repeat clientele?

TERMS TO KNOW

Define or briefly explain the following:

Furnishings	Point spread
Dress shirt	Stays
Sport shirt	Windsor collar

Collar bar

Double cuff

Pinned collar

Gauntlet

Front placket

Locker loop

French cuff

Barrel cuff

Tone-on-tone

Broadcloth

Pinpoint oxford

Split size sleeve

Fitted cut

Regular cut

Tapered cut

Single needle tailoring

Cervical point

Shirt-tail hem

Ascot

Foulard

Regimental tie

Club tie

Conversational tie

Four in hand

Half windsor

Truman fold

Hosiery

Clocks

Braces

Paddles

Monk strap

Cap-toe oxford

Wing tip

Dress slip-on

CHAPTER 8
FORMAL WEAR

The average man today does not have the need or occasion for formal wear as in years past. Our society has become much more relaxed in terms of appropriate clothing for social or evening events. When very formal events are planned, however, the rules revert to tradition and are to be followed fairly strictly.

BLACK TIE VERSUS WHITE TIE

There are basically two types of formal attire in the U.S.: *black tie and white tie*. These two terms define two basic outfits. They are coupled under the retail classification of formal wear, though technically *semiformal* wear includes black tie and formal wear equates to white tie. There are areas where individuality can be shown, but the parameters in formal dress are not very wide. In the 1930s white-tie dress was favored by the sophisticated. Black tie has since become the style of choice for many events.

"The black and white color scheme was a mid-19th century development." It was for practical reasons that men moved away from the previously colorful formal wear. During this industrial age, the streets were thick with soot and colorful clothing was less than practical.[1]

Black Tie

An invitation to a event may state "black tie," "black tie optional," or "semiformal" on it. The invitation is indicating the degree of formality of dress. The term actually relates to menswear; however, women also take their cues from it. *Black tie optional* and *semiformal* are synonymous. In either case, the man may choose to wear a tuxedo, dinner jacket, or dinner suit. "Black tie" means that the tuxedo or dinner jacket is expected attire; the dinner suit would be deemed too informal.

Sometimes an invitation or a description of appropriate attire for an event may use "black and white," as in a black-and-white ball. The indication here is that all who attend, including women, should wear apparel that is black or white in color. The implication is that the men wear traditional black tuxedos and white shirts. Often the black-and-white theme is carried out in the decorations used for the evening.

In the past, only the wealthy would have occasion to own a tuxedo. Today they are much more common. Though not seen in every closet, business men have more events calling for black tie, and price ranges at retail are much more reasonable than in the past. Let's look at the elements of black-tie dressing (Figure 8 –1).

SEMIFORMAL TUXEDO: STYLING AND ACCESSORIES

Tuxedo Jacket

The tuxedo gets its name from its birthplace, Tuxedo Park, New York, where it was first worn by Griswold Lorillard in 1886.[2] Initially, the term *tuxedo* related solely to the black, or midnight navy, dinner jacket, but has come to represent the entire outfit. The tuxedo lapels may be notched, but peaked or shawl collars are dressier. The coat may also be single-breasted or double-breasted. The most elegant pocket is the besom variety. Tuxedos are available with besom and

---

[1]Greg Collins, "The Tuxedo Turns One Hundred," *Gentlemen's Quarterly*, September 1986.
　　[2]Ibid.

Figure 8–1. Semiformal dress—tuxedo.

flap, but have a less elegant look. And they may have a single or double vent, or have no vent. The single-breasted coat front may be a one- or a two-button model. There are variations in style of the coat, just as in day wear. However, it is usually made from a fine fabric such as all wool, with satin or grosgrain lapels.

Tuxedo Pants

The tuxedo pants are distinguished by a fabric strip running down the sideseams. This fabric originated with military uniforms to cover and reinforce the sideseams. It still can be seen in many uniforms, as those worn by cadets. This strip is made of the same fabric as the lapels.

Otherwise, pant styling may be somewhat similar to day wear. The man has a choice of a plain or pleated front. Pockets are usually on seam or quarter-top style. The tuxedo pant is beltless as it will usually be worn with a cummerbund. Also, tuxedo pants are to be hem finished, not cuffed. The historical significance of cuffs precludes them being worn for evening.

Black is the color of choice in a tuxedo. It is the most traditional and sophisticated. It will *always* be appropriate, and every man will look elegant in a black tuxedo. In the 1960s and 1970s other colors were popular, and some are still available. However, they are best served by those in entertainment and, by today's standards, look gaudy on most others. Because some wedding parties will use colored tuxedos, rental firms still carry them.

Tuxedo Shirts

Tuxedo shirts have some variation in styling. The wearer may opt for a wing collar or a straight-point collar. The wing collar is the dressier of the two, because it is a style not seen in day wear. If the man opts for the wing-collar style, the wing-collar tabs should be positioned to sit behind the bowtie, not in front of it. The front of the shirt is pleated—the width and number of pleats being optional. The pleats end above the waistband of the pants to avoid the shirt bowing out when the man sits down. French cuffs are traditional on a tuxedo shirt.

Again, in the 1960s and 1970s all manner of colors were available, and today you will still see many hues in shirtings. Regardless, the most elegant shirt is crisp white. This may seem boring, but black and white are the most refined and classic color choices for formal menswear.

Shirts are made with buttonholes on both front edges. This is because studs are used instead of buttons for closure. But for packaging purposes, manufacturers use a separate strip of buttons to keep the front closed. Once the shirt is purchased, the strip is removed, and when the shirt is worn the studs are used for closure.

Tuxedo Accessories

Studs and cufflinks are a very individualized part of the tuxedo. For example, the man may choose black onyx stones, or he may purchase black silk knots, or gold knots. There are many offerings in cufflinks and studs. As far as taste goes—large, flashy stones, or excessive amounts of gold are considered ostentatious and should be avoided. In any stud set, there are usually three studs. Studs may also be bought as part of a set with matching links.

A *cummerbund* is a pleated, wide sash belt that is adjustable and closes in the back. It is to be worn with the pleats pointed upward, some say to "catch crumbs," but originally was used to hold theater or opera tickets (Figure 8–2).

The waistband of the tuxedo pant should not be seen, and the cummerbund serves that purpose when the man is wearing a single-breasted coat. Or the man may wear a vest and omit the cummerbund.

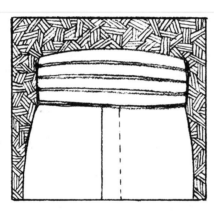

Figure 8–2. The cummerbund is the traditional waistband "belt" for formal wear.

Traditionally the cummerbund and bowtie were made of the same fabric as the lapel of the coat—black satin or grosgrain. In recent years, men have added their own flair by choosing color or fancy patterns in the cummerbund and tie. This is well accepted in many circles. Among the most traditional, though, you will still see the classic black being worn.

The *bowtie*, though perhaps deemed idiosyncratic for day wear, is de rigueur in formal wear. The most sophisticated dressers buy real bowties. It is considered an art to tie a bowtie well, and those men who frequent many formal events have learned to do so. Conversely, many men resort to the "prefab" variety of two sorts.

The *pretied* bowtie is by far the preferred of the two. It has the bow already tied and attached to an adjustable strap, which then clasps together in the back or on the side. The shortcoming of this style is that the clasp is quite evident when the man is wearing a wing collar shirt.

The *clip-on* variety is a real faux pas in most circles. It looks somewhat "plastic" in its perfection of bow and smacks of the little boy dressed by his mother for Sunday school.

Either case is identifiable because the real tied bow has the bow loop on the top on one side, and the free end on the top on the other side. It also has the charm and character associated with "hand made" that one doesn't get with the "prefab" style (Figure 8–3).

Figure 8–3. Pleated wing-collar shirt with bowtie.

Tuxedo Vest

The formal vest is different from the day vest. It typically has a shawl lapel and is cut very low in the front to show off the shirt front. Like the shirt, it uses studs instead of buttons for closure. Of course, the vest front is made in the same fabric as the coat and pant. The formal vest is backless, which makes it more comfortable than the traditional day-wear vest. It has a strap along the waist at the back, which is adjustable and ensures a close fit. Because the tuxedo coat is seldom removed, the full back as seen in a day vest is unnecessary.

Tuxedo Shoe: The Pump

The classic shoe of the tuxedo is a *pump*. It may also be called a *dress pump*. The most traditional style may resemble a little girl's flat with a grosgrain ribbon on the front. It is worn by the most sophisticated male dressers. Because it may appear feminine to some men, however, it is not worn as often as a dress oxford. If the man often dresses formally, he may purchase a patent leather oxford, solely for formal wear (Figure 8–4).

Figure 8–4. The pump is dressiest when offered in patent leather with a grosgrain bow.

Hosiery

Because this is a very refined look, the sock should also be of a finer material—not the woolly short sock please! If you are working with a very cosmopolitan man, he might like a silk or sheer lisle over the calf sock. This would work well with the dress pump. If the man is more conservative or mainstream, he may prefer a fine wool, over the calf sock with a black oxford shoe with a high shine.

Dinner Jacket

The other option the man has for black tie is the *dinner jacket*. This coat is most appropriately worn in summer and affords the man some variety in his formal wardrobe. The most classic dinner jacket is white or midnight navy, though pastels and some fancies are available. White is, of course, only worn for summer or resort. With the dinner jacket, the man wears a pair of plain, fine-wool slacks in a dark, formal color. He might choose a pair of navy or burgundy slacks with the white jacket. But the furnishings are the same as with the tuxedo.

Also, because the man is making a statement here, he may bring in some additional color via a tinted, pleated shirt. This must be done with real care. For example, an icy pink shirt could be striking with a white jacket and a navy pant. He could choose a cummerbund and tie that pick up both the navy and pink. It would be stunning but also could be a real mistake if everyone else is dressed in very conservative formal wear. The man must have a good feel for the group in attendance and the mood of the evening.

Though the dinner jacket is well accepted in some areas and for some functions, by far the most popular choice for black tie is the traditional tuxedo. The man who wears the dinner jacket will almost always be making a stronger fashion statement than the average man attending the function. When assisting a man, bear in mind his personality and whether he can pull off the look confidently.

What about the man who detests wearing a "monkey suit," the term often demeaningly used to indicate a tuxedo. Some men just dislike wearing one and may even avoid a function if it means they have to wear one. Many times the man will be acceptable in a dark suit, though he will not have the formality of those dressed in tuxedos. This is where it is important that the man have a very basic, fine-wool, solid-color suit (midnight navy or a dressy black fabric). Some men will keep a more formal *dinner suit* just for that purpose. He should wear a fresh, crisp white shirt in a straight-point collar with French cuffs. Either necktie or a bowtie will be acceptable.

Leathers should be excellent quality, black and as plain as possible. A good shoe style would be the plain oxford or cap-toe oxford. A more casual slip on or wing tip would be inappropriate. A cummerbund would be inappropriate with the suit. He can dress up this look with a crisp linen or soft silk pocket square and perhaps a flower on the lapel.

Formal White Tie: Styling and Accessories

If your invitation says "white tie" expect the height of formality. This level of formality is often referred to as *full dress* and is a much more formal look than black tie. Only the full-formal, white-tie outfit is appropriate in this situation. Today, white tie is worn for affairs of state and very formal balls. It is possible that

Figure 8–5. Formal white-tie dress.

the only time a man may ever wear white tie is if he is the groom in a very formal wedding.

The coat of the white-tie outfit has its origins in formal horseback riding coat with its sweeping *cutaway* style. The front curved edges were cut away, and the split tails allowed for ease of wear while on horseback. This "swallow-tailed" coat is often referred to as a *tailcoat*, and called *tails* for short (Figure 8–5).

The most traditional color of full dress apparel is black. The tailcoat is worn with black trousers and a white piqué vest. The backless vest, or *waistcoat*, has lapels and is cut low in the front to show off a stiff, white shirt bosom which usually sports a wing collar. The vest may be single- or double-breasted and the bottom of it should be covered by the coat. The white butterfly bowtie is typically piqué also. No cummerbund is worn because the vest covers the waistband. White gloves used to be obligatory with tails. If worn today they are made of kid or very fine cloth (Figure 8–6).

Figure 8–6. Top hat and gloves.

Most often we associate full dress with evening occasions. Formal dress, however, may also be worn in daytime, such as at weddings, and the elements take on a different look. For example, for very formal daytime wear the man may choose a striped or paisley ascot. His coat and vest may be gray instead of black, and he may wear black and gray striped pants. If he wears gloves, they also will be gray.

Furnishings for Formal Wear

Suspenders, otherwise known as braces, are sometimes worn with formal wear. The best formal braces are white or black silk, or a rayon, woven fabric. It goes without saying that clip-on braces are totally out of the question here. Braces are appropriately seen when combined with a cummerbund in relation to black-tie wear. The pocket square adds a bright touch to formal wear. The white linen pocket square, worn with points up, gives a crisp look to either the white-tie or black-tie outfit. Color may also be added for semiformal wear, perhaps picking up shades from the tie. A flower adds a festive air; known as a "boutonniere," it is to be positioned on the left lapel and may be used in conjunction with a pocket square for black-tie events.

Jewelry should be simple and tasteful. We have already addressed the need for studs and cuff links. Because they make a strong statement, wearing much more jewelry will be overkill. Men should stick with wedding ring, or one simple ring and a plain elegant watch. Avoid the digital, or sports variety as they are too large and clumsy looking for formal wear. A simple gold face with black skin band is by far more elegant. When it comes to jewelry, less is more!

OUTERWEAR FOR FORMAL OCCASIONS

The most appropriate style coat is the solid-color chesterfield. Coats that may be worn with suits for day wear are often too casual for the elegance of formal wear. The man may add a white silken scarf for additional warmth as well as style.

FORMAL WEAR RENTAL

Many men today opt for garment rental if their needs for formal wear are infrequent. From a practical viewpoint, this is a viable option. The man must be aware of several problems that can arise, however.

Because rental garments are in frequent use, you will not find the same quality level of maintenance as if the man owned his own suit. Fabrics are often blends of polyester, and construction is not the top level. Also, the man is relying on alterations to bring the suit fit up to standard. Seldom are alterations made as accurately as if they were being done on a purchased garment. The man may not know the pants are too short until he picks them up, and it may be too late to do anything about it then.

If the man rents a tuxedo two to three or more times a year, it may be more cost effective for him to buy his own, and get better quality and fit. If, however, he must rent, he should avoid renting the accessories. He can purchase relatively inexpensively a shirt, stud set, and cummerbund and tie. This way he doesn't scream "rented" when he walks into the function. And he will feel more of an individual because he's added his own personality to the rental items.

CASE STUDY

Fred Johnson received an invitation to a black-tie dinner. He knew that "black tie" indicated a tuxedo would be appropriate for the occasion. However, he neither owned one, nor had he rented one in the last 15 years.

With a recent management promotion, Fred knew that such invitations would be more frequent. He could expect two to three such events a year in his new position. His quandary was whether to rent a suit or to buy one. His choice was somewhat made for him. He was in the process of losing weight and felt that it would not be cost effective for him to invest in one at this time, then have it not fit him next year. So it was settled—he'd rent a tuxedo till his weight stabilized, and then he'd buy one.

- How could Fred make his rented tuxedo look more personal and individualistic?
- What are some of the garment choices Fred will need to make before he even enters the rental store?
- What fabric and style tuxedo will get the most mileage for Fred on an all-year-round basis?

TERMS TO KNOW

Define or briefly explain the following:

Black tie
White tie
Tuxedo
Studs
Cummerbund
Dress pump
Dinner jacket
Dinner suit
Cutaway
Full dress
Tailcoat
Waistcoat

CHAPTER 9
SPORTSWEAR

Though the emphasis in this book is on tailored apparel, we must look at sportswear as an important classification of menswear. Just as clothing has an impact on the styling of sportswear, sportswear certainly has a significant influence on the styling and merchandising of tailored apparel. And this impact can be felt more today than it could in the first half of the century.

Our society has become more informal on the whole than in the past. In the 1930s and 1940s the man's closet showed greater differentiation between sportswear and clothing than it does today. What he wore for business was quite different from what he might wear for leisure. Two factors have helped to bring the two classifications a little bit closer together. First, our society has become more relaxed in its attitudes. Not only does the man not have to keep his suit coat on while in the office, he may be able to wear sportcoat and slack without a tie, which is far more informal than in the past. Many offices now have a "casual" day, and employees may dress in a more relaxed manner than through the rest of the week.

The second factor is financial. Apparel is so expensive that the consumer is searching for ways to stretch usage of his purchases. If he can take a dress pant and wear it both to work and for dressy casual, social events, his money has gone much farther. He does not require such an extensive and specialized wardrobe. This is certainly a more sensible and financially practical approach.

So what we see happening are more garments which have multiple uses in the wardrobe. These are referred to as *crossover elements*. The more sophisticated dresser may come home from the office in the evening, change his shirt, remove his tie, and go out to a casual restaurant in the same sportcoat and pant he wore during the day. In 1991 this is how the noted American designer, Joseph Abboud, saw the trend: "More men are really using their clothing and taking advantage of them. With the old rules, a man buys a suit and wears it to business and then comes home and hangs it up. That's his uniform. Not now. The new way is to take that suit and wear it as sportswear with a sport shirt. What's even more chic is wearing a dress suit this way."[1] Likewise, the young clerk may be able to take the khaki pant he wears on the weekend, pair them with a navy blazer and knitted tie, and wear the outfit to work. The bridge department in many department stores even specializes in offering these crossover items.

During tight economic times business drops off in the clothing departments and picks up in sportswear and furnishings. Garments from the sportswear classification are typically less expensive than that of clothing. If the consumer can buy an item that crosses over, then he has made a truly cost-effective purchase.

There are many similarities between men's sportswear and womenswear. Retailers have learned much about merchandising menswear from observing womenswear successes. Walk into any men's sportswear department and you will see many of the same fixtures and display techniques as used in womenswear. Even more important, men's sportswear has traditionally taken its cues in styling from womenswear. Many of the "new" colors seen in womenswear one season will soon be interpreted in menswear. Style and proportion in menswear also follows womenswear; if broad shoulders and highly decorative pockets are "hot" in women's sportswear, the concepts will be interpreted in appropriate looks for men the next season. There is one more similarity that exists between these otherwise disparate areas: the speed with which styles change. Because sportswear takes many of its styling cues from womenswear, each season offers men's retailers new looks for the customer.

Sportswear is more recent on the menswear merchandising scene, and clothing and retailers have had the opportunity to watch and learn from womenswear retailers. Many of the merchandising techniques seen in men's sportswear are the same or very similar to womenswear. The concepts of coordinates and related

[1]Stan Gellers, "Designers Add New Rules to Dress Code Book," *Daily News Record*, July 15, 1991.

separates come directly from womenswear. Some sportswear manufacturers are now offering groupings, or collections, of separates designed to coordinate and be worn specifically with each other. These items are merchandised and displayed in the same manner as womenswear. Other manufacturers offer related separates in basic colors and fabrics. The consumer may opt to purchase several items from the same line, or he may buy a single item that will work with garments already in his wardrobe.

Many women do a large percentage of the purchasing of men's sportswear, and women like to see a wider range of colors on men. Increased sale of brighter sportswear has encouraged menswear manufacturers to continue to produce such items. Sportswear is also easier to buy for others because there are fewer fit concerns. For example, a loose jacket, oversized sweater, or fashionable, big top have far fewer fit requirements than a man's tailored sport jacket or dress pant. Even jogging shorts or drawstring pants may be sized as small, medium, large, or extra large, which facilitates purchase for others.

Before we investigate the sportswear of today, let's look back at its origins so we can better understand the history and progress of this apparel classification.

HISTORY OF SPORTSWEAR

Apparel has always and will always reflect the events of the period. We can almost read the economics and politics of an era by its garments in style, cut, and color. But this is even truer in sportswear than in clothing. Apparel worn in leisure time more accurately reflects the attitude of the wearer and his avocations than the dictated business dress code of the day.

By 1920 World War I had ended, and Prohibition was in force. The returning veterans had newfound freedom, as well as legal restrictions. They also had leisure time, and the opportunity for sports and relaxing activities. The young man of this period was truly ready for change. But he needed apparel appropriate for his leisure interests. Before the war, there was little differentiation between work and casual apparel. The man wore the same garments in his leisure hours as he did to work. But after the war, his traditional business apparel was inappropriate for dancing with flappers and driving the horseless carriage. Spectator sports were enjoyed in greater numbers than ever before. Tennis was being played by novices now, not just the pros. Golf became the sport of the day. And this sport required special apparel that afforded the wearer greater ease of movement. The highly starched, removable collars of business dress shirts were too rigid and uncomfortable for these veterans. It was a combination of the additional free time, release from the pressures of wartime, and the desire for a more relaxed and comfortable styling that led to the popularity of sportswear.

The influence of active sports became clear as the apparel used for these sports started to reach the masses and move into street wear. *Knickerbockers* (*knickers*, for short) were worn often for golf. These pants were also called *plus-fours* because their full legs allowed the fabric to fall 4 inches below the knee band. In 1920 the Prince of Wales, subsequently to become the Duke of Windsor, wore knickers, as he toured a South American cattle ranch. His apparel made headlines![2] Knickers became extremely popular. Once worn only for golf, their message of easy style was enjoyed in every day apparel. Suits of the day included the sack coat, vest, long trouser, and plus-fours. By the mid-1930s knickers had evolved into the casual pant, which was more comfortable. This new look was called "slacks," named after the slack time during which they were worn.

[2]Marcia Vanderlip, "The Duke Defined the Classics," *Dallas Morning News,* May 15, 1991, p. 9E.

It was in the 1930s that sportswear really gained a following by men in the United States. The Duke of Windsor was a most important figure in spreading the appeal. He was royalty by birth, but seen as more of a popular, celebrity personality around the world. His dashing life-style resulted in a great deal of press coverage. His interest in fashion and his personal style played a part in the spread of sportswear. International travel by the wealthy brought back sophisticated, casual fashions from the French Riviera and a countrified, gentry look from Great Britain. Newsreels of international topics that accompanied movies in local theaters aided in a greater acceptance of sportswear by the American public. At this time men began wearing a separate coat, which was called a "sportcoat" with their slacks to the office.[3]

The broadcast media mesmerized the American public in the 1940s. While World War II gripped the United States with fear, Hollywood offered relief and escape. California was seen as the new frontier, a free-wheeling, glamorous one with an easier life-style. The West Coast style influenced men across the country, and they began wearing more expressive colors and patterns. Hawaiian shirts and large plaids were worn by the more adventurous.

The postwar 1950s brought a renewed conservatism in businesswear, but a growing sense of regional sportswear style. The Northeast reveled in apparel

The Duke of Windsor (*left*) and French professional golfer, Aubrey Boomer (*right*) at the St. Cloud golf course near Paris in 1938. Knickers, the classic golf wear of the day incorporated a jaunty style while allowing for ease of movement. UPI/Bettman.

[3] Alan Flusser, *Clothes and the Man* (New York: Villard Books, 1985), p. 144.

associated with British sport like croquet, rugby, and tennis. On the golf course and at the country clubs men could be seen wearing outspoken madras plaids and bright slacks. The Southwest played with the cowboy influence, seen in all manner of western styled pants and shirts with scalloped yokes, arrowhead designs, and snap closures. The West Coast further defined its look by becoming identified with pastels and softer fabrics. And in Greenwich Village in New York the beatnik intellectuals rebelled against society by wearing all black pants, turtlenecks, and berets. Their bohemian apparel spoke of a serious outlook on life[4] and a rejection of society's mores.

The 1960s was a tumultuous period politically and economically. The Viet Nam War raised the consciousness of the country, and the American public became quite outspoken on the subject. Sportswear strongly spoke of the political position of the wearer. It was at this time that the T-shirt came so strongly into vogue. Here was a walking billboard that could visually and verbally speak the sentiments of the wearer. Hippies, with their love beads, ragged jeans, sandals, T-shirts, and psychedelic accessories spoke of their opposition to the war. Preppies were still in evidence. This traditional, Ivy League look was interpreted by some as involvement with other matters.

At the same time, the English music craze began. The Beatles, the Rolling Stones, Herman's Hermits, and so many other bands brought with them a strong interest in English style. There was often a costume appeal to this look with floppy, newsboy hats, hip-hugger pants, fringe, and bright colors. Many adopted the Neo-Edwardian style with narrow jackets reminiscent of their grandfather's style. The female model Twiggy and London's *Carnaby Street* became synonymous with the latest fashions. "On the backstreet of London in 1966 there were seventeen boutiques, of which no less than thirteen were for menswear." Designers and retailers of this area and period did not care about how Savile Row or British royalty felt about style. The Carnaby look was the rage representing youth and a "mod" street look.[5]

But no matter the political bent, the blue jean came into its own. Jeans had always been worn, but they really claimed their position as classic during this period. Toward the end of the 1960s it was worn, not only by the young man, but by his father as well.

The 1970s spawned all manner of sportswear style. The diversity of the period was perhaps best seen through the singing group, the Village People. Their song "Macho Man" reflected the same message as their garments. Each singer wore styles representing different careers and ethnic groups, such as construction worker, cowboy, Indian, policeman, and so on. Sportswear of the day varied from disco duds to designer jeans to English punk to active wear for the health enthusiast. There were two very important trends to come from this period. One was the popularity of designer garments, and the second was the birth of the fitness craze.

For the totally fashion conscious, one had to wear designer apparel. Logos were now a status symbol, and proudly displayed on garment chests and seats. Every manner of apparel from head to toe sported logos. Designers became household names, and brand awareness was at an all time high in sportswear. Men were now wearing designer jeans with sportcoats to restaurants in the evening, a major change from their informality with which they were worn in the 1950s and 1960s.

As part of what was perceived as a craze in the 1970s, the health "nut" jogged or exercised instead of going to the disco. This consumer group, which needed specialized apparel, grew slowly and steadily in importance at retail during this period.

[4] Alison Lurie, *The Language of Clothes* (New York: Vintage Books, 1983).

[5] Diana de Marly, *Fashion for Men, An Illustrated History* (London: B.T. Batsford Ltd., 1985) p. 132.

From the mid-1980s to the early 1990s a national conservatism brought sportswear back to more traditional styles. The preppie look was now called "updated traditional." It had the same classic roots, but with more style and sophistication. Active wear continued to grow, encompassing a much larger audience. Now it was not just the "real" athlete wanting the look of fitness. This active look garnered great appeal by those who appreciated the appearance of a fit, healthy lifestyle and the colorful, comfortable apparel that went along with it. Brightly colored jogging suits were being worn on weekends and evenings. Some of the dressier sportswear items were being worn to the office, such as more colorful sport shirts and updated slacks.

LEVELS OF FORMALITY OF SPORTSWEAR

There are basically three levels of sportswear in terms of degree of formality: active-leisure, casual, and dressy casual. Any piece of sportswear found at retail will fit into one of these categories. The *active-leisure* group is the most informal. It consists of apparel for sports participation, and very informal leisure times for home, the grocery store, or car maintenance. These items would be considered too casual for wear to most informal social events. The grouping of *casual* would include those items that would take the man to informal, social gatherings with friends, like a barbecue, golfing, Saturday shopping, and so on. And the last group is *dressy casual*. This is the level that many men have a difficult time relating to. This is also the level that is typically least in evidence in the man's wardrobe. And when he has a social engagement that calls for something from this grouping, he is often at a loss. It is the level of formality that bridges from casual to dress or business wear. Think of this as evening casual or dating clothes. It is a level above casual wear and may actually combine elements from the man's business wardrobe with more forward or more casual sportswear items. For example, the man may take his basic, navy blue blazer, combine it with a pair of dress slacks, and dress it up with a special sport shirt that he would not otherwise wear to the office. This concept gains in importance when evaluating the best wardrobe purchases to make based on the life-style of the customer (see chapter 12).

STYLE INFLUENCES OF SPORTSWEAR

Sportswear styles change much more dramatically and much more quickly than the classification of clothing. Therefore, we will not look at individual aspects of sportswear styles, rather at the sources for those styles. There are many sources of inspiration for the wide range of styles, fabrics, patterns, and cuts of apparel seen in sportswear departments. Styles may range from the basic 100 percent cotton, gray sweat suit to the tailored golf slacks and classic tennis sweater, all the way to the very avant-garde, Japanese separates. We may look at the differences in styling and fabrics, but also must consider the type of stores where these garments are sold, the differences in customers, actual uses of the garments, and origins of the styles. Much is to be considered, and one can see why sportswear is such a melting pot of creativity and practicality!

These sources of sportswear inspiration are a separate concept from the levels of formality already addressed. The following influences may be seen at any of the three sportswear levels. Much depends on the sophistication level of the designer, the fabric the design was interpreted in, and the quality of the construction. A sweat pant that has an active sports origin or influence may be found at all three levels. In its most basic form, the standard, heather gray, 100 percent cotton fleece sweat pant that is associated with very active sports would be categorized in the active-leisure group. If this same style were interpreted as a lined, workout pant in brightly colored nylon with decorative zippers it would be a part of the casual level. How would such a sweat style pant work into dressy casual, you might ask? Consider the gray cashmere, men's sweat pant designed by Donna Karan, which sold for $1,300 at Barneys! It was a very sophisticated rendering a man might wear to an avant garde, informal social event. All three garments have the same origin of style, yet they are interpreted at different formality levels. The primary approach to be taken here is to investigate the origins of the styles seen, so we might better recognize trends and ultimately identify the best possible choices for our customers. Here are 7 origins for sportswear style. There are actually endless sources of inspiration, but those listed are usually available at any one time in some form at retail.

Activewear often sports logos of the maker. Tim Davis/Photo Researchers.

Health, Fitness, and Professional Sports Influence

This category of active sportswear infers that the wearer is actually going to partake in a physical sport. Garments are designed for ease of movement, ease of care, and practicality, which can apply to any sport in general. Whatever purpose the item is purchased for, the design of the garment communicates to others that the wearer is an active person or wishes to be perceived as one! Certainly, the impact of fitness is dramatic in influencing the colors used, the fabrics, the body-conscious shapes, and the function of active wear.

Brighter colors are often used signifying high energy, but they also afford a measure of safety. The jogger, wearing bright yellow and red shorts, will more easily be seen by motorists. Design and construction elements take into consideration the movement of the body. For example, a tennis shirt may be designed with diamond-shaped gussets under the arms to allow for greater ease of movement. Elastic waistbands may be used to increase comfort for the runner. Seam construction is often double and triple reinforced to accommodate the strain put on the garment during activity. The garments must be easy care and made of hard-wearing fabrics. A workout suit that will take abuse in the form of perspiration, abrasion from movement, and frequent washings will need to be a fiber that can hold up to the wear and tear. Fibers that may be perceived to be of inferior quality in street wear are often quite practical when interpreted in active sportswear. Though the 100 percent cotton sweatsuit will be very absorbent, the suit with some percentage of nylon or polyester may well last longer. A fabric like a 100 percent nylon tricot knit washes well, retains color purity, dries quickly, is lightweight, and requires no ironing. What could be better for hard-playing active wear? In this sense, this level of sportswear must play first to practicality and then to style.

Popular with the customer of health and fitness apparel are the perforated, nylon mesh tops. Knitted fabrics that have been prewashed and have a worn look that says "I really have been working out hard" are appreciated by those who *have* worked out, as well as those who want to *look* as if they have. Workout apparel that is identified with athletic activities are preferred by many, like Everlast products, which are associated with boxing. Gold's Gym, haven of fitness for the serious athlete, is now emblazoned across the chest of many men. But the desired psychological association is often not reality. "Most of our retail customers are *not* guys who go to the gym and work out," says Joe Bozich, president, Gold's Gym Apparel.[6]

Manufacturers like Reebok, Nike, and Izod, who had previously produced a narrow range of items for the sportswear market, have now branched out considerably to gain a greater market share. Some of the active sportswear manufacturers, through contracts with high-profile sports figures, have their company names and logos seen in television competitions every weekend. These agreements, while highly lucrative for the sports figure, have resulted in a high degree of brand recognition by the public (see also chapter 3).

Professional sports is often a source of style in sportswear. Sometimes the sport is the theme, as in the casual pullover that has a generic theme with footballs, goal posts, and football players as the printed design on the back. The garment may be a team replica jersey or an item licensed by the major league for retail sale. All types of *professional sports licensing* agreements exist in sportswear. Major League Baseball Properties (MLBP), for example, handles all the licensing for major and minor league baseball teams. Top-name designers are even getting involved with this type of licensing. Alan Flusser and Nicole Miller, both well-known American designers, are now licensees of the MLBP[7]. This category has become so popular

[6]Robert Parola, "Sportswear Takes Cue From Sports," *Daily News Record*, September 18, 1991, p. 1.

[7]Jeff Black, "Stores See Extra Innings from Spring Baseball Apparel," *Daily News Record*, October 14, 1991.

that many urban malls now include retailers that specialize in offering local and national team sportswear.

This category has enjoyed the greatest growth of any area of sportswear, and has become more and more important at retail. Department stores have devoted far larger floor space to active wear than in past years. J C Penney now offers athletic apparel in its store-within-a-store concept called "Simply for Sports." In addition there has been an upsurge in specialty stores devoted to active wear and retailers marketing to participants of specific sports. *Sport specific manufacturers* produce apparel or accessories for particular active sports. We see specialty stores devoted just to sports shoes and offering shoes engineered for requirements of specific sports. Now that is the kind of retailer who is truly consumer specific! And retailers that in the past sold just sporting goods have included apparel in their mix. The customer has certainly considered style, as well as function, to be a part of his sports persona.

Classic Influences

The classic influence is derived from both the category of clothing and traditional pastimes. Upscale sports like golf, polo, tennis, and sailing are often sources for the styles seen here. The lines are usually simple and clean. Sometimes themes are seen in the styling, as in the sailboats associated with Nautica sportswear, or the polo player that is the logo of the classic Ralph Lauren designs. Colors may be bright or muted. Styles often hearken back to the refined details and proportions seen in garments of the 1930s and 1940s. Fabrics are more often wovens in natural fibers or blends. Active wear can bridge into this grouping as evidenced in apparel for golf.

Some sportswear manufacturers, like E. McGrath Golf, design their apparel to be worn both on and off the golf course. Pants with traditional multiple pleats, sophisticated tonal colorations, and fine, natural fiber fabrics offer a much dressier look than had previously been associated with the sport and allow the pants to be multifunctional. This concept certainly increases their value to the wearer. But golf is one of the very few sports that can make this transition. One cannot easily go out to dinner in tennis shorts, but a classically styled golf pant can!

In the past, a golfer had to find golf apparel in a pro shop, located near a golf course. However, today, sport-specific manufacturers like Sporthompson or Bobby Jones are now available in many department stores. Likewise, resources like Polo by Ralph Lauren and Izod are making inroads into the pro shop markets.[8] And other sportswear manufacturers, like Wilson, have started to sell to the *green grass shops* located in golf settings. It is an expanding marketplace, and manufacturers and designers are reaching out to gain greater market shares. At the same time the consumer of classic-influenced garments benefits by the ability to wear his apparel both in casual and in dressy casual levels.

The classic influence is often thought of as the "all-American" look, clean cut, fresh, and smacking of a wholesome life-style. Manufacturers who specialize in garments in this genre often associate themselves with endeavors that reinforce the image. Nautica is a high-quality line that sports sailing as a common theme in its designs. In 1991 it sponsored both the Soviet and American youth sailing teams in the World Youth Sailing Championships where the Nautica Cup was awarded. This was an opportunity to affiliate with their theme sport in an international goodwill gesture.

Some designers who are strongly associated with this influence also branch into other categories to broaden their offerings to retailers. Ralph Lauren's Polo line, so traditional in styling, has broadened to include some garments of the athletic influence, such as racing numbers on pullovers and gym shorts. But the look here is that of a retro-inspired, upper-crust athlete.

[8]Jeff Black, "There's War in the Golf," *Daily News Record*, July 22, 1991.

Sweaters as well as casual outerwear are also important in this grouping. We can see the influence of tradition in form of the V-neck cardigan tennis sweater with red and blue stripes on the neck and cable-knit body. British traditional styling may be seen in the Fair Isle and shetland wool sweaters. Styling in outerwear reflects the uncluttered lines so typical of this influence. One may find hats, shirts, pants, jackets, shoes, socks, belts, and all manner of accessories to outfit the man completely in a cohesive classic sport look.

Levi Strauss, the epitome of Americana, has brought the look to the masses through their Dockers line. And they have done this by completely outfitting the man from head to toe in all areas of sportswear. No one company or designer has managed to reach all economic levels of consumers, all age groups, internationally, as well as this organization. And their influence can be seen throughout this classification of apparel.

Even the *way* a man wears his sportswear can add emphasis to the message of his apparel. For the man preferring the clothes of classic influence, wearing a slightly oversized shirt, blouson at the waist and buttoned all the way to the top, signifies an awareness of current style and a confidence to carry it off.

Some designers and manufacturers that typically represent the very best of the classic American influence include Polo, Nautica, Tommy Hilfiger, Ruff Hewn, Perry Ellis America, and Levi Strauss. They offer clean, classic lines and add freshness through sophisticated, muted colors, or bright colors and theme concepts.

Military Influence

As we have seen in the category of clothing, military influence in detailing, color, and fabric has long been a source of inspiration to designers. Garments of military influence often bridge into the classic area, as in sport shirts with epaulets, sleeve straps, and flaps over patch pockets. But there are other military influences that do not send the same tailored message. Consider, for example, the camouflage wear which invariably becomes popular during times of war or political upheaval. Its roots are military, but from the rank and file, not the officers! So it has a more relaxed, informal look than the tailored variety. At the leisure level of sportswear we may see khaki jackets with military emblems on them. Nautical looks which derive from navy apparel also fall into this category. Casual horizontally-striped shirts with slash, "boat necks" are often associated with French sailors and when combined with white pants are very popular in summer. Some consumers want the real thing and may even frequent army-navy surplus stores for authenticity.

Garments often associated with a safari look fall in this group also. The styling of the bellowed pockets, strapping and belting on the coats, khaki color, and the oft-used bi-swing back hearken back to military roots.

Any item that has a sense of uniform to it probably has its roots in military styling. It is clear that there is a very strong correlation between clothing and military design as we have seen. And uniforms for many professions also have their roots in formal or practical military design. The head waiter's jacket in an upscale restaurant points back to the tailored uniforms and formal wear of the 1800s. Garments that are so tailored will fall into the higher level of dressy casual sportswear because of the fabric and the formality of the tailoring. More military-influenced options will be seen at the dressy casual level at retail. At the leisure and casual levels, military-inspired sportswear tends to fluctuate in popularity depending on national and world politics.

European Influence

In the past, most of the apparel from this category fell into the dressy casual level of sportswear. But with diffusion lines becoming so important, both American and European designers are making offerings that move down both in price point

The nautical style has strong ties with military influence. C. Rob Lang/FPG.

and in level of formality. Though European designers are certainly influenced by American style of sportswear, the Europeans have a certain style that truly originates in their own lands. France and Italy lead the way for European styling of sportswear.

European influence is subtle. It is the elements of the garment that give them the special flair. One sees a subtlety of color, unusual tonal shades used, as well as superior fabrics both in wovens and in knits. Proportions and scale of the garments may be more forward than in American or British sportswear, as seen in a sophisticated oversized, drop-shoulder sweater. The point spread on a sport-shirt collar may be narrower with collar points that are longer and slimmer than in a more conservatively styled shirt. The dressy casual pant may be made of rayon, or fine, lightweight wool which moves with the breeze.

European influence may be seen in all variety of sportswear and in garments that derive their style from other influences. It is an almost indefinable look that gives the garment or the outfit a slight edge in sophistication. This edge, more often than not, is built on fine fabrics, unusual colors, and a fit that shows an understanding and appreciation for fluid body movement.

Giorgio Armani, leading Italian clothing designer, is fast becoming a leading sportswear designer as well. His diffusion line, A/X: Armani Exchange, brings his style to the masses. A few of the more avant-garde designers include Claude Montana, Jean Paul Gaultier, Gianni Versace, and Karl Lagerfeld.

Ethnic Influence

During the 1960s, ethnic influence was at its peak. Perhaps one of the most ill-fated styles of ethnic influence was the *Nehru jacket* of the mid-1960s. It was fitted, with a collar band, and was similar to the jacket worn by the Nehru, India's prime minister at the time. The style received great fanfare when it first came out, was manufactured by many companies, but lived a very short life. Throughout the 1960s and into the 1970s, the world saw African, Indian, Native American, middle eastern, oriental, Mexican, and South and Central American styles inspiring designers. The more exotic the outfit the better, and if it were authentic apparel from an emerging country, all the better. The interest in other cultures and the opportunity to understand them better can partially be expressed by wearing apparel of ethnic origin or style. Many individuals wear garments of their own ethnic origin to show pride in their roots.

The man who is wearing natural materials, made by natives, shows that the commitment of the wearer is greater than when they are merely copies.[9] Those garments that are made by mass manufacturers, or current designers, indicate an interest in other cultures, or an interest in the latest style by the wearer, but not the same degree of commitment as the authentic styles.

World issues have an enormous impact on which ethnic styles are in vogue. Ethnic styles lend themselves to natural fibers because they appear more "authentic," whereas some of the high-tech, man-made fibers are not as readily associated with developing countries. Colors are often in the range associated with natural dyes available to the culture. Rick-rack, embroidery, applique, fringe, lacing for closures, drawstrings, leather, and beads are all style details commonly used in ethnically influenced garments. Regions of the country also lean toward certain ethnic looks on a consistent basis. For example, Texas, with its neighbor of Mexico, often favors a Latin American theme in sportswear.

Historic Influence

What's old is new again. And so goes the styling of sportswear. There is very little today that is truly an innovation in apparel style. Designers have always drawn from the past, as well as sources in the present, in presenting a new line. The most daring, and often high-priced, designs may well draw on earlier garments for inspiration. Italian designer, Gianni Versace, indicated his inspiration for his spring-summer line for 1992: "I looked at history. There are 18th century jackets, high button pants that look new, influences from [ancient civilizations like] Babylon, Egypt and Greece."[10] Certainly garments like this are not mainstream. But as we have seen it is often from the most fashion-forward designers that trends filter down to reach what is eventually seen on the street.

Period dress revival is most common among young men and women, rather than the set entrenched in their careers and upward mobility. Those interested in the more authentic form of period dress are often searching for a manner of self-expression or a method to set themselves apart from the commonplace.

Some of the more classic historical looks in menswear include the bomber jacket, knickers, and riding apparel. The *bomber jacket*, a World War II survivor, is a short, blouson style made of leather or imitation leather style. It sports a large, pull-up collar. It was a warm jacket and allowed for ease of movement. This coat weathered hard use. Also a classically popular style is the *Eisenhower jacket*. Another short, banded-bottom style, it is typically made of cloth, is close fitting, and is usually seen in GI colors. Knickers, mentioned earlier, are still seen by the daring

[9]Alison Lurie, *The Language of Clothes* (New York: Vintage Books, 1983) p. 93.

[10]Amy Spindler, "Good-Time Gianni," *Daily News Record*, June 24, 1991, p. 15.

on the golf course. And traditional English riding apparel is a source of classic sportswear: jodhpurs, the hip-flaring riding pants, and the hacking jacket, designed for riding, influence modern-day traditionalists like Ralph Lauren.

Media and Art Influence

Entertainment arts like television, the movies, and concerts have had tremendous impact on fashion. In evaluating the effect there are two factors to be considered: (1) personal styles of the movie stars and TV celebrities, and (2) styles that designers create specifically for the television show or movie.

The huge popularity of the TV series "Miami Vice" in the 1980s resulted in an easy, fashionable look worn by women as well as by men. PhotoFest.

The public enjoys following the private lives of their favorite movie and television personalities. How these people dress offstage has a part in influencing fashion styles seen on the street. Whether it is a rock star or a movie heartthrob, we feel we know a little bit more about these personalities based on their choices of apparel. And the glamour associated with them may also be ours, in some small way, by donning a similar look to theirs.

Movies and television garment designers carefully craft the look of their characters via the garments worn. Style trends are often set in motion by the items worn by a particular character. For example, Bill Cosby wore many beautiful sweaters in his television comedy series of the 1980s and 1990s. It became his signature look for the show, and communicated the easy-going nature of the television persona. In the 1980s, the television show *Miami Vice* initiated a major sportswear trend in a more forward, casual style. The movie, *Urban Cowboy*, took the western look to every city. New Yorkers sported cowboy hats and boots in their off hours. Michael Douglas, as Gordon Gekko in the movie *Wall Street*, created real interest in a more formal, polished business look. In particular, a horizontally striped dress shirt he wore became exceedingly popular with clothing cognoscenti.

This area of influence often interrelates with the other areas of influence, like history, military, ethnic cultures, and so on, and is a most important conduit to spread style. That is, a period movie, like *Gone with the Wind*, uses historically influenced styles in apparel. Popular movies and television shows provide a source of color, texture, and design line for the designer. The movies of the 1930s and 1940s still provide designers today with a rich source of style ideas.

Since the 1970s traveling art exhibitions have brought art insights into major cities nationally. King Tut, one of the first mega-exhibits, received incredible press nationally. Its influence was seen in apparel colors, design lines, and even spread to interior design.

These seven style origins are just a few of the sources of inspiration for designers. There are many, many more. Subjects that are of interest to the public, such as the environment and political issues, can be seen reflected in sportswear trends. In the summer months, a recurring theme in young men's sportswear is the surfer and the beach of the West Coast. Career themes are periodically in vogue, and the more authentic they are the better, such as the medical scrubs being worn for leisure wear.

Sportswear is a constantly changing, and therefore challenging, classification for the retailer. The consumer has many, many choices and needs guidance in determining the very best styles and fabrics. The more active the man is, the more choices there are to be made.

CASE STUDY

Herb Robins' life had been pretty simple and easy. He had been living on a sailboat for 4 years and cruising the Mediterranean as a charter captain. He was now back in the states, however, and was about to go to work as a salesman for a sailboat manufacturer. His work would require him to travel throughout the Southwest, calling on the dealers for the sailboat line. This meant he would often be in boat yards, on and off boats in the water during the day. He would attend and work at some boating industry trade shows. And he would often be invited to dressy receptions and parties for those in the sailboat business. Periodically he would take clients to lunch or dinner at upscale restaurants.

- In making such a life-style change, what problems would Herb be presented with in terms of his wardrobe?
- What style influences would most readily conform to his new work?
- What basic elements in the wardrobe do you think would be truly necessary for him to have, considering all the different types of situations he would be in?

TERMS TO KNOW

Define or briefly explain the following:

Knickerbockers
Plus-fours
Crossover elements
Carnaby Street
Active-leisure level
Casual level
Dressy casual
Professional sports licensing
Sport-specific manufacturer
Classic influence
Green grass shops
Military influence
Ethnic influence
Nehru jacket
Bomber jacket
Historic influence
Eisenhower jacket

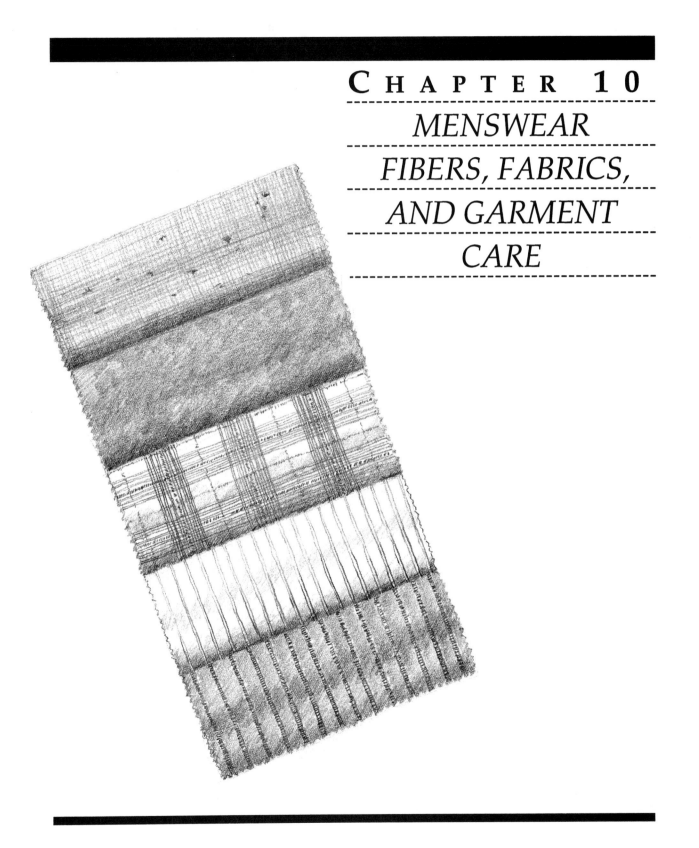

CHAPTER 10

MENSWEAR FIBERS, FABRICS, AND GARMENT CARE

The purpose of this chapter is to acquaint the reader with some basic terms of fibers and fabrics. There are many fine texts that go into great detail on the study of fibers and textiles. That is not the purpose of this book, or this chapter. This is a very important topic in the discussion of menswear, however. The student of menswear must be knowledgeable of fabrics, be able to identify them, and know their properties and how to care for them. What follows are some of the basics as well as some terms that apply specifically to menswear.

FIBERS AND FABRICS

It is important to use the terms fiber and fabric correctly. *Fibers* are the smallest component of a fabric, and these fibers are spun into *yarns*. The yarns are then woven or knitted to produce *fabric*. Natural fibers, being of limited length, are twisted or spun together to form continuous yarns for weaving or knitting. In the case of man-made fibers, chemical *filaments*, continuous-length strands are created and are the basis for yarn formation. Silk is the only natural, continuous filament. It is produced by a silk worm in its cocoon. When the term *fiber content* is used in relation to a fabric it is defining the fiber source(s). Often the fiber content may be a *blend* of two or more fibers.

There are two main classifications of textile fibers: natural fiber and man-made fiber. Natural fibers fall into three subcategories: animal, vegetable, and mineral. Man-made fibers have two subcategories: cellulosic or noncellulosic. *Cellulosic* fibers are chemically processed fibers that have the base of a natural plant or are from plant protein. *Noncellulosic* fibers are totally man-made or "from a test tube," and are chemical compounds. Examples that are quite common from each of these subcategories as well as their sources include the following:

Natural Fibers

Animal
　Wool (sheep)
　Silk (silkworm)
Vegetable
　Cotton (cotton plant)
　Linen (flax plant)
Mineral
　Asbestos (rock)

Manmade Fibers

Cellulosic
　Rayon (chemically processed wood pulp and cotton linters[1])
　Acetate (chemically processed cotton linters)
Noncellulosic
　Polyester (totally chemical compound)
　Spandex (totally chemical compound)

---

[1]*Linters* are fibers that adhere to cotton seeds.

When you use the term *fabric* you are addressing both fiber and the construction of the fabric—whether it is a knit, a woven, or a nonwoven (like felt). The type of knit or weave is defined by the fabric term. For example, "wool gabardine" indicates that the fiber is wool and the fabric construction is woven with a gabardine twill.

Properties of Commonly Used Fibers

To be of greatest service to the customer, it is imperative to understand the properties of fabrics and understand the best end uses of certain fibers, as well as pros and cons of those fibers. Only the most commonly used fibers in menswear are addressed here. For additional information on other fibers or fabrics, consult one of the textile resources listed in the bibliography at the end of this book.

An important point about blends: When evaluating fabrics of blended fibers, the characteristics of each fiber will have some bearing on the characteristics of the fabric itself. Let's look at how this works in the classic blend of polyester and cotton for a man's shirt. The polyester will add some warmth, will aid in resisting wrinkles, may hold stains, but will wash and dry easily. The cotton will absorb moisture away from the body and dry quickly, be cool, and have a soft hand. Blending these fibers together means that some qualities of each will exist in the finished garment. The degree depends on the percentage of polyester to cotton. A man who likes the look of linen, but hates wrinkled clothing, can opt for a pant that is a blend; add to the linen some polyester, and the fabric will resist wrinkling yet have the look of linen.

Acetate.   Acetate is a man-made fiber from cellulose base. The process was patented in 1894 and was first produced commercially in the United States in 1924.

> *Pros*: Resilient, returns to original shape, excellent drape, luxurious hand
> *Cons*: Poor conductor of heat, not absorbent, hot in summer, clammy in winter, abrades easily, weakens when wet, poor elasticity, not washable, shrinks easily, and usually requires professional dry cleaning
> *End uses*: Slacks, sportswear, underwear, garment lining fabrics, and used often in blends and linings

Acrylic.   Acrylic is a man-made chemical fiber. It was commercially produced in the United States in 1951.

> *Pros*: Soft hand, drapable, lightweight, warm, washable, dries quickly, wool-like hand with similar characteristics, resilient, returns to original shape, resists abrasion, excellent resistance to sunlight
> *Cons*: Static and pilling problems
> *End uses*: Sweaters, fake furs, sleepwear, lining for outerwear, used in blends

Cotton.   Cotton is a natural vegetable fiber. It has been in use for more than 5,000 years. Cotton is commonly used in many garments, and is stable and versatile. Egyptian cotton, Sea Island cotton, and Pima Cotton are the very finest quality cotton available.

> *Pros*: Cool fabric, conducts heat away from body, absorbent, dries quickly, abrasion resistant
> *Cons*: Little elasticity, loses strength in sunlight and when wet, shrinks easily, does not typically drape well, subject to attack by mildew and silverfish

End Uses: Shirtings, sportswear, handkerchiefs, socks, pajamas, robes, and underwear; often used in blends

Linen.   Linen is a natural vegetable fiber produced from the plant flax. It is an ancient fiber that was used by Stone Age man.

Pros: Cool fabric, conducts heat away from body, absorbent, dries quickly, resists dirt, strengthens when wet, dry cleans well and softens with washing, second in strength to silk fiber, somewhat resistant to sunlight
Cons: Least elastic of natural fibers, not resilient, brittle fibers wrinkle easily, does not drape well, white linen yellows with laundering and dry cleaning, shrinks with washing, subject to attack by mildew and silverfish
End uses: Shirts, slacks, sport coats, handkerchiefs; used in blends for summer wear

Nylon.   Nylon is a man-made chemical fiber. It was first produced in the United States in 1939. Nylon is the second most widely used man-made fiber, behind polyester. It is used widely in blends to stabilize other fibers.

Pros: Lightweight, excellent durability, abrasion resistant, highly elastic, returns to original shape, drapes very well, washes easily
Cons: Nonabsorbent, hot in summer, clammy in winter, static and pilling are problems, poor resistance to sunlight
End uses: Sportswear, hosiery, outerwear; often blended with other fibers

Polyester.   Polyester is a man-made chemical fiber. It was first commercially produced in the United States in 1953. Polyester is the most commonly used of all man-made fibers and can be made to simulate many other fibers.

Pros: Abrasion resistant, fair to excellent drapability, very resilient, returns to original shape, nonabsorbent, water repellent, resists dirt, washes easily, resists shrinkage, excellent pleat and crease retention
Cons: Hot in summer, clammy in winter, some fabrics pill easily, can stain easily (particularly oil)
End uses: Blended with other fibers for almost any type of garment; 100 percent polyester for active sportswear and outerwear

Rayon.   Rayon is a man-made fiber with cellulose base. The first manmade fiber, it was developed in Britain in 1892 and was produced in the United States in 1910. It was originally created as "artificial silk"; there is a wide variance in quality levels and resulting properties. Modern rayons are greatly improved and far more stable than early versions. (Most common form of rayon processed is Viscose Rayon.)

Pros: Excellent drape, absorbs moisture, but dries slowly
Cons: When wet can lose strength, shrinks easily, not resilient, wrinkles easily, feels hot and heavy in humid weather, seldom washable, requires frequent dry cleaning, little elasticity, abrades easily
End uses: Shirts, pants; blended with other fibers for all other types of garments

Silk.   Silk is a natural animal fiber. This luxury fiber comes from silkworm cocoons and has been in existence since 2640 B.C. Silk fabric is available in a wide range of qualities depending on how fiber is processed. It is the thinnest of the natural fibers.

> *Pros*: Strongest of natural fibers, second (to wool,) most elastic of natural fibers, but when stretched may not regain shape, luxurious hand, drapes well, resists dirt, some silks may be hand washed
>
> *Cons*: Deteriorates more quickly than wool or cotton in sunlight, some shrinkage but not as bad as rayon or wool, subject to attack by moths
>
> *End uses*: Shirts, sportcoats, ties, pocket squares; blended with other fibers for all types of garments

Wool.   Wool is a natural animal fiber. It is an ancient fiber that has been used since before 400 B.C. Wool is considered the highest-quality fiber for tailored clothing. Some wool fabric constructions especially popular in menswear include worsteds, woolens, tweeds, and flannels.

> *Pros*: Most elastic of all natural fibers, excellent drape, durable but loses strength when wet, resilient, returns to original shape, resists wrinkles, highly absorbent without feeling damp, tends to retain body heat, warm in winter, tropical weight is cool in summer
>
> *Cons*: Loses strength in sunlight or when wet, attracts dirt and dust, requires professional cleaning, tends to pill, wide range of shrinkage, subject to attack by moths and silverfish
>
> *End uses*: Suitings, dress slacks, sport coats, sweaters, hosiery; blended with other fibers for all types of garments

Fabric Suggestions for the Customer

The style and fit of a garment are key elements to match to the needs and likes of the customer. But the fabric is another critical element that may determine the customer's happiness with his purchase. The average consumer has only a very basic, sometimes naïve, understanding of fibers and fabrics. Some customers will buy on style alone, and only later realize that the fabric is too hot, wrinkles too easily, has to be pressed after washing, and so on. It is what happens in the wearing and in the required care of the garment that will in part determine how often the item is worn. It is critical to evaluate closely what will be the best fabric choice for the client, and to advise him on the pros and cons of each fabric being considered.

Here are some questions to ask and considerations to make in working with the consumer.

Questions to Ask the Consumer.

1. *Are you warm natured or cold natured?* If the man is warm natured, he will respond to natural fibers that allow the skin to breathe and that absorb perspiration. Cotton, lightweight, worsted wool, and linen will all be cool fibers; however, they do wrinkle easily. If wrinkling is of concern, the man may require a blend with a small percentage of polyester to help resist wrinkling. Loosely woven fabrics that breathe are effective for sport coats. In suit coats and sportcoats avoid fully lined garments if possible. Hosiery of 100 percent cotton will be most comfortable.

   A cool-natured man may appreciate blended fibers in shirts; the polyester fiber is warm and will be more comfortable for him than 100 percent cotton. In suits, slacks, and sportcoats, he will respond to heavier-weight worsteds and woolens. Wool flannel, cashmere, camel hair, and lofty fabrics that retain body heat will work well for him. Hosiery may be 100 percent wool, a blend of wool, or nylon, which are lightweight but warm.

2. *How do you feel about fabric wrinkling*? Many men feel quite strongly about this and will be unhappy with a garment that wrinkles easily. In this case, consider shirting fabrics that have some polyester fiber to resist wrinkling. A shirt with a percentage of 55 percent cotton and 45 percent polyester will really resist wrinkling, but will tend to be warm. In addition, it will not have as long a life as the 100 percent cotton shirt. No matter how much polyester fiber there is in the shirt, it will still need some touching up with an iron to look truly crisp and professional.

In suit or sportcoat and slack, this man may opt for 100 percent wool or wool-polyester blends. Though 100 percent worsted wool may show some wrinkling after sitting for a while, it is the nature of the fiber to throw off the wrinkles with a little steam. If the man travels, a quick steaming in the humidity of the hotel shower will do wonders to spruce up his apparel.

Rayon and linen are fibers that do not fare well for the man who hates wrinkles. These fabrics are best avoided. Also, real care should be taken in considering blends that contain high percentages of cotton, linen, rayon, or any fibrous plants. A good wrinkle test is to grasp the fabric tightly in the fist for a few moments, and the results will be clear.

Light colors tend to show wrinkles much more easily than dark colors. A light-colored linen pant, for example, will show its wrinkles much more clearly than a dark-colored linen.

3. *Do you have any strong feelings about garment laundering or dry cleaning*? Regardless of the fiber content, the care label that is attached to the garment must be followed. A consumer has absolutely no recourse but to take responsibility if garment failure occurs when care instructions are not observed and followed.

If the man does not want to take his shirts to the laundry, then he really should consider purchase of cotton-polyester blends. He must be advised that these shirts, regardless of the percentage of polyester, will require some maintenance in terms of pressing. If he has his shirts professionally laundered, he can purchase 100 percent cotton or blends. It is advisable to avoid heavy starching in shirts as they will wear out more quickly than a lightly starched garment.

Linen, silk, and rayon in most cases will require frequent professional care. Shirts and slacks in these fibers will wrinkle easily. It is not advisable for the consumer to try to spot clean a stain in a garment of these fibers, as a ring will often remain.

Wool fiber tends to attract dust and dirt, but it is very resilient and with proper airing may last several wearings before professional garment care is required. The only wool that may be washed at home with great care is a wool sweater. It may be washed in cold water with a product like Woolite, and then hand blocked and dried flat.

FIBER AND FABRIC GLOSSARY

All wool: This is an often misunderstood term. It means that the garment is made of all wool fiber. However, it doesn't indicate the quality, type of wool used, or whether it is new wool, or reprocessed wool.

Basket weave: This is a plain weave fabric similar to what is found in oxford cloth shirting or hopsacking.

Bird's eye: In worsted fiber, it has small, diamond-shaped indentations with little dots in the center that look like the eye of a bird. This is a classic, high-quality suiting.

Broadcloth: A fabric that got its name because it was woven as a very wide cloth. It is most often made in cotton, silk, or wool. It is a most common type of shirting, most often associated with a straight-point collar style.

Camel hair: Hair that comes from the Mongolian camel, where extremes of weather cause a very thick coat to grow on the animals. It is usually associated with sportcoats and overcoats as it is very warm yet lightweight.

Cashmere: A luxury fiber from the underbelly of the Cashmere goat. A very expensive and delicate fiber. It is a finer fiber than mohair or wool. Because of its very limited supply it is frequently blended with wool, which also adds some durability to the fabric.

Cavalry twill: A rough, hard-finished woven fabric with a deep diagonal rib design. It was originally used by the army—hence its name. This is a very sturdy fabric and can be made of cotton, wool, or a blend of fibers.

Chambray: Named after the French town of Chambrai. It is a plain-weave cotton or cotton blend. The warp, or lengthwise threads, are colored, and the fill, or crosswise threads, are white. The color is usually a light blue and looks somewhat like a denim but is lighter weight. It is often thought of as the "work-shirt" fabric.

Challis: A lightweight, finely spun, worsted fabric that usually has a printed design. Challis is often used for ties.

Cheviot: Woolen or worsted wool with a slightly rough texture in a twill weave. Often used in men's suiting.

Chino: A cotton twill weave originally used by the army for summer wear. It is lighter weight than the cavalry twill.

Corduroy: A ribbed, woven fabric with a high, lustrous pile. In 100 percent cotton, it can produce a very soft hand. Also woven in fiber blends, its hand may not be quite as soft to the touch. In menswear, it is most often seen in sportswear including slacks, shirts, and casual outerwear.

Cotton: For shirtings, the top fiber choice is 100 percent cotton. There are many different grades and qualities of cotton. Some feel as soft as silk; others have a rough hand. Egyptian cotton is considered the best in the world. Sea Island is also a top grade of cotton, as well as Pima cotton. These fine-quality cotton fibers are long staple, from 1/2 inch to over 2 inches, and produce a soft, fine hand.

Covert: Woolen fabric closely woven with two yarns of different colors.

Denim: A very strong, durable twill weave. The lengthwise, or warp yarns, are typically blue and the fill yarns, white. Heavy weights are used for work clothes and sportswear. Light weights are available in various colors, and seen in sportswear and shirts. The most common association with denim is the blue jean pant.

Double knit: A knitted fabric that is relatively heavy weight. It stretches in two different directions and therefore is very comfortable. It can be made in almost any fiber but is often associated with polyester. Polyester double knits were very popular in the 1970s.

Douppioni: This is an Italian, textured silk fabric. It is often used in expensive summer suits. It has noticeable slubs, or thickened yarns, which add to its visual interest.

Drill cloth: This term is used to describe the sturdy cotton twill fabric often seen in military garments.

Felt: A fabric made by compressing loose fibers together instead of knitting or weaving. Wool produces the best felt. In mens hats, beaver hair is added for durability. The higher percentage of beaver hair, the more expensive is the hat.

Flannel: Flannel is a woven wool fabric with a soft, napped finish. Though usually associated with warm woolen garments, it can also be produced in cotton.

Gabardine: A sturdy fabric with a 45-degree diagonal twill line. It is made of a twisted yarn and can be made of wool or a blend of fibers. Excellent, long-wearing fabric for pants and coats. Available from light weight to heavy weight.

Glen plaid: A Scottish clan plaid often found in men's suitings. It was a favorite of the Duke of Windsor. Its pattern is a large, distinctive overplaid made up of a basic houndstooth check.

Hand: The term used in the industry to describe the feel of the fabric. For example, a "beefy" or full hand might relate to a fabric that is thick and heavy.

Harris Tweed: A hand-woven, woolen fabric produced as a cottage industry in the Outer Hebrides islands off the northern coast of Scotland. The name "Harris Tweed" is protected by a trademark and each garment produced with authentic fabric has such registration indicated on the garment label. Expensive, quality, heavy fabric for sportcoats and outerwear.

Herringbone: A design in a twill weave fabric that looks like repeated rows of zig-zags. Often found in woolen fabrics for sportcoats.

Hopsacking: A rough, loosely constructed, basket-weave fabric most commonly found in sportcoats. Can be any fiber content. Usually middle to heavy weight.

Houndstooth: This is usually a woven fabric, which at first looks like a check. But on closer investigation, the pattern has a pinwheel effect to it. It is often found in a two-color pattern.

Khaki: This is the Hindu word for "dusty." It was a color worn by the British in India to protect them from the sun. The term "khakis" is often used to refer to this color pant or summer suit.

Knit: This type of fabric is distinguished by a series of interlocking loops. The loops allow the fabric to stretch and give, making knits very comfortable fabrics.

Lambs wool: This wool is from the first shearing of a sheep at about 8 months. It produces a very high-quality, soft fabric.

Linen: This is an ancient fabric, made from flax, a stalky plant. Seen in spring and summer clothes, it is a cool and comfortable natural fiber. Typically made into woven fabric, it wrinkles very easily. Many men do not like this aspect of linen and are resistent to wear it.

Lisle: This is a high-quality, fine, cotton yarn made from long-staple cotton. It is used in men's socks and undershirts. It was first made in Lisle, France.

Lycra: A common brand of spandex. It is a man-made fiber that offers a very high degree of stretch. Frequently used in active sportswear.

Melton: A solid-color, heavy woven fabric that has a matted, napped finish. Used in overcoats, it was traditionally a wool fiber but can be a blend. Very warm and insulating. Often used in outerwear.

Merino: This is a breed of sheep that produces the highest quality of wool—resembling cashmere in softness. This sets the standard for wool quality. Merino sheep are largely raised in Australia.

Microfiber: A yarn made up of exceptionally fine filaments. Initially produced in nylon, then polyester and rayon. Yarns made up of microfibers produce a fabric with a soft hand, excellent drape, and great crease retention. Frequently used in blends with cotton or wool. Used more in sportswear and rainwear than in clothing.

Nailhead: Small, dotted design, suggestive of the head of a nail. A traditional suiting fabric.

Nonwoven: A fabric that is neither woven nor knit. It is like a superlight felt that has a binder added to the fiber, which holds it together. In apparel it is usually associated with interlinings.

Oxford: Shirting in a basket weave, with slight variations in thickness. Often associated with button-down shirts (see pinpoint oxford).

Percale: A plain-weave fabric most often associated with sheets but sometimes found in shirtings and pajamas.

Pilling: Little balls of tangled fiber that stick to the surface of a fabric and are produced by friction or rubbing against the fabric. Pills may be removed from some fabrics with a razor.

Pinpoint oxford: This is a finer gauge of oxford cloth for men's shirtings. It produces a smoother, finer hand, and results in a more luxurious and more expensive fabric.

Polyester: A man-made fiber, it is a petrochemical byproduct and has some of the same properties as plastic. It will not absorb water, and therefore 100 percent polyester fabric can be clammy to wear in winter and hot in the summer. It is often blended with other fibers for top- and bottom-weight fabrics and assists in making wrinkles fall out more quickly. Some men prefer polyester blends for travel because the fiber resists wrinkling.

Poplin: A hard finish, tightly woven fabric, which is light weight and associated with spring and summer goods. Because this fabric is so tightly woven, it does not tailor well and tends to pucker easily.

Rayon: Rayon was the first of man-made fibers in 1884. It is made from chemically treated wood pulp or cotton byproduct. It was originally produced to simulate silk and had been referred to as "artificial silk." In its early days it was unstable and subject to shrinkage in washing. In more recent years, mills have produced rayon fibers that are much more stable, some of which may be washed, though all dry clean well (see viscose).

Reprocessed wool: Wool that has been reclaimed from scraps of cloth or the wool combing process. This wool has never been used in actual garments, as opposed to "reused" wool.

Reused wool: Wool fiber that has been salvaged from old clothes, blankets, and so on. Fabrics are shredded and the fiber is respun.

Saxony: A wool flannel with a tweed effect that is very soft, luxurious, and expensive. Used in suitings and coats.

Seersucker: A very cool, lightweight cotton or blend in a woven fabric for spring or summer. It is most often a vertically crinkled stripe with a puckered look. Often found in pastels, light blue is a common seersucker color in men's summer slacks or suits.

Serge: A popular twill weave, worsted fabric. Originally made of silk, then offered in wool and silk blend. Today it is most often all wool. This fabric tailors but can get shiny with much wear. It is a common suiting fabric.

Shetland wool: Originally a fine, soft woolen made from the sheep from the Shetland Isles. Now the term is used much more broadly to mean any woolen which looks and feels like authentic Shetland wool. It is associated most often with sweatering.

Silk: The luxury natural fiber produced by silk worms. One silk cocoon can produce up to one mile of silk filament. It has a very soft, lustrous hand and may be made into any variety of fabrics. It may be woven or knitted.

Slub: A thickened place in a yarn. It can be artificially created to duplicate the look of a natural fiber. Some silk and cotton fabrics have slubs and are not necessarily considered imperfections.

Spandex: A man-made fiber that offers a high degree of stretch and is often used in sportswear (see lycra).

Sponging: This term refers to a process where fabric, usually wool, is wet and preshrunk before garment manufacture. This ensures that the finished garment will not have excessive shrinkage. Also referred to as "London shrinking."

Tartan: A plaid, usually wool, fabric. Each scottish family has its own plaid, that historically only they were to wear. It is often associated with blankets and kilts. In menswear it's seen in sportswear—especially flannel shirtings.

Tattersall: A bold check that was originally used in horse blankets. Today, this is used in shirtings and some sporty vests.

Tencel: A new, advanced form of rayon introduced to the American market in 1992. It may be washed, doesn't shrink, and is stronger than the most common form of rayon on the market.

Tropical weight: A light-weight suiting traditionally made of wool but can also be a blend. The term "tropical weight" is often applied to those light weight (7–10 oz.) wools made for the warmest of weather.

Twill weave: A woven fabric which has diagonal lines. Typically a stronger, heavier, and more durable cloth than a basket weave. Used for work and casual wear (denim) and suitings (serge).

Virgin wool: This is a fiber that has never been spun or woven. It is not necessarily an indication of high-quality level.

Viscose (or viscose rayon): The process for making the most common type of rayon fiber. The terms viscose, viscose rayon, and rayon are often used interchangeably.

Washable woolen: Wool fiber that has been coated with a microscopic film of nylon resin. Woolens treated this way can be machine washed and dried, and need no ironing.

Woven: Fabric created by interlacing yarns at right angles to each other. Many fabric variations are constructed through different methods of weaving.

Windowpane: Horizontal and vertical lines crossing over background color giving the impression of window panes.

Wool: By far the best choice of fiber in men's clothing is wool. Many people think of wool as only a winter fiber, suitable for heavyweight fabrics. On the contrary, wool is available in lightweight fabrics for summer weather. In warm climates, where winters are mild, the man is served well by the tropical weights and midweight fabrics. For cold winters, the heavier woolens (see woolen) are appropriate in sportcoats, and flannels in suits and slacks.

Woolen: Fabrics that are made of short, fuzzy wool fibers. They are softer and thicker than worsted wools.

Worsted: Wool fiber made with long-staple yarns that are tightly twisted. Worsted fabric is tightly woven and produces a flat finish.

GARMENT CARE

To lengthen the life of a garment, it is key that the consumer care properly for the item. There is no reason for a customer to lose a garment through moth infestation, poor general care, or for garments to lose shape because of the manner in which they are stored.

How a garment is pressed has an impact on its life. Use of appropriate heat, moisture, or steam must be adhered to. Care labels within a garment offer such information. Additional precautions, such as using a press cloth instead of applying heat directly to the fabric can avoid excessive shine on some napped fabrics or those with high man-made fiber content. Likewise, excessive heat can actually scorch fabrics such as 100 percent cotton shirtings. Steamers that are readily available to the public are especially effective on wools and those fabrics with polyester or nylon content. They cause the wrinkles to fall out and require no pressure on the surface of the fabric. Do not press any garment which has spots on it or has retained perspiration or body oils. Pressing will only drive the stains deeper into the fabric causing deterioration.

Garments must be clean before any type of storage. The longer a stain sets, the less likely that it can be removed. Food stains are an attraction for insects. Dirt, perspiration, and body oils will degrade fibers.

Garments may be stored at the dry cleaners in special vaults for the summer months. The consumer may either leave individual garments with the dry cleaner or request *box storage*. With box storage, the consumer brings garments to the dry cleaner in a box. The garments are dry cleaned before being stored in the box for the summer. In the fall the garments are unpacked, pressed, hung, and made ready for the customer.

The International Fabricare Institute (IFI) in Silver Spring, Maryland is a trade association of professional dry cleaners. Its goal is to maintain high standards within the dry cleaning industry. Besides working closely with dry cleaners internationally, they have strong interests in working with retailers and manufacturers on garment care concerns. IFI offers membership to retailers also. Both dry cleaner and retailer members have access to a highly sophisticated garment analysis laboratory. This laboratory can analyze garments which have failed the process prescribed on the care label and determine where the failure lies: with the consumer, the manufacturer, or the dry cleaner. IFI can then suggest a more suitable care process for similar garments in the future.

It is crucial that retailers notify their vendors as soon as possible to any manufacturing or garment care problems. It is only through such communication that the manufacturing pipeline can be adjusted to avoid increased production of garment failures. Lack of such communication results in spiraling numbers of unhappy consumers and frustrated retailers and dry cleaners. Here are some tips to help the consumer preserve his wardrobe.

Suits, Sport Coats, and Slacks

- Remove all items from pockets and remove belt from pants before hanging garments.
- Hang the coat on a curved, wooden *wishbone hanger*; the shoulders should be fully supported by the hanger. Wooden wishbone hangers may also be purchased that have large wooden knobs at the ends to support and retain the shape of the shoulder.
- Suit pants may be hung on the wishbone hanger crossbar, with the fly unzipped.
- Slacks may be hung on clamp-type pant hangers. By hanging the pant by the hem or cuff, the weight of the pant will help to retain the pant crease.
- Dry clean suits, sport coats, and slacks whenever there are spots on the garment. Sometimes there may be an "invisible" spot of a clear liquid such as a beverage or food which the wearer spilled. It is important to tell the dry cleaner that there was a spill and what it was, even if it is not visible. It is also critical to advise the dry cleaner what the consumer may have done in an attempt to remove any spot. Either the original spill or the consumer's "treatment" may require "pre-treating" to remove a stain.

Otherwise, the spot may "set" and become visible after the cleaning process. If dirt, perspiration, or body oils have come in contact with fibers, cleaning should not be delayed. These stains will worsen with time and may permanently damage the garments.

As much as possible let garments air out after wearing and before putting back into the closet. If garment has retained a high degree of perspiration clean as soon as possible to avoid textile deterioration. This is especially important with wool and other natural fibers.

- Wool garments may be spot cleaned with club soda, but it is far better to get the item to the dry cleaner as soon as possible with an explanation of what the stain is.
- Be sure to store wool items in an airtight area with some type of moth-insect repellent. Never store dirty garments; stains can set permanently over a period of months, and food stains are an invitation for insects.

Shirts

- If professionally laundered, the less starch used, the better. Pressing a very highly starched shirt can result in the fabric breaking down and wearing out more quickly.
- Launder shirts as soon as possible. Perspiration that remains in the fabric for a long time will cause the fabric to deteriorate more quickly.

Ties

- At all costs, try to avoid dry cleaning ties. Because of the bias-cut lining, they never look quite the same after going through the dry cleaning process. Use club soda to treat spots if possible. There is also an aerosol that can be sprayed as a stain repellent for silk ties. This product is available through many retail stores.
- Keep ties rolled in drawers or hung vertically in the closet. Do not store ties with knots intact.
- Wool ties are just as attractive to moths as any other garment. Store them carefully when not in use.

Sweaters

- Fold and store in drawers, or fold and hang over a pant bar on a hanger. Sweaters often are heavy, and hanging them like a shirt will result in them becoming misshapen.
- Store wool sweaters for the summer folded and, like other fine wools, with some type of insect repellent. Cedar blocks or chips are particularly effective as they have a pleasant smell, take up little room, and last indefinitely.

Shoes

- Good leather shoes are expensive and deserve special care. Keeping them polished with wax will help to retain their suppleness and resist water damage.
- Use wooden shoe trees to maintain shape and draw moisture out from the shoe.
- Avoid wearing the same pair of shoes two days in a row; alternating shoes will extend their life.
- Good shoe care, along with sole and heel replacement, can result in a life of many years.

Fiber: Resistance to Perspiration

Perspiration may affect the color of fabrics and may stain some; it also causes deterioration of textile fibers. Frequent cleaning is advised.

Natural fibers. All natural fibers can be degraded by perspiration, but silk left uncleaned is especially likely to have permanent damage.

Man-made fibers. These fibers resist perspiration except for rayons, which may be degraded.[2]

SELECTING A DRY CLEANER

The quality of the dry cleaner's work has an enormous impact on the life of the consumer's apparel. How does one confirm that the correct cleaner has been chosen? Norman Oehlke of the International Fabricare Institute makes these suggestions: Ask others in the neighborhood, especially those who show attention to detail in their own appearance. Visit the dry cleaners. Does the shop appear clean, and well organized? Do they ask the right questions of the customer? Do they understand any special requests? Is there good, clear verbal communication with them, with no language barriers which could result in misunderstandings? Do they display membership in IFI or the state dry cleaning association? Membership will indicate an awareness of, and attention to, maintaining high standards in their work. Are their rates reasonable for the quality of results desired, neither too high nor too low? Consider it a warning if they display information which indicates they will not honor claims!

The retailer should also consider developing an alliance with a high quality dry cleaner. There are many benefits to both in discussing new fibers, unusual garment construction, how to handle garment failures, how to build stronger relationships with manufacturers, and how to best meet the changing needs of the consumer. The retailer-dry cleaner-manufacturer relationship is one which can be strengthened through better communication and will result in higher quality for all and fewer customer complaints.

CASE STUDY

John Juniper traveled frequently in his executive position with a real estate company. His preferred style was mainstream traditional, and he didn't want to have to fuss taking care of his wardrobe. Simple styles, easy care, and easy to pack for travel were his main concerns.

His real estate firm had sportcoats in a standard style and color for uniformity and consumer recognition. However, he needed some slacks, a few shirts, and perhaps one suit for more formal meetings. He lived in the Southwest, and his region spanned from Arizona to East Texas.

One other factor that was important to John is that he was very warm natured, and the heat of the Southwest was often overwhelming for him. He disliked clothing that was too warm.

- With a limited budget, what would your suggestions be for him as to type of fabric and fiber content? Bear in mind his concerns for easy care and his dislike of clothing that is too warm.

[2]Barnard P. Corbman, *Textiles: Fiber to Fabric* (New York: McGraw-Hill, 1983) p. 484.

■ Identify the pros and cons of the following fabrics in relation to John's budget and life-style:

100 percent cotton shirts versus 65 percent cotton/35 percent polyester shirts

100 percent tropical weight wool suit/pant versus 100 percent polyester suit/pant versus 85 percent worsted wool/15 percent polyester suit/pant

■ Considering the preceding choices what would your suggestions be as to garment care?

TERMS TO KNOW

Define or briefly explain the following:

Fiber
Fabric
Filament
Fiber content
Blend
Cellulosic fibers
Noncellulosic fibers
Man-made fibers
Wishbone hanger
Cotton linters
Box storage

CHAPTER 11

SPECIAL-MAKE CLOTHING AND THE TAILOR

Often special-make clothing is thought to be a luxury for the wealthy. For the man of unusual proportions, however, special-make clothing may be a necessity. For some, it is almost impossible to find off the rack clothes that will fit or can be altered to fit. Whatever the perception, the field of custom apparel has been growing and taking more dollars away from the traditional retailer and putting them into the pocket of those who offer special services. Let's look at the different options this man has. There are three main categories of special-make clothing: *made to order, made to measure, and custom-made*. Each has its pros and cons, and the choice must be made by the client based on his particular needs and his budget.

MADE-TO-ORDER CLOTHING

This category may or may not work for the man of unusual size. Some stores and some manufacturers enable customers to special order items already in their line. In this case, the customer picks a fabric, color, and style already being produced by the company, or offered via swatches seen in the store. The company makes the garment to the customer's request *in their stock pattern*. In other words, there are no special accommodations as to size or fit. This might be done because the store doesn't regularly carry that size in their stock, like a 36 regular, even though the manufacturer does offer it. Conversely, some men like made-to-order clothing because it allows them variety and individuality in choice. Made-to-order garments may be available from many different garment classifications, not just suits. They can include sportcoats, slacks, shirts, and shoes.

Usually, higher-end manufacturers, like Oxxford and Hickey-Freeman, are more likely to offer made-to-order apparel. The retailer will be familiar with policies for each of their suppliers.

Sometimes, the manufacturer has the desired garments in their warehouse, and this becomes a *special order*; it is not specifically made for the customer. Special orders must be placed through an accommodating retailer, often a specialty store, that carries the desired line. Many manufacturers will work with retailers in servicing customers with special orders.

Who Will Benefit?

The man of average proportions whose size is one not stocked heavily at retail, such as a 36R, 38S, 48R, and so on will benefit. This is also an option for the man who needs only minor fit alterations.

Source

Some investigation will need to be done as to the stores that will offer this service. It is best to do this by telephone. You will be most likely to find this option at specialty stores or very service-oriented, high-end department stores.

> *Pros*: The customer may be able to get exactly the color and style he wants even though it is not presently in the store's stock in his size. If his proportions are average, this is an excellent option without paying for custom work.
>
> *Cons*: It will not be adjusted to fit him exactly; alterations will still need to be made if he has unusual proportions. There might be a small surcharge for a special order; this is up to the manufacturer and retailer.

MADE-TO-MEASURE CLOTHING

Here the customer chooses from a wide variety of fabric swatches and colors. He is shown pictures of different styles, or actual sample garments to determine preferred cut, pocket style, lapel style, and so on. Then he is measured. Measurements are sent to a company that specializes in made-to-measure clothing. Their stock patterns are then adjusted to those measurements and style variations. The pattern is not created from scratch for that man. Existing patterns are altered to agree with his measurements. The company that makes those patterns may have many retail outlets representing them all over the country, or perhaps just in their state. In any case, they mass market this semi-custom suit.

The manufacturing operation adjusts the pattern and makes the suit, coat, or pant. On completion the garment(s) are shipped back to the retail outlet, and the customer tries on the apparel. If alterations need to be made, the adjustments are done on the premises by a tailor. Notification of any alterations made to the garment(s) is sent to the manufacturer, who will then adjust the pattern. In this way, future orders will produce better fitting garments.

This service extends to shirtings as well as suits, sportcoats, and slacks. And many offering the service have furnishings available from other resources for wardrobe coordination. There are many traditional retailers who also offer shirtings made-to-measure through high-quality shirt manufacturers. You will find, for example, a wide variety of offerings at Brooks Brothers nationally as well as the highly specialized Custom Shop (refer to chapter 7).

Made-to-measure clothing has become a very important segment of clothing sales for some retailers. It is now possible for retailers to install computer operations that are on-line with the system garment manufacturer. The retailer puts measurements into the computer, along with fabric and styling choices, and the finished made-to-measure garment is sent to the store within a couple of weeks. This retailer is now able to service the customer whom he previously had to "walk" because he couldn't fit the customer.

This is probably the fastest-growing segment of the three special-make varieties. Its price puts it in the realm of the affordable for many who have been purchasing higher-end merchandise. But its attraction comes via the special service and ease of shopping that accompany the process. For many, there is a real benefit to having the service person come to the consumer's office, show swatches, and have measurements taken without ever having to leave his place of business. For today's busy executive, the price is well worth the service and time gained.

An unusual option in this category that is available in some larger cities nationally is the *Hong Kong tailor*. A representative of a made-to-measure operation from the Orient schedules measuring sessions for several days while he is in a particular city. Usually the representative sets up "shop" in a central hotel. He displays fabric swatches of suitings and shirtings. The scheduled client then is measured, chooses from available styles and fabrics, and pays for the finished garments in advance. The orders are then sent to the Orient where the garments are made. In 6 to 8 weeks the finished garments are then shipped to the customer. If alterations are required, these may be done by a local tailor with the bill and adjustment information sent to the Hong Kong operation. Suit costs are typically less than the U.S. made-to-measure garments. Style is not the forte of the Hong Kong tailor.[1] If one is interested in a mainstream fabric and style this avenue is an option.

[1]Marc Frons, "Custom Tailors from Seoul to Savile Row," *Business Week*, November 7, 1988, p. 184.

Who Will Benefit?

The man of unusual proportions, who cannot find garments at retail to fit him will benefit. This same man may not be able to even get made-to-order garments to fit satisfactorily because of the extensive alterations he needs.

The man who likes unusual fabrics, individualized styling, and personalized service may also prefer this route even if he is a standard size.

Source

In any major city there will be several tailors who represent organizations like this. The telephone book will list them under "tailors" but will not identify them as made-to-measure tailors. Therefore, it is best to do investigation by telephone. Because quality can vary widely, it is best to get some references to qualify the company. An example of a national made-to-measure organization is Tom James, although the local retailer may operate his shop under a different name.

> *Pros*: Endless range of colors, fabrics, and style combinations. Because they make garments to the man's measurements, there is the opportunity for greater satisfaction and less frustration for the customer. If the man does not have really severe fit problems, this may be a viable option.

> *Cons*: This is understandably more expensive than made-to-order clothing, but this man is used to paying more also. Because the garment is sent back to the retailer already completed, there are no intermediary fittings that might otherwise ensure better fit as is done in traditional custom work. If the man has a really unusual build, he may need the intermediary *fittings* of a custom tailor to get the fit just right. Realize that these garments come out of a production shop and therefore will not have the detail work from a custom tailor, and the price may not differ that much from custom.

CUSTOM-TAILORED CLOTHING

This is the height of luxury in getting quality and fit. The beginning process of garment creation goes beyond that of made-to-measure. The options are endless here as the tailor's shop does all the design. So the customer may create his own style if so desired.

The man is measured, and his concerns and history of fit problems are discussed at length. Traditionally the pattern and garment is made on the premises by the same tailor who measured him. In many shops, there are assistants who work with the tailor on each garment. There are several fittings during the manufacturing process. The client sets up an appointment for a *fitting*, or the tailor will call when the garment is ready for a try-on. This is a very critical aspect of custom work. When a garment is altered as it is being made, there is far greater likelihood that it will fit well. Once the garment is completed, it is difficult, if not almost impossible, to make some alterations. So the concept of several fittings is key to the value and satisfaction with custom clothes.

For many men, there is a satisfaction that comes from these fittings. The man learns more about quality and fit, and has an integral part to play in the look and fit of his clothing. It is with the custom tailor that the man develops a relationship over the years, resulting in a very personalized look. Of course, the time and detail involved with the make of these clothes is understandably going to cost more.

Both the time and the cost of the custom suit vary greatly with the expertise of the tailor. The least time to receive the finished suit is two weeks and that is extremely fast. It can take as long as 3 months in some tailor shops. Costs can range anywhere from $1,000 to $4,000, depending on the type of fabric used, and, again, the expertise and reputation of the tailor's operation.

Like the other categories, the accomplished custom tailor goes well beyond suitings in his offerings including sportcoats, outerwear, slacks, shirts, and so on.

Who Will Benefit?

Any man who has the financial means to afford a fine custom tailor will reap the benefits. However, the man who has consistently had trouble finding at retail clothing that fits may most appreciate the results of the custom tailor.

Source

Though tailors are listed in the yellow pages of the telephone book, real care must be taken in choosing one. Tailors may be top rank or be novices. Some tailors do mostly repair work and alterations. It is best to locate a tailor who specializes in custom clothing and makes a living producing these clothes.

Another source of custom tailors is through retailers. Ask knowledgeable sales people or tailors in specialty stores. They will be happy to refer you to a tailor if they are not able to fill your needs from their stock. You still need to take care in checking out these references; it could be a brother of the shop tailor or a cousin of the store owner. It is always possible that bias exists here.

You may locate several tailors who do specialize in design and make of clothing, but then you must learn more about their particular look. Just as big name designers have a "look" synonymous with their name, like a Ralph Lauren or a Giorgio Armani, tailors also have their own look. It is best you find one who has similar style and fit preferences as you do.

The best way to do this is by reference. It is similar to finding a hair stylist—a very personal matter indeed. Asking others who are knowledgeable about clothing or who use a custom tailor is the first step. Then visit the tailor, see some of his work, and get a sense of his philosophy. There must be a rapport between the tailor and the client. There is a great deal of time and money that can be spent in producing a custom-made suit. So effort must be placed in determining the custom tailor who can fill the customer's needs. If personalities don't click, the results may not be satisfactory.

It is also important to understand that tailoring is an art, a dying art. And the excellent tailor is an artist. The stereotyped tailor is high strung and hot tempered. This is not necessarily the case in reality. Tailors are in a service business, and they try to accommodate the client's needs and wants. The best tailors will value the client's attention to detail, as well as his appreciation of the tailor's work.

Pros: Garments individually designed and garments that fit. Scheduled fittings during the make of the garments that ensure quality and precise fit. Personal relationship with the person making the garments, resulting in greater attention to details. Custom-designed features that cannot be accommodated in made-to-order or made-to-measure clothing.

Cons: Expensive. More time must be taken in finding the *right* tailor for the client's style and personality. It does take more time to produce these garments because of the fittings required.

BACKGROUND OF TAILOR

It is important to understand the roots of today's tailors to relate to and communicate better with them. Tailoring is somewhat of a mystery to many people. It is an old-world art, which historically was learned as an apprentice working under a master tailor.

The well-designed and executed suit is an act of design engineering. The tailor must understand how the body moves, how fabric responds, the different properties of a variety of fabrics, the impact of heat and moisture in pressing, and so on. It took years for young apprentices to learn all aspects of the trade. Once learned and practiced, the tailor was understandably proud of his accomplishments. In today's society, we no longer regularly practice apprenticeships in the true sense of the word. Those entering garment design today more often learn high-tech methods and lose some of the high touch associated with old-world tailoring.

The work of the experienced tailor is a true art-form. Alberto Cercone, named by Esquire as one of the best tailors in the U. S., learned his trade in Pacentro, Italy. He still uses old-world methods to create the fine detailing found in custom clothing. (Courtesy of A. Cercone.)

The very best tailors come to the United States from areas where apprenticeships are still served. Italy unquestionably produces the finest tailors in the world. England is well known for its bespoke, or custom, clothing. Countries that produce fine fabrics are often known for their tailoring as well.

It is understandable that the best tailors consider themselves a unique breed. So it is important to "sense out" the tailor you will be working with to determine how to communicate the most effectively.

PROCESS OF WORKING WITH TAILOR

The first step in working with the tailor at retail is to gain his or her respect. This can best be done through knowledge of the product, understanding of your customer, appreciation of the tailoring arts, and a desire to communicate effectively. You must be clear in your communication and use the appropriate menswear terms discussed throughout this book. Speaking the same language will go a long way in cementing a working relationship.

If you are going to be working frequently with a particular tailor it is a good idea to meet with him before meeting with the customer or client. This gives you the opportunity to start building a relationship before the fitting. It is very difficult, if not impossible, to get the tailor to understand your relationship with a customer or client once you are all together. So this initial meeting with the tailor is essential.

Let him know what your working relationship is with your client. This is especially important if the customer is relying on you for directions on sleeve length and pant length, for example. This is important to emphasize to avoid awkwardness for either you or your customer during the fitting. If you have any particular questions or concerns of the tailor, discuss those with him in private.

Be sure to acknowledge the tailor's position and expertise when you are with the client. The client will feel more secure in knowing that you admire the tailor's work. Conversely, remember that your concerns should always be for the client, and if that means that you must ask the tailor for an additional fitting or rework of some sort, then that is your responsibility. The client should not always be the one to wear the "black hat"; rather you should be a buffer between the client and the tailor if need be.

FITTINGS

There may be from one to five fittings or more, depending on whether working with a retail tailor or a custom tailor. If you are working with a tailor at retail, remember, the customer's satisfaction comes first. If the hemmed pants are not just right, then they should be redone. If the customer is talked into accepting a garment that is slightly off, and he hears about it from family or friends, he may never be a customer of that store again. When pains are taken to meet the needs of the customer, however, you can expect repeat business.

If you are working with a tailor in a retail store, as the store's sales associate, you may be involved in the fitting. The tailor may ask you to write down measurements on the store form. In some cases, the sales associate may actually take the measurements and mark the garments instead of a tailor doing so. The tailor then picks up where the salesperson left off, in terms of actual alterations being made. In this situation, if fit adjustments are still required when the customer returns for garment pick up, the tailor would be involved in the process.

At retail, the customer should always try on an altered garment before taking it home. He may be coming in only to pick it up after alterations have been done, but he should still be encouraged to try it on. Once home, the customer will be less likely to return it to the store for adjustments. When you suggest trying on the garment(s) before leaving the store, you are saying that you truly care about his satisfaction. You want to be sure that the work coming out of the shop is quality, and that will help to build repeat business for you and the store.

Make sure the customer sees himself in a three-way mirror. If he is trying on a suit, he needs to have on a correctly fitted shirt. If he is not wearing a long-sleeve dress shirt, many stores have extras available for suit try-ons. This is much preferred to trying on a coat over a knit polo shirt, which may have an impact on the fit of the coat. The man should have on shoes representative of the heel height and style he will be wearing with the suit. In addition, he needs to put everything he usually uses in his pockets.

After purchase, ask the client if he wishes you to remove tickets. Carefully take off all the tickets, remove the stay tacks at the back vent(s) of the coat, and open the coat pockets if they are sewn closed and the customer wants them opened. Note, it is best to do this from the inside of the garments. *Extreme care* must be taken to avoid clipping the fabric! Be sure to give the tickets to him or put them in the pockets.

If there are any further fit concerns, they should be brought to the attention of the tailor at this time. If you will be working with this tailor repeatedly, *your* attention to detail early in the relationship will reinforce *his* attention to detail in making future alterations for you and your customers.

CASE STUDY

Stephen Laska had high, broad shoulders with bone spurs protruding on the top of each one. He had preferred American natural shoulder styles, and every coat he had ever bought resulted in bumps along the shoulder line. No matter how much altering the store tailor did, the coats never looked right. He had even tried made-to-order suits before, and the results were not satisfactory.

In desperation he contacted a fashion consultant for direction. The consultant suggested a custom tailor. The tailor created special shoulder pads that had an indentation right where the spurs were. This produced a shoulder pad that camouflaged the bump and resulted in a smooth shoulder line. The tailor also designed a special pattern that would accommodate Stephen's full, square shoulders.

Though the expense was greater than he had anticipated, the aggravation was far less. Stephen's confidence level also benefited by a suit that fit him perfectly.

- Would Stephen have been better off in a European-cut suit than an American suit?
- Why did the made-to-order suits not make any difference in the problem?
- Would a made-to-measure suit have been a better choice than custom-made?

TERMS TO KNOW

Define or briefly explain the following:

Made-to-order
Stock pattern
Special order
Made-to-measure
Hong Kong Tailor
Custom made
Custom tailor
Fitting

CHAPTER 12

GARMENT SELECTION FOR THE CONSUMER

Even with all the technical details in place, determination of appropriate style can be difficult for the consumer. And coordination is a very complex part of the issue. It is here where the fashion professional has the ability to use all natural talents for the art of fashion. Combining that with an understanding of style, cut, and make will prove a real benefit for the consumer. This process is often much easier for the fashion consultant than the consumer himself, as the consultant can be much more objective about style and proportion.

Apparel is so much more expensive today than in the past; each purchase must be made carefully, especially for those on a budget. Apparel selection is now serious business for those investing in a wardrobe, and the sales assistant must help make the right choices, or risk loss of a customer.

GARMENT PROPORTIONS AND THE CUSTOMER

Having looked at individual aspects of menswear, it is extremely important to look at how the parts interrelate to the whole and how that whole relates to the consumer. We may study fashion and follow the trends, but then we have to be able to connect this to each customer we serve. For example, let's say our customer is 5 feet 5 inches tall and is wearing cuffed pants that are too short, and show his light-colored socks. His bold plaid sport coat has a lapel width of 3 1/4 inches, a traditionally conservative width, but his tie is 10 years old, and it's 5 1/2 inches wide. It is out of sync and ruins the look of the suit. The tie becomes the focal point of the outfit because of its lack of proportion to the rest of the outfit. Individual aspects of this outfit do not work with each other, nor is the outfit appropriate for the physique of the customer in question.

We must balance the proportion of current style with the physique of the customer. Then a new element must be injected into the decision-making process. What is the personality type of the consumer, what is his life-style and career track, and what styles are appropriate for this individual? This is a sizable issue and must be evaluated step by step.

First, let's back up just a bit and look at the factors that tend to influence menswear proportion. When the country is in conservative times politically and economically, the lapels tend to get narrower. In very liberal times, the lapels tend to widen. The lapel of the coat tends to be like a barometer in relation to the political and economic climate. There are exceptions, of course. At times of economic or political upheaval or in times of war, the concept falls by the wayside. In conservative times, not only is the lapel narrower, but there is a smaller shirt collar, narrower tie, slimmer pant silhouette, narrower cuff, and so on. And the reverse holds true of liberal times. Of course, this relates to mainstream menswear, not the fashion-forward looks that will always be experimental.

So when we look at proportion on the man we must look at total proportion of all the parts. Does the tie balance with the shirt and the coat with the pant, and so on? The next step is to look at how the proportions look on him.

The average style and proportions of the day may not work for every man. For example, a very large man better upgrade the scale of his apparel, or he will look like he's bursting out of his clothes. Most manufacturers and designers keep this in mind as they size their garments. For example, the lapel on a size 48 coat is wider than the lapel on the same model size 38 coat. Likewise, the small man should be very sensitive to total proportion, or he may look like a little boy in his father's clothes.

This is a matter of being objective in looking in the mirror. It sounds a lot easier than it is! This is where the fashion professional must have a trained eye to assist the customer. Does the collar look too large for the man's face? Does it balance with the size of the lapel of his coat? It is easiest to evaluate this at a distance rather than in front of the man. Stand back about 8 feet to 10 feet and look at total proportion.

Though this is very subjective, one can learn what looks balanced. This can be done by constant study of ads, store windows, television, and catalogs. By consciously looking at proportion, you will be training yourself to recognize what looks right and what looks wrong. An excellent place to evaluate proportion of collar, tie knot, and lapel is by observing newscasters on television.

PHYSIQUE OF THE INDIVIDUAL CONSUMER

Apparel creates an illusion on the body—it can add weight, increase perception of shoulder size, shorten appearance of long legs, and so on. What is perceived as the ideal build is the inverted triangle, or the wedge, where the chest and shoulders are broad and the waist and hips are slim. Some garment styles lend themselves to this silhouette, like a sportcoat that has a strong shoulder line and a slim sweep. Also, the elements of a coordinated outfit may result in the "wedge" silhouette, like a sportshirt that has shoulder-broadening epaulets with a slim silhouetted pant. The following concepts may be applied with color and texture to create the illusion of a more ideal physique for the customer.

In the process of doing this, also look at the messages of the elements of the outfit. Do they say the same thing as the whole? If the man is wearing a natural shouldered Ivy League style suit, does he have on a very forward tie? They don't send the same message. If he is wearing a sophisticated low-gorge, Italian double-breasted suit, has he worn a sporty, oxford-cloth, button-down collar shirt? There is a subtlety here. But it is well understood by the sophisticated dresser.

PERSONALITY TYPES

A primary tool to help in proper choice is understanding of personality expression and application of that concept to your clients. This is a matter of looking at the man's life-style, profession, build, and personality, and combining them all together to give garment guidance in shopping.

There are five basic personality types. Although all men are a blend of several styles, one category usually surfaces as the primary personality type. Clothes in this category already form the mainstay of the man's wardrobe. Men generally also have a strong secondary type. Their casual clothes and their evening wear cluster in this subsidiary group.

It is foolish to put a man in sophisticated European clothing, even if that style is the height of fashion, if his personality, build, life-style, and career point to a more conservative style. He might like the look initially, but ultimately he'll learn it doesn't fit his personality or his life-style and shouldn't be in his closet. He'll be less likely to look to you for direction in the future with a poor choice made here.

Even though the types have been narrowed down, there are many variations and a lot of flexibility in each group. The scope remains limitless within the confines of the category despite the definite boundary lines between each group. Given the unspoken taboos of the workplace, the man may have no control over the options on facial hair or the requirement to wear a white shirt in his business. But the man does have total control over the suit and tie, which can speak volumes about who he really is.

A personality quiz has been included at the end of this chapter to assist in personality-type determination.

To Look Taller and Slimmer	*To Look Shorter and/or Heavier*
Do wear the following:	Do wear the following:

Do wear the following:

- Solid colors, preferably in the same color range on top as on bottom
- Flat-finish fabrics
- Narrow stripes
- Hemmed, not cuffed, pants
- Pants that reach the counter-heel seam of the shoe
- Tie that at least touches top of waistband
- Monochromatic coordination in shoe, sock, and pant
- V-neck sweaters

Don't wear the following:

- Many different solid colors in same outfit
- Busy patterns
- Mixture of textured fabrics
- Short, cuffed pants
- Vests
- Full, large tie knot
- Many busy accessories

Do wear the following:

- Contrasting colors in separates and sportswear
- Mix of patterns
- Sportcoats with patch pockets or styling details
- Oversized sweaters
- Layers in sportswear
- Highly textural fabrics
- Full-cut double-breasted coats
- Cuffed pants
- Pants with deep pleats and full silhouette legs
- Contrast or patterned hosiery

Don't wear the following:

- Monochromatic look from head to toe
- Vertical stripes
- Coats that have narrow shoulders, slim silhouette
- Overly long, hemmed pants
- Plain front, slim silhouette pants
- Tie that extends longer than the waistband or belt buckle
- Very narrow ties and lapels
- Monochromatic coordination in shoe, sock, and pant

BEST STYLES BASED ON PERSONALITY TYPES

Conservative Classic

This style is the most traditional of all types. This man favors the classic American look, which has its roots in British clothing. The short man in this group must avoid overly full-cut clothing because it may emphasize his short stature. The athlete in this class may also have some fit concerns as he'll require a lot of alterations or may need to buy custom apparel in some cases.

This man is conservative. Politically he may vote in the mainstream. He values tradition and appreciates quality. You will find a lot of the professionals in this group: physicians, lawyers, bankers, politicians, and mid-management to chief executive officer level form the career core. Men in positions of authority and responsibility gravitate to this personality style.

Former President Ronald Reagan's classic style represents the very subtle and traditional approach to apparel as seen in the conservative classic personality expression. Other well-known personalities in this group include Donald Trump, John Glenn, and Phil Donahue. UPI/Bettman.

Clothing message. This man wants to communicate that he is trustworthy and stable. He creates the impression that he is a careful decision maker. Men who wear conservatively classic clothes are more concerned about being appropriately dressed than they are with making a bold fashion statement. They never want their choices to cause any undue attention. Examples are Ronald Reagan, Donald Trump, John Glenn, and Phil Donahue.

BUSINESS WARDROBE

Suits: British or traditional American full cut, two- or three-button single-breasted suits with a center vent. He'll prefer solids, but does like some subtle patterns including pinstripes, chalk stripes, and very reserved plaids.

Sportcoats: The navy blazer is a must, and he may have one for winter as well as summer. Solid colors are preferred, though some traditional tweeds or herringbones work well in the wardrobe. Outspoken colors may be chosen for evening hours or in the clubhouse after a round of golf. This man likes raw silk, fine wool serge, gabardines, and some hopsacks. He'll often wear seersucker and poplin in warm weather and flannels in winter.

Slacks: He prefers the traditional beltloop style. He will often wear conservative pleats and may also opt for cuffs. Pleats and cuffs are a very personal matter, however, and preference can vary widely here.

Shirts: Both button-down and spread collars are found in this man's wardrobe. In the northern industrial cities, particularly the Northeast, there is a leaning toward the button-down. This hearkens back to the strong Ivy League influence there. In the South and West more straight-point collars are worn. He prefers the full-cut shirt, but if he is exceptionally slim, he may want a tapered cut. Both solids and stripes are worn, but emphasis is on the traditional white shirt. When he is feeling more outspoken, he may bring in a few wider stripes with white collar, typical of the British shirting.

Ties: He leans toward the traditional foulards, clubs, and stripes. The smaller the pattern the better. On stripes, the colors should be pure, and the stripe lines should be well differentiated, not blending into one another. He also may like knitted ties, but they should be saved for the weekend because of their informality.

Shoes: The most conservative of this group will wear only tie shoes like wing tips, cap-toe oxfords, and plain oxfords. Slip-ons like tassel and penny loafers are preferred with sportcoats and slacks.

Furnishings: This man feels less is more. If a silk pocket square is used, it will be in subdued colors. Many prefer a crisp white linen handkerchief. These men should use patterned pocket squares sparingly. If he wears French-cuff shirts, cuff links should be small, classic, and unobtrusive. Save collar bars for evening. Conservative hats wear well with this look. British-style caps and mufflers look good in the winter.

Outerwear: There are just two real choices here: a single-breasted raglan sleeve, tan rain coat (or all weather coat), and a traditional reefer topcoat in a long length.

SPORTSWEAR

Slacks: Beltloop models predominate, some beltless models for leisure. Favored fabrics include twills, poplins, gabardines, khaki, and denim.

Shirts: Button-down collars are favored here, and now the man will bring in a wider variety of patterns and colors. He will like plaids, checks, and windowpane patterns. Even for leisure this man would prefer his shirts pressed and lightly starched.

Sweaters: He loves sweaters, cardigans, pullovers, sweater vests, and he prefers them in shetland wools, lambswools, and subtle cashmeres. Because he is basically conservative, he will lean toward solid colors. His favorite sweater may well be a beefy wool, shawl-collar cardigan with roomy pockets.

Shoes: He loves loafers, deck shoes, and tennis shoes for casual wear.

Outerwear: The lightweight, solid-color stadium jacket is the coat of choice. Or he'll buy a solid-color parka with a plaid wool lining for cold weather.

FORMAL WEAR

The traditional black tuxedo is always this man's first choice. His tuxedo shirt has straight-point collars. But he will wear a dark suit with a white shirt if he doesn't own a tux.

Updated Traditional

This is the younger, more upbeat version of the conservative classic. The "Big Chill" and "Wall Street" crowd, in movie terms. It is the sartorial training ground for America's future gray-headed power brokers.

A true updated traditional, athlete and sportscaster O. J. Simpson reflects a classic look balanced with expressive style. Others representative of this group are Dick Cavett, Rob Lowe, and Joel Grey. PhotoFest.

Any build or size may fall in this category, though there is a leaning toward the slim to average. This man often works out and stays in shape. The big or heavy-set man may feel and look more at ease in the conservative styles. For the athletic build, more options will be found here than in the conservative classic.

This man tries to be open-minded about new ideas. Politically he sits right in the middle. His clothes show he doesn't take himself too seriously, and he will be somewhat adventuresome with fashion.

Clothing message. He is interested in his clothing and appearance, and pays attention to detail. His appearance also says, "I work hard but I also like to have fun, and I have a sense of humor." He is a risk taker, and he's willing to try new things. His clothes say confident, with an appreciation for tradition with a new twist. Examples are Joel Grey, Ryan O'Neal, Dick Cavett, Rob Lowe, and O. J. Simpson.

BUSINESS WARDROBE

Suits: This man prefers the modified American (European) or Drape cut. Jackets have a two-button, single-breasted front with center or side vents. He is open also to double-breasted styles. This man likes to buy patterned suits more than his conservative classic counterpart. He likes subtle plaids, houndstooths, tick weaves, heathers, and herringbones. But he has not forsaken solids. Some in this group will gravitate toward the slightly oversized, traditional-cut suit, which makes more of a fashion statement. The updated traditionalist prefers an "interesting" look and favors a wide variety of colors as well as mixing textures.

Sportcoats: Blazers of all colors and sportcoats of all fabrics and textures are used freely. There may be greater flexibility for sport coats used in business in this category. Some sport coats may take on a European look in cut and fabric.

Slacks: These are usually a beltloop model. Many are pleated and cuffed in a longer length. The silhouette may sport a fuller cut to express an interest in style. Favorite fabrics include gabardines all year long, worsted wools in winter, and linens in summer.

Shirts: Though button-downs are found in his wardrobe, the straight-point collar looks best with his more fashionable appearance. Fancies are used more here because this wardrobe employs a greater use of separates. The shirt fit may be full cut, tapered, or fitted. A lot more color and pattern variation will be seen here.

Ties: Stripes are strong, clear, and traditional. Regimental stripes and foulards hit the top of the list. Paisleys and some printed patterns exhibit an outgoing nature. Colors are expressive with an unusual blending of sophisticated colors with traditional patterns. Knit ties are used with sport coats for leisure. He will experiment with theme ties, florals, and conversationals.

Shoes: This man likes the clean look of a cap-toe oxford in a tie shoe. If he opts for a wing tip, it has a leaner, more European look to it. He also likes tassel loafers for business or an updated loafer with a low vamp for wear with slacks and blazers.

Accessories: This man likes to add flair with accessories. He will update the traditional look with unusually patterned suspenders. He may express his personality also in his choice of socks, patterns, and colors. Pinned collars and French cuffs with cuff links are seen both during day and into the evening. He often wears hats all year round.

Outerwear: Once again, it's the traditional raglan sleeve raincoat or perhaps trench coat. He may select a topcoat for winter. If he has the build to carry it off, he may choose a double-breasted style.

SPORTSWEAR WARDROBE

Slacks: He leans toward the conservative classic in similar styling, but they have a more updated silhouette. He may be open to a stylish full or very narrow leg. They may also sport cuffs and pleats.

Shirts: Same as the conservative classic.

Sweaters: He prefers solid colors. He also likes the feel of Shetland wool, lambswool, and cashmere. His sweaters lean to the cardigan and pull-over styles. When he "lets his hair down," he will buy strongly patterned sweaters in argyles and stripes. He loves the Scandinavian ski sweaters and knitted looks with a specific motif.

Shoes: Deck shoes, soft soled loafers, jogging shoes, and huaraches, or Latin American sandals, are good choices. He's likely to wear cloth or leather espadrilles at home as well as to the resort.

Outerwear: He'll wear the standard stadium jacket, but it may also be a more expressive style—oversized or with unusual detailing on it. He's also an avid reader of the sporty L. L. Bean catalogue, and may enjoy a parka or rubberized foul-weather gear for sailing.

FORMAL WEAR

Dark suit, white shirt, and expressive tie are his way of looking elegant. He'll wear a traditional black tuxedo, but jazz it up with a wing collar and colorful tie and cummerbund.

Sophisticated Continental

This man picks up where the updated traditionalist left off. He is more adventuresome in color, fabrics, coordination, and proportion. His clothes often have a European look. They are a study in contrasts; they either hug the body or they are oversized. He likes to create charisma through unusual patterns, colors, and textures. And his clothes are an important avenue to self-expression.

Politically he may fall somewhere between moderate and conservative. He has a worldly air, and is supremely confident in any business or social situation. This personality type lends itself to older men who have some years under their belts to breed this unshakable self-confidence. The younger man who tries to adopt this look may appear contrived—much depends on his bearing to determine if he could carry the look off.

Actor John Forsythe represents the elegance and worldliness in his choice of sophisticated continental apparel. Others representative of this group are Harry Belafonte, Gianni Agnelli, and Tom Wolfe. PhotoFest.

His build is usually medium to tall and slim to average in weight. The athletic build will find some selection here.

This gentleman is often found in the worlds of finance, advertising, and the media; top executives and business owners also enjoy these looks. Of course, the look applies itself directly to those in fashion or design.

Clothing Message. He is in control and very sure of himself. He likes to dress up and enjoys the refinement of elegant clothes. He is used to getting what he wants! Examples are Cary Grant, Fred Astaire, Harry Belafonte, Gianni Agnelli, Douglas Fairbanks, Jr., and John Forsythe.

BUSINESS WARDROBE

Suits: This man prefers European styling. He can wear the cut with no problem. Many men in this group like the inverted triangle silhouette with a fashion-forward look. He may opt for an oversized Italian silhouette. The style may be single- or double-breasted with one- or two-button fronts. He will like the basics or worsteds, gabardines, and flannels, but also will wear unusual blends of fibers in sophisticated textures. He likes fabrics that have a high sheen and will wear those suits for dressy occasions or evening.

Sportcoats: They will wear either single- or double-breasted coats in either long, sleek silhouettes, or easy, unconstructed, oversized looks. Textures span from fine wool serge to raw silk and linen in summer. The basic navy blazer is made more elegant by the cut, fabric, and accessories. Though the basics are necessary here, this man generally avoids the mundane. He prefers unusual pieces that express his personality.

Slacks: This man buys lightweight, soft fabrics that move easily with the body. He likes beltloop models that have either a pleated or plain front. The silhouette is sleek and longer, giving the illusion of height. If the pant is cuffed, there is a healthy break in the crease, to keep the pant long. Pant fabrics include wool faille cloth, lightweight gabardine, and tropical-weight worsteds. He will experiment with unusual colors and textures for dressy casual.

Shirts: This man leans toward the formality of the French-cuff shirt for both day and evening. This can become a signature look for him using very special cuff links. His cuff links are understated and communicate an old-world elegance. He seldom wears a button-down shirt except for very casual wear. He much prefers straight-point and wide-spread collars. You will find him wearing broadcloth, swiss voile, and fine batiste shirtings. He prefers solids and uses unusual color combinations with his ties and suits. However, he also likes the elegance of top quality tone on tone and crisp, narrow stripes.

Ties: Nothing in the ordinary for this man. He likes unusual patterns typical of Italian and French ties. He feels at ease with florals, free-flowing, nonobjective patterns, conversationals, pin dots, elegant foulards, paisleys, and subtle stripes.

Shoes: There's a definite European influence; the man selects thin-soled shoes with low vamps. He will also opt for the simple elegance of a plain oxford. For business he might wear a lightweight wing tip, though he prefers a cap-toe oxford. For more casual meetings, he will step into a simple slip-on, like a loafer with an unobtrusive buckle.

Accessories: He uses them with panache. Pocket squares, collar bars, tie tacks, and suspenders are standard fare for him. This man also favors unusual socks. He will select subtly patterned socks of fine cotton, silk, or lightweight wool. Scarves and hats are worn with aplomb. He manages to use these accessories so they blend together and heighten the sophistication level without looking overdone.

Outerwear: This group likes trench coats in an oversized proportion or wrap raincoats in a high-fashion look. When winter sets in he will wear a top coat in a long, sleek style, perhaps a chesterfield.

SPORTSWEAR WARDROBE

Slacks: He'll wear the same silhouette as for business. Fabrics are fine cottons, linens, and silks for casual and resort wear. But here he enjoys clothes of unusual colors. He'll wear pastels and brights as well as the basic neutrals.

Shirts: Spread and straight-point collars are preferred. In addition to cotton broadcloth, he likes rayon, linen, and silk shirts. He may still use his French-cuff shirts with more casual pants and shirts to continue his signature look.

Sweaters: He loves sweaters, and he wears them all year for leisure. He likes cotton and linen sweaters for summer. He wears them loose and easy without a shirt underneath. In cool weather he likes the softness and luxuriousness of lambswool and cashmere. He also likes unusual sweater blends incorporating silk and mohair and those with suede sewn on to the garment in sophisticated patterns.

Shoes: Once again, these are European in origin with thin soles and low vamps. Slip-ons predominate, running the gamut from lightweight penny loafers in dark, shiny leathers to a slim and elegant sandal for summer. The key here is to avoid a heavy shoe that would contradict the refinement of the rest of the outfit.

Outerwear: This man will buy dramatic and oversized jackets as well as those lightweight and starkly simple in design. He stays with solid colors and timeless fabrics.

FORMAL WEAR

This man may well have a crowded social calendar and therefore needs greater variety in this category than men of other types. He likes to get dressed up. So he will forego the dress suit for the tuxedo in black or midnight navy. He prefers a wing-collar shirt with an expressive bowtie and cummerbund. He may also want the flexibility of a dinner jacket.

Arty Eclectic

This man creates his own unique style. He is a real individualist and is less concerned with what others think than with what he likes. His clothes are fun and give him pleasure. He sometimes enjoys shocking those around him by what he wears.

He is liberal and open-minded, a creative thinker who is seldom intimidated by the attitudes of others. You will find all sizes from small, slight stature to tall and thin. There are fewer heavy-set men in this group, however.

He is often associated with the arts, entertainment, the media, political and human rights issues, fashion, and retail. This category also draws a lot of entrepreneurs.

The category of arty eclectic lends itself to the broadest range of styles. Mick Jagger represents just one of many looks from this group. Some purposely choose offbeat apparel, and others take a very laissez-faire approach and may wear an odd mix of whatever is available at the time. Whatever avenue taken, the look is totally unique to their personalities and life-styles. Others include Woody Allen, Mickey Rourke, George Carlin, and Anthony Perkins. *Left*: Brigitte Lacome/Liaison Agency. *Right*: Perrin/Campion/Tardy/Gamma.

Clothing message. This man wants to communicate that he is not afraid of bucking the system. He wants others to know that he is open-minded yet has strong opinions and will stand his ground. He wants others to know that he is an interesting person and he stands out as different in a group. Examples are Woody Allen, Anthony Perkins, Mick Jagger, Mickey Rourke, and George Carlin.

BUSINESS WARDROBE

Suits: This man seldom wears suits. They are physically and psychologically too restrictive for him. They are also not required because of the nature of his work. When hard pressed to do so, he leans toward a full-cut, unconstructed easy fit, which has a fashion look to it.

Sportcoats: He wears many older sportcoats—they are often thought of as "old friends" of quality fabrics made more comfortable by the years. He will also fill in the gaps with a modern oversized, unconstructed jacket. Because this man mixes colors and textures easily, you will find solids in unusual colors and fancies in all variety of sizes and textures. He has been known to haunt the Salvation Army and antique clothing stores for unique pieces.

Slacks: Comfort is the buzz word here. The pants are often oversized and tend toward the long side. They are almost always beltloop models, allowing him to seek out interesting belts and buckles. Favored fabric choices stretch from good wools to a rumpled linen look.

Shirts: He offers himself lots of latitude here. He loves the rayon fabrics reminiscent of the 1940s. But he may also wear a French-cuff shirt or a tuxedo shirt with an old-wool flannel pant and a deck shoe! He wears as many fancies as solids and has no fear in mixing patterns at will. He is less worried about rules than in the aura he creates. He may wear his shirt buttoned up at the neck with a western bolo or a string tie.

Ties: Because they are a symbol of the establishment and tend to make him feel uptight, he would prefer not to wear them. He has learned how they can be fun, however. He likes skinny string ties, especially in leather. These he likes to wear with an open, loose four-in-hand knot. Color, texture, and the way the tie is worn is most important to him. He also loves the ties of the 1940s and 1950s. Each of his ties is chosen with great care and strongly reflects his personality. You won't find this man in a regimental stripe or a neat foulard.

Shoes: Again, comfort comes first. He loves jogging shoes and soft-soled casual shoes, even with dress slacks and jackets. In summer, he prefers sandals. He will concede to a sensible oxford or a traditional loafer when he has to. He may well be seen without socks, regardless of the shoe style.

Accessories: He loves offbeat, antique, and somewhat trendy accessories to add visual texture to his look. He may wear a bolo with a dress shirt or have a collection of belt buckles to use as a focal point in his outfits. He will tuck in an elegant pocket square periodically or revert to a Truman fold white linen handkerchief. He loves hats of all sorts and also wears scarves much of the year. He enjoys suspenders from a functional viewpoint as well as from an aesthetic one.

Outerwear: Anything goes so long as it's not too tailored. Ease of wear is primary. He doesn't like anything fussy.

SPORTSWEAR WARDROBE

Slacks: These are much the same as business slacks, only the options include old blue jeans and khaki pants. Sweat pants and old army fatigues are de rigueur.

Shirts: These are much the same as the business attire.

Sweaters: The comfort and coziness associated with sweaters make them a favorite of this man. He likes all kinds, especially those that are full and easy to wear. He may still wear some of his father's old sweaters, yet he also enjoys the beauty of the Italian knits. Because of his artistic bent, he likes the hand-knit imported sweaters that are like individual works of art. He collects these and wears them year after year. He will wear sweaters all year long. In summer they may be made of cotton and linen.

Shoes: Sneakers, espadrilles, sandals, huaraches, and thongs are favored. He will wear any unusual relaxed shoe as long as it is comfortable.

Outerwear: Anything goes including sweater jackets.

FORMAL WEAR

The concept of formal cuts against the grain of everything he believes in. He will avoid wearing formal wear if possible. If he can't get out of it, he will try to personalize his look in some way. He may opt for an unusual second-hand tuxedo from an antique store, or he'll add a unique accessory that makes him feel more individualistic in an otherwise uniformed social situation.

Adventurous Sportsman

This type communicates the message "rugged individualist." His appearance is that of a man who has the strength to test the elements. He is natural and unassuming. His political bent is moderate. He understands the importance of flexibility, yet is quite decisive in his personal life. He likes animals, the out of doors, and sports.

In build, this man is quite often muscular. He may be average in size to big and tall. The small man is less frequently found in this group.

Burt Reynolds typifies the adventurous sportsman both on and off the screen. A relaxed attitude and real-world approach to apparel are reflected in his look. Others from this group include Robert Redford, Bruce Willis, Bruce Jenner, and former President Carter. PhotoFest.

Typical careers in this group include writers, members of the media, salesmen, travel consultants, small business owners, builders, athletes, and entrepreneurs.

Clothing message. His clothes tell others that he is pretty much mainstream politically because they are traditional in style and color. His choices are also those of comfort and function, typical of the sportsman. Lacking in artifice or excessive decoration, his apparel says "no nonsense" in a direct way. He also prefers a simple, easy look with a leaning toward the comfortable and informal. Examples are Burt Reynolds, Bruce Jenner, Robert Redford, and Jimmy Carter.

BUSINESS WARDROBE

Suits: Like the conservative classic, this man likes American or British cut clothing. Jackets typically are single-breasted with a center vent and natural or padded shoulders. Because this man intrinsically prefers sportcoats and slacks to suits, his suits are never too formidable. This man likes soft, easy woven fabrics in solids, plaids, and checks. Pinstripes are not seen too often here. In winter textured wools, tweeds, and flannels are favored. In summer, traditional khakis and poplins as well as tropical worsteds are in favor.

Sportcoats: Natural shoulder blazers with easy fit are a must. Patterns like checks and plaids are appropriate. Interesting surface textures represent this man better than silky, shiny fabrics. In fall there will be some detailing like elbow patches, throat latches, and gun patches.

Slacks: Again, textures are important. Flannels are key in cool weather; heathers and tweeds are also acceptable. For warm weather he wears cavalry twills, khakis, hopsacks, and gabardines. Plain front or pleated styles and cuffs lend themselves to this personality type. The silhouette is a straight leg worn fairly close to the body. No fashion forward or oversized look here. He usually wears a beltloop style.

Shirts: He prefers the more casual air of a button-down collar in oxford-cloth fabric. For more formal business occasions, he may choose a straight-point collar. Because he wears a lot of separates, he likes to include patterns in his shirt family. These patterns include tattersalls, stripes, checks, and plaids.

Ties: He leans toward the traditional in his choice of ties. Regimental stripes and foulards communicate his personality type well. He likes club ties, particularly those that relate to sports and outdoor activities, but he should be reserved in his use of those for business. Because texture is important in his wardrobe, his ties often have a surface texture. Dressy, shiny silk ties do not coordinate well with the rougher textures of his sport coats and slacks. Knitted ties can be worn in some business situations and certainly in leisure.

Shoes: Because of the more relaxed attitude of his personality, he prefers slip-ons. The traditional penny and tassel loafers work well for him. His tie shoes may be wing tips and cap-toe oxfords. Lightweight European style shoes may not work for this man because the more fashion-forward look does not coordinate well with his apparel.

Accessories: This man is not overly enthusiastic about accessories. In fall and winter, he will wear woolen scarves and hats that complement his outdoor look. He doesn't like to deal with the fussiness of accessories; he likes the look, but has never felt comfortable wearing them himself.

Outerwear: The traditional single-breasted raglan sleeve raincoat or all-weather coat is a basic. This man does not like to deal with a topcoat, so he prefers the flexibility of the all-weather coat.

SPORTSWEAR WARDROBE

Slacks: He will wear a beltloop, straight-leg model. He may opt for pleats or select a plain front. The fabrics are usually crisp, such as khakis, or soft, like 100 percent cotton corduroy. He loves denim all year round. He may shop the army-navy store for his most casual wear.

Shirts: Plaids are a mainstay in his closet. They reflect a friendly, outgoing, and adventurous nature. Sometimes he likes western styles. Flannel shirts, chambrays, and chamois looks are his comfortable "friends" and his preference on weekends. For more casual wear, he saves those old work shirts from years ago. This man does not care for short-sleeve shirts.

Sweaters: He would prefer to wear a heavier shirt than don a sweater. If weather calls for it, however, his sweaters are usually heavy-knitted pullovers in solid colors, allowing him to make the most use of his patterned shirts. His favorite sweater might have a large shawl collar.

Shoes: Because of his outdoor activities, he is well serviced by a good walking or hiking shoe—a sensible lace-up model. A lightweight shoe would contradict everything else he has done in his sportswear. He enjoys jogging shoes and also likes comfortable, soft-soled loafers.

Outerwear: The hooded parka is a staple for fall and winter. A lightweight, solid-color stadium jacket is a basic for warmer weather. He may also have the need for a quilted down jacket for cold-weather outdoor activities.

FORMAL WEAR

This man really feels like a duck out of water in formal wear. He will concede to wearing a tuxedo if absolutely necessary; however, he prefers a straight point collar rather than a wing collar. If he feels he can get away with it, he would rather wear a dark business suit with a white shirt for those formal occasions.

DETERMINATION OF PERSONALITY TYPE

As you work with a customer, especially in the early stages of a transaction, you need to be evaluating the verbal and nonverbal messages he is sending you. Sometimes a customer may want to wear the clothes of the arty eclectic, yet his build and personality communicate a sportsman type. Though most people feel comfortable dressing true to their own personality type, periodically you may encounter an individual who desires to be other than he is. He may have been influenced by television or a charismatic personality. He will ultimately be less happy, however, wearing the clothing of the incorrect personality expression. In addition, those around him will tend to be confused by this contrast in nonverbal messages.

Most people have a primary and a secondary personality type. Seldom will you find a person who is thoroughly one type. Sometimes there may be a blending of several. However, for the purpose of effective wardrobe building and coordination, it will be wise to determine the primary and secondary types.

The *primary personality expression* is the one that will reflect his career and goals. Typically the largest portion of his wardrobe budget is spent in this area. The *secondary personality expression* relates to his personal life and his leisure-weekend wear. It is in this area where he can show the greatest amount of expression and individuality in choice of apparel.

The self-scoring quiz that follows can aid in both understanding the differences among the types, and in typing primary and secondary categories. Instructions and evaluating results follow.

QUESTIONNAIRE: WHAT IS YOUR PERSONALITY TYPE?

1. Starting with build, work across the page from left to right. Circle each answer that seems appropriate for you. You may circle more than one item per line.
2. When you are finished, add the items you have checked in each column. Put the total in the space at the bottom of the column.
3. Look at your two highest numbers. The category with the highest number that is congruent with the attitudes of your superiors and your clients should be your primary personality type. The other category signifies your secondary type.
4. If your scores tie, reevaluate your answers to narrow the results.

PROCESS OF WORKING WITH EACH PERSONALITY TYPE AT RETAIL

Though there will be many exceptions to the traits and tendencies in shopping habits of each type, some generalities can be made. These generalities become important when considering the needs and preferences of each customer you work with. The effective sales associate or wardrobe consultant will consider the individual's personality rather than work with each customer in the same manner. It is this understanding of personality that will turn a customer into a repeat client.

Conservative Classic (Column I)

This man will tend to be both frugal and quality conscious. He will be interested in the investment quality of his clothing. Style factors may not rank so high on his list, but he will want to be sure that he is not inappropriate in any of his choices. Trust in the sales person is critical to repeat business. The sales associate must be straightforward and establish trust through honest direction on garment quality and value. This man will not want to spend a lot of time shopping and will appreciate the efficient, no-nonsense approach.

Updated Traditional (Column II)

A more open-minded approach to clothing will allow for some experimentation with coordination and color by the sales associate. If this man has already developed a strong sense of style in his business wear, he will appreciate the sales associate updating him as to new stock and current trends in incoming stock shipments. This customer will value the salesperson who lets him know when unusual items or special sales are available. He will also be interested in the opinions of others and what items his peers are buying.

Sophisticated Continental (Column III)

This man has a seasoned approach to clothing and the impact his appearance has in relation to his persona. His sophisticated appearance may be attributed to the excellent assistance of a wardrobe professional, either consultant or salesperson. In this case, he will be open to suggestion, yet at the same time, may be comparing the quality of the advice to his "tutor." Conversely, he may just have a

PERSONALITY EXPRESSION CATEGORIES

	I	II	III	IV	V
Build	All builds, from short to tall, slim to heavy-set	All heights but slim to average in girth	Average to tall in height, slim to average in girth	All heights; usually slim to average in girth	Average to tall in height; average to full in girth
I am often perceived as...	Straightforward, thoughtful, sometimes serious	Approachable, fun loving, dynamic	Worldly, self-confident, poised	Open-minded, off-the-wall, sometimes shy	Energetic, outgoing, enthusiastic
Career/ profession	Finance, politics, business management, physician, lawyer	Advertising, sales, management, young professionals	CEOs, International businessmen, media, fashion	Retail, fashion, the arts, entertainer, grass-roots politics	Consultants, real estate, athletes, entrepreneurs, writers
Favorite sport	Football or baseball	Sailing or tennis	Soccer or skiing	Basketball or hiking	Football or soccer
Favorite publication	*Wall St. Journal*	*Newsweek*	*The New Yorker*	*New York Times*	*Sports Illustrated*
Favored dinner partner	Meryl Streep or Jaclyn Smith	Mary Tyler Moore or Candace Bergen	Catherine Deneuve or Audrey Hepburn	Nastassia Kinski or Katherine Hepburn	Sally Field or Cheryl Tiegs
Favorite music	Classical, easy listening	Oldies, rock and roll	Classical, jazz	Jazz, rhythym and blues	Top 40, country, oldies
I would rather...	Pilot my own Lear jet	Race in the America's Cup	Own a vineyard in France	Own a loft in New York City	Own a ranch in northern California
I would like to look like...	Charlton Heston or Sidney Poitier	Ryan O'Neal or Frank Gifford	Cary Grant or Ricardo Montalban	Billy Crystal or Mickey Rourke	Jim Palmer or Burt Reynolds
Preferred car	Mercedes or Cadillac	Volvo or BMW	Ferrari or Bentley	1956 MG Convertible or any Porsche	Land Rover or 36' Holiday Motorhome
Total Items checked	_____	_____	_____	_____	_____

Primary personality type: _____
Secondary personality type: _____

very good understanding of fit, quality, and what looks good on him. In either case, the sales associate must show a high level of product knowledge and a refined understanding of color, fabric, and textural coordination. The novice will not fare as well with this customer and will "fill orders" rather than offer guidance.

Arty Eclectic (Column IV)

For this man, shopping can be a serendipitous adventure, or it can be perceived as boring and a waste of time. The sales person must be very creative in approach to this man. Does he have something very specific in mind, or is he just "browsing" and hoping to trip over a wonderful new addition to his collection? If he's looking specifically for a Santa Fe-type bolo, for example, once he locates what he's looking for he may be open to your showing him other unusual items that have just arrived. Realize that his imagination is always at work, however, and your efforts at wardrobe coordination may not be appreciated as much as the ideas he has floating around in his head. He may only need to see an unusual item to know how to use it and coordinate it himself. So, show and not necessarily tell, may be the best approach for him.

Adventurous Sportsman (Column V)

Adventure for this man is getting out of the store and to his real interests, which don't include shopping. He cares little for style and more for function. The sales person should get straight to the point, find out what specific items he's looking for, and help him solve his concerns in wardrobe. If he is making a purchase in the area of clothing, he may want some guidance in coordinating furnishings, but leave it at shirt and tie; the frills will not be of interest here. He prefers that his clothes require little effort for him. His life-style is so active that "less is more" and "simpler is better" are important philosophies for him. Keep the basics in mind when assisting this man.

COORDINATION OF WARDROBE FOR CLIENT

You have now worked with the client and know his size requirements, personality type, and are ready to coordinate his wardrobe or his new purchases. The following forms will assist you in three ways:

1. To ensure that there are elements in the wardrobe that are being used in outfits
2. To ensure that the client knows how to use and coordinate his new purchases
3. To determine that no needed items have unwittingly been omitted

In reference to the last point, it becomes very clear in the process of coordinating his apparel when there is an item that is still needed to round out the wardrobe. This is sometimes not evident until you get to the point of truly analyzing his options. The benefit of the forms to the client is that he feels confident in how to put the elements together for a complete, well-coordinated look. This form then becomes his resource for dress and aids tremendously in packing for business trips.

The forms are self-explanatory, except for the terms "misc." or "statement." "Miscellaneous" might be a special sock, collar bar, cuff link, and so on needed for that outfit. "Statement" helps those clients who are concerned about the message that this outfit sends to others. They can then have defined for them a "high-powered" look, "friendly" look, and so forth.

These forms may be photocopied for repeated use.

CASE STUDY

Brian Pinty had his own business, which required that he spend 90 percent of his time on the telephone. His clientele were international financiers, most of whom he had never met face to face. This situation allowed him to work in an informal setting. His "business" wardrobe consisted of jeans and chambray workshirts. As his business grew, however, his client base included more United States executives. In addition, several of his European clients scheduled visits to the United States and meetings with Brian.

SPORTCOAT/SLACK
WARDROBE CHART

CLIENT: _____   DATE: _____   REV: _____

COAT	PANT	SHIRT	TIE	SHOE	BELT	MISC.	STATEMENT

CLIENT: _____

SUIT: _____

DATE: _____ REV: _____

SUIT
WARDROBE CHART

SHIRT	TIE	SHOE	BELT	PKT. SQUARE	MISC.	STATEMENT	

As a result, Brian found himself with greater wardrobe needs. Because he was handling the financial portfolios of some very powerful and sophisticated business people, he realized that he could not meet them in such casual apparel. He contacted a wardrobe consultant to assist him in putting together a professional base wardrobe as soon as possible.

Brian's conception of a "professional" look was a very mainstream, conservative cut with traditional patterns in ties and shirts. His clients were more worldly and sophisticated in style, however. His build was slim, and his physique could bear almost any cut of suit. His personality was that of an offbeat intellectual, his interests were eclectic, and his home and office decor was very varied and unusual. His perception of what was "right" for him was based on the business looks of the previous generation and did not really mesh with his present world. In his early days of working with the wardrobe consultant, he insisted that he emulate the looks he'd seen in Brooks Brothers catalogs, yet those same looks were not in sync with his personality.

After buying several suits in this traditional style, the wardrobe consultant realized the amount of money being invested in a wardrobe that would ultimately prove unsatisfactory to Brian. In shopping with him one day, she managed to get him into a more fashion-forward specialty store. Once he slipped on a well-tailored European suit he understood the look that was really appropriate for him. At that point, his standard suits just never felt quite right to him.

- What do you think was Brian's primary personality type?
- How could the wardrobe consultant have worked with John to find his personality type more quickly?
- How could Brian most easily convert his traditional wardrobe to a more sophisticated wardrobe without enormous expense?

TERMS TO KNOW

Define or briefly explain the following:

Personality type
Conservative classic
Updated traditional
Sophisticated continental
Arty eclectic
Adventurous sportsman
Primary personality type
Secondary personality type

BIBLIOGRAPHY

Batterberry, Michael and Ariane. *Mirror Mirror: A Social History of Fashion*. New York: Holt, Rinehart and Winston, 1977.

Bolen, William. *Contemporary Retailing*. Englewood Cliffs, NJ: Prentice Hall, 1988.

Boyer, G. Bruce. *Eminently Suitable*. New York: W. W. Norton, 1990.

Carlsen, Peter, and William Wilson. *Manstyle*. New York: Clarkson N. Potter, 1977. Copyright by *Gentlemen's Quarterly Magazine*.

Cobrin, Harry A. *The Men's Clothing Industry*. New York: Fairchild Publications, 1970.

Corbman, Barnard P. *Textiles: Fiber to Fabric*. New York: Gregg Division/McGraw-Hill, 1983.

deMarly, Diana. *Fashion for Men: An Illustrated History*. London: B. T. Batsford Ltd., 1985.

Fenton, Lois. *Dress for Excellence*. New York: Rawson Associates, 1986.

Flusser, Alan. *Clothes and the Man*. New York: Villard Books, 1985.

Flusser, Alan. *Making the Man*. New York: Wallaby/Simon & Schuster, 1981.

Hardingham, Martin. *The Fabric Catalog*. New York: Wallaby/Pocket Books, 1978.

Hix, Charles. *How to Dress Your Man*. New York: Crown, 1981.

Horn, Marilyn J., and Lois M. Gurel. *The Second Skin*. New York: Houghton Mifflin, 1981.

Levitt, Mortimer. *The Executive Look*. New York: Atheneum, 1981.

Lurie, Alison. *The Language of Clothes*. New York: Vintage Books, 1981.

McGill, Leonard. *Stylewise*. New York: G. P. Putnam's Sons, 1983.

O'Hara, Georgina. *The Encyclopaedia of Fashion*. New York: Harry N. Abrams, 1986.

Pizzuto, Joseph J. *Fabric Science*. New York: Fairchild Publications, 1980.

Russell, Douglas A. *Costume History and Style*. Englewood Cliffs, NJ: Prentice Hall, 1983.

Stone, Elaine, and Jean Samples. *Fashion Merchandising: An Introduction*. New York: McGraw-Hill, 1985.

Tolman, Ruth. *Selling Men's Fashion*. New York: Fairchild Publications, 1982.

Wingate, Isabel B. *Textile Fabrics and Their Selection*. Englewood Cliffs, NJ: Prentice Hall, 1970.

GLOSSARY

A

activewear: A subdivision of sportswear that includes apparel worn for exercise or active sports.

all-weather coat: A raincoat with a zip-out lining making it serviceable all year long.

arrowhead: A small, triangular design in either leather or decorative stitching. Often used at the ends of pockets or darts in westernwear.

ascot: A wide tie worn for dressy day wear, or dressy casual events. It doubles over and is held in place by a decorative stick pin positioned vertically on the tie.

athletic cut: A suit that is cut for the highly developed physique where the drop is greater than average. The typical athletic cut suit has an 8-inch drop. See also *drop* and *young man's cut*.

B

balmacaan: A heavy outerwear coat, usually overcoat weight. It is looser and fuller than other styles, with a raglan sleeve and a rounder, standing collar. It gets its name from an estate in Scotland.

barcodes: The vertical lines and spaces that, when read by a laser scanner, electronically identify a product.

barrel cuff: The most common form of sleeve cuff. It may have one or two buttons for closure. See also *split size sleeve* and *French cuff*.

besom: A pocket opening with a very narrow welt on both top and bottom sides. Often a flap is inserted into the besom for suitings. A besom may be used on coats or on pants. Also referred to as an inset pocket or a slash pocket.

bespoke: The British term for custom-tailored apparel. See also *Savile Row*.

bi-swing: A back treatment on sportcoats designed for ease of movement. A vertical flange on right and left side of the back beside the armholes allows forward movement of the arms without restriction. Often associated with hunting coats or safari jackets.

black tie: The semiformal level of formality. Black tie is most often associated with the traditional tuxedo, though dinner jackets and dinner suits may also be worn. See also *tuxedo*.

blazer: A solid-color sportcoat. Traditionally it is navy blue with metallic buttons. It may be single or double-breasted. Today, the term blazer has broadened to include other solid-color sportcoats. The term blazer comes from HMS Blazer of the British navy, which originally wore this style.

bluff edge: The edge of a lapel and pocket or flap that has no topstitching.

boutonniere: The French term for buttonhole. The small buttonhole is placed at the top of the left lapel. Originally its function was to hold the lapel closed in cold weather. A button was placed under the right lapel. This is still functional on some outerwear. Often the term is used in reference to a single flower pinned on the buttonhole, or positioned where a buttonhole would be.

braces: British synonym for suspenders.

break: The additional fabric that softly drapes at the bottom crease of the pant leg when the pant falls longer than the top of the shoe at the front. See also *clean crease*.

breast welt: The rectangular-shaped pocket opening positioned on the left front of a sportcoat, suit coat, or on outerwear.

bridge department: A department that offers merchandise in price point and style between clothing and sportswear including inexpensive sportcoats and middle- to lower-end slacks. The bridge department is often merchandised with goods for the young man.

British warmer: A traditional cut of outerwear. It can be made in either overcoat or topcoat weight. It is usually double-breasted with set-in sleeves.

broadcast media: Form of disseminating information over a broad area, most often associated with radio and television.

button-down collar: A soft collar that has a button at the bottom of each point. Originally worn in playing polo, it is associated with a traditional apparel and may be seen in both dress shirts and sport shirts.

C

cap-toe oxford: A classic tie shoe that has a seam running horizontally across the toe.

care label: A permanent label that, by law, must be sewn inside a garment to instruct on proper cleaning and care method.

Carnaby street: A street in London where boutiques started the "mod" look popular in the 1960s. The look retained the name of the street where it started.

catalog: Printed matter, often in magazine format, that offers merchandise by mail. An updated form of catalog is in video format. See also *mail order* and *video shopping*.

celebrity sponsorship: An agreement with a manufacturer whereby a well-known personality lends his or her name for a fee for promotion of merchandise.

cervical point: The point at the base of the neck identified by the dominant spinal column bone. This is the starting point for measurement of shirt-sleeve length.

chain stores: A group of centrally owned stores handling similar merchandise and controlled by a central office.

chesterfield: A classic outerwear coat. Typically it is a long, slim cut with set-in sleeves and a black-velvet collar. The most traditional chesterfield is gray in color.

clean crease: The unbroken crease line of the pant from the knee to the bottom. This occurs when the pant just touches the top of the shoe at the front, or is shorter than the shoe. See also *break*.

clocks: A vertical striping design on the sides of a sock.

clothier: Traditionally defined as a maker or retailer of tailored apparel. Originally the term was used to describe a finisher of wool cloth.

clothing: Technically, a classification in menswear that includes suits, tailored sportcoats, dress slacks, and tailored outerwear.

club tie: A small, repeated representational tie pattern. Originally, the tie represented membership in a particular club, and the club crest was the pattern used. Today, the interpretation has broadened to include representational patterns such as golf clubs, sailboats, birds, and so on. These patterns often represent the interests of the wearer. See also *school tie*.

consumer publications: Printed matter, usually magazines, which address the needs and interests of the ultimate consumer. Examples include *M*, *Gentlemen's Quarterly*, *Esquire*, *Man*.

conversationals: Ties that have unusual patterns, often large in scale or bold in pattern and include subgroups like theme ties and art reproduction ties. They are attention getting, resulting in the name of "conversational."

counter card: An advertising placard used by retailers on display counters. Most often positioned at point of purchase.

counter, shoe: The hard leather portion of the shoe at the back of the heel.

couture: A very high level of apparel in quality, style, and cost. Associated with high-fashion designers, the term is used more often with womenswear than with menswear.

crossover element: A piece of apparel that can be used in more than one way or for more than one level of formality. For example, a navy blue blazer can cross from business to dressy casual to casual wear depending what is being worn with it. Items that cross over help to make a wardrobe more serviceable.

cuff links: Decorative closure mechanisms to be worn with French-cuff shirts. This piece of jewelry is inserted through all four buttonholes of the double cuff and keeps the cuff in place.

cummerbund: The wide, pleated belt that is worn with formal wear. Pleats are to be worn pointing upward.

custom tailored: A method of manufacture where a single garment is made according to the specifications of the customer including fabric, color, and some design features. The customer is measured, and patterns are made according to those measurements. Fittings are conducted throughout the construction process to ensure accurate and precise fit. This method of construction produces the highest quality and typically highest cost to the customer. See also *made to order* and *made to measure*.

custom tailor: An artisan who has the skill to create clothing from raw goods. The custom tailor, through several fittings, creates apparel that fits the customer more precisely than apparel that is available off the rack.

cutaway: The portion of a coat front that has been "cut away" or rounded at the opening edges below the waist. A single-breasted coat typically has a rounded cutaway at the front opening edge. The term is also used to describe a formal tailcoat that supports a dramatic cutaway and tails. See also *tailcoat*.

D

Daily News Record (DNR): The "brother" paper to *Women's Wear Daily*, DNR is the "bible" of the menswear industry and the most important trade journal for menswear apparel manufacturers, retailers, and affiliated industries.

dailies: The daily newspapers published in towns and cities across the country.

darted front: A suit coat or sport coat that has a long vertical shaping seam on each front panel.

department store: A retail establishment that employs twenty five or more people. It offers merchandise in the categories of home furnishings, general apparel, and dry goods.

designer: The definition varies widely but most commonly is associated with the individual who creates the concept of a style and, either individually or through others, implements its production.

diffusion concept: A method of increasing production and a designer's business through adding more lines under different labels and at different price points. See also *price point spread*.

dinner jacket: A jacket that may be used in place of a tuxedo for special occasions. It may be a color other than black. The white dinner jacket is classic for summer wear. It may also be a patterned fabric. Dinner jackets are most often worn with black or midnight navy formal pants.

dinner suit: A classic suit that is made of a dressier fabric than the traditional business suit. For some occasions it can take the place of tuxedo or dinner jacket.

discount store: A self-service, single-store operation, a chain store, or a subsidiary of a department store where merchandise is offered at greatly reduced prices.

double-breasted: A coat opening that is asymmetrical, overlaps itself, and has double rows of buttons. See also *single-breasted*.

double cuff: The term the British use for French cuff. See also *French cuff*.

drape cut: A full, softly cut suit that follows the shape of the form without being tight. Accent is on a broader shoulder and a full chest.

dress shirt: A classically styled shirt, devoid of decorative details, which is traditionally worn for business. It is usually long sleeved, with one left breast patch pocket or no pockets at all. The collar style may vary as well as the fabric. It is sized by neck measurement and sleeve length. See also *sport shirt*.

drop: The difference in inches between the waist and the chest. Average drop of the American man is 6 inches. Also see *athletic cut* and *young man's cut*.

drummer: Early term for a traveling salesman. He used a drum to gain attention to his wares, and he "drummed up business."

E

elbow patch: An oval leather patch sewn on sportcoats in the elbow area. Originally this was to avoid excessive wear in the elbow area when the coat was worn while working at a desk. Today it is more decorative than functional.

electronic data interchange (EDI): The electronic technology of communications as well as the electronic practices by which business is conducted.

endorsement: Approval for use of an individual's name in promotion of a product line. Most often, a well-known personality receives monetary compensation for use of his or her name.

engineered plant: A manufacturing plant that uses sophisticated, specialized machinery to produce mass manufactured apparel in a highly efficient manner.

English spread: A collar style made popular by the Duke of Kent, brother of the Duke of Windsor. The point spread of this collar falls between the straight-point collar and the wider, Windsor collar.

epaulet: A short shoulder strap associated originally with military coats to hold rifle straps and, as in officer's shoulder boards, they held decorative roping. Epaulets may be seen in sport shirts or on casual sport coats.

F

factory outlet: Typically a manufacturer-owned store that sells company products at reduced prices.

fitted shirt: A shirt that fits close to the body, most often incorporating back darts to aid in shaping and to reduce bulkiness. This is the closest-fitting shirt cut.

fitting: A meeting between customer and tailor to determine alterations necessary to produce a well-fitting garment. Most often used in conjunction with custom tailors. Several fittings occur during the manufacture of a custom garment to ensure excellent fit. See also *custom tailored*.

fly front: A coat-front closure style where the buttonholes are covered by a flap as a protection from wind and rain.

fly tab: The fabric extension on the inside of the pant at the zipper. This extension has a buttonhole in it which buttons to the inside of the opposite front panel of the pant and keeps strain off of the zipper. See also *French fly*.

formal wear: Apparel worn for evening or formal occasions. Includes apparel from subcategories of black tie and white tie. See also *black tie* and *white tie*.

four-in-hand: Originally this term was used to signify a type of tie, today known as the necktie. It is now most often used to signify the long, cylindrical knot that was used with the earlier tie of the same name. This tie and its knot were first worn by the drivers of the four-in-hand carriages of the eighteenth century.

French cuff: A sophisticated, wide, double cuff that is folded over and requires cuff links for closure. See also *double cuff*.

French facing: A lapel that extends to the inside of a coat front as a very wide facing.

There is no lining in this style and the construction is often used for informal coats or summer-weight garments.

French fly: The fabric extension on the inside of the pant at the zipper. This extension has a buttonhole in it that buttons to the inside opposite front panel of the pant and keeps strain off of the zipper. The French fly is a more expensive version of the fly tab as it extends the full length of the fly opening. See also *fly tab*.

full cut: See *regular cut*.

full dress: The most formal level of dress that includes tailcoat, accompanying dress pants, and formal shirt. Full dress is worn only for those occasions that indicate "white tie" on the invitation.

furnishings: A classification in menswear that includes shirts, ties, underwear, socks, pajamas, and accessories.

G

gauntlet: A shirt sleeve placket that has a reinforcement of an additional strip of cloth along the opening edge. A long gauntlet often has a buttonhole on it that keeps the sleeve vent from opening.

gorge: The seam that joins the collar to the lapel on a coat.

grade numbering: A system of ranking the quality or make of clothing based on the number of hand operations. Grades range from "x-make," which is totally machine made, to "6-plus make," which is the highest quality of tailored menswear, with a high percentage of hand operations. See also *make*.

green-grass shops: Retail shops located on or adjacent to golf courses.

gun patch: A leather patch typically sewn on the right coat front in the shoulder area for rifle recoil. A style treatment associated with hunting coats or casual sportcoats.

H

half Windsor: A triangular-shaped necktie knot that uses one less wrap than the full Windsor knot.

hard news: Issues of major interest that affect the direction of, and may have bottom-line significance to, the industry.

Harris tweed: A strong hand-woven, woolen fabric produced in the Outer Hebrides of Scotland. The name is protected by a trademark.

heavy outerwear: A U.S. Bureau of Census classification that includes windbreakers, snowsuits, ski jackets, and heavy sportswear.

hosiery: The traditional term for men's socks.

I

imports: Raw or finished goods that come into the United States from foreign countries. Imports may include items that are cut or partially constructed in the United States and then completed offshore.

inseam: The distance from the crotch seam to the finished bottom of the pant. See also *prehemmed/precuffed* and *unfinished*.

inset pocket: See *besom*.

Ivy League: A style of apparel often associated with the traditional, conservative look of the 1950s. The term is also used to describe the soft, or natural shoulder associated with the Ivy League coat of the period. See also *natural shoulder*.

J

jobber, retail: A middle person who buys from manufacturers and sells to retailers.

K

knickers, knickerbockers: A loose, baggy pant that is held in place by a band just below the knee. Originally worn for golf. See also *plus fours*.

knock off: A lower-priced copy of a high-end style.

L

Laver's law: Fashion historian James Laver's concept on the evolution of fashion. His theory defines the way we look at fashion based on how it changes with the years preceding and following its popularity.

licensee: The manufacturer who produces garments under another company name or designer name.

licensing: A formal agreement to produce and market merchandise under another's name, typically a highly recognizable designer's name. A percentage of sales, or royalty, is given to the owner of the name being used.

licensor: The designer or company that has contracted with a manufacturer to make product under the licensor's name.

locker loop: The small loop often positioned in the yoke seam at the center back of a dress or sport shirt. Originally this was used to hang up a shirt on a hook. It is more decorative than functional today.

logo: The shortened term for "logogram," which is a visual element or symbol representing a company name. Logos are sometimes used for decorative effect on clothing, such as the Izod alligator on knitted shirts. Prominently placed logos were extremely popular during the 1970s and 1980s.

long run: A longer manufacturing period within which many similar items are manufactured. High numbers of manufacture may result in greater efficiency, higher quality, and lower costs.

M

made to measure: A process of making a garment to the style and fit specifications of the customer including fabric, color, and some design features. The customer is measured, and garments are manufactured according to those measurements. Fittings are not typically a part of this process. See also *made to order* and *custom tailored*.

made to order: A process of making a garment to the style specifications of the customer including fabric, color, and some design features. The garment is made in the stock pattern of the manufacturer.

mail order: A retail firm that offers merchandise by mail, usually through catalogs. See also *catalog*.

make: The manufacturing methods used to construct apparel.

make number: See *grade numbering*.

mass manufacturer: A manufacturer that produces in large quantities and sells through retailers.

matrix buying: The process by which suppliers are selected for retail stores by committee or team buyers.

monk strap: A shoe with a plain tip that closes with a buckle and strap.

N

natural shoulder: A very lightly padded shoulder that has a rounded appearance at the shoulder to armhole seam. Also known as a "soft shoulder." See also *Ivy League*.

nested suit: A coat and pant of the same fabric that are merchandised on the same hanger, with the pant "nested" inside the coat.

norfolk straps: A style treatment that incorporated vertical strapping on coat fronts and back. Combined with a sewn-on belting, the coat style was called a Norfolk jacket. It was popularized by the Duke of Windsor and was one of the earliest sportcoat styles worn in the United States.

notch lapel: The most common collar/lapel treatment. Also called "notch collar," the notch forms a 45-degree angle or less and is in a direct line with the gorge seam. See also *gorge seam*, *peaked lapel*, and *shawl collar*.

O

off-price store: A retailer that buys goods directly from a manufacturer at reduced prices and offers them to the consumer at a special price break.

offshore production: Garments that have been partially made or totally constructed outside the United States.

outerwear: Apparel designed and constructed for use over street wear and for various types of weather. See also *overcoat, topcoat, rainwear*.

outlet store: See *factory outlet*.

overcoat: A heavy weight outerwear coat. Classified as a part of the clothing category. It is more often sold and worn in the north. See also *topcoat*.

oxford shoe: A shoe that uses shoelaces for closure, like a cap-toe oxford or a wing-tip style.

P

paddles: The loops, usually leather, which are at the ends of suspenders. The paddles have holes in them, like buttonholes, which attach the suspenders to the pant buttons inside the waistband.

paisley: A classic pattern shaped like a curved tear drop. Originally an Indian design, it was later produced in Paisley, England, and the pattern retains the town's name.

peaked lapel: A lapel that forms a sharply angled point higher on the coat front than the more common notch lapel. It is most often associated with double-breasted styles. See also *notch lapel* and *shawl collar*.

personal shopper: An individual who assists clients in making wardrobe selections at retail stores. An independent consultant accesses a variety of stores. An in-store consultant is an employee of a particular store and accesses merchandise only in that store, or branches of the store. See also *wardrobe consultant*.

pick stitch: A form of topstitching that originally was done by hand. Stitches were small and widely spaced to create a distinctively elegant look. Today the appearance of pick stitching can be created by specialized machinery.

pinned collar: A straight-point collar with a hole in each point. The hole allows a decorative metal pin to pass through and hold the collar firmly in place. This forces the tie into a more prominent position.

placket: A finished opening edge of a garment that usually unbuttons to allow a body part to pass through. For example, the front opening edge of a shirt often has a placket as well as the shirt-sleeve vent placket. See also *gauntlet*.

plus-fours: Another term for knickerbockers. Popularized in the 1920s and often worn for golf. This style of pant had the fabric cut to the knee plus 4 inches, which resulted in the distinctive full drape below the knee.

pocket square: Handkerchief used in a decorative manner in a suit coat or sportcoat pocket. The most traditional pocket square is made of white linen. Also seen in all colors of silk and many multicolor patterns.

point spread: The distance between collar points.

point to point: The distance across the back from the right shoulder where the shoulder seam intersects with the armhole seam to the same point on the left side. The point to point is an important fit and style feature as it indicates the breadth of the shoulder and affects the fullness in the coat chest.

polo coat: Outerwear style that is somewhat similar to the British warmer, but slightly more casual. Historically it is made of camel hair. It has a belted back, patch pockets, and is double-breasted with heavy topstitching.

prehemmed/precuffed: A pant that is merchandised with the bottoms prefinished. The manufacturer offers the pant with the bottoms already hemmed or cuffed. The price tickets will indicate the inseam length as a part of the size, the second number reflecting the inseam length. Example: size 32 x 30 has a 32-inch waist and a 30-inch inseam. See also *inseam*.

price point spread: A method of increasing production and a designer's business by incorporating more styles at varying price point levels. In this concept, the same label name is used for all price points. See also *diffusion concept*.

private label: Merchandise that is offered by a retailer and available only through that organization. Often called "store brand," the retailer frequently specifies the design of the items and produces it through contractors.

pump: A slip-on shoe for formal occasions. Often seen in patent leather or high-quality leathers. There are many styles but the most classic sports a grosgrain bow on the top.

Q

Quick Response: Strategy of U.S. manufacturers for responding more quickly to the retailer's needs than foreign manufacturers can. Use of electronic data interchange in Quick Response helps to shorten the manufacturing and retailing pipeline.

R

raglan: An armhole/sleeve treatment that is associated with outerwear and very casual sportswear. The raglan sleeve has a slanted seam on the front and the back. This allows for great ease of movement. See also *split raglan*.

rainwear: Outerwear designed specifically to be worn in inclement or rainy weather. It has been coated with a water repellent that must periodically be retreated. A raincoat may also be designed with a zip-out lining and is then called an "all-weather" coat. Trench coats are often treated for water repellency and classified as rainwear. See also *all weather* and *trench coat*.

ready to wear: Apparel that is mass produced and is available on the rack or from mail order and is ready for immediate wear. Garments are not made to specific customer needs or measurements.

reefer: The single-breasted version of the British warmer. It fits closer to the body and has a slimmer silhouette. Usually topcoat weight.

regimental stripe: A traditional striped tie. Its broad, bold stripes represented different British army regiments. The fabric used is most often the heavily ribbed "repp" that lends itself to stripings. See also *repp*.

regular cut: In suits a regular cut indicates the traditional full-cut, 6-inch drop. In shirts this is also the most traditional cut and is also called full cut or box cut.

repp: Also spelled "rep," this is an old word for "rib." It is a closely woven fabric with a distinctively ribbed surface. A fabric that is often used in making traditional striped ties. See also *regimental stripe*.

rise: The distance from the crotch to the waistband of a pant. A long rise is typically found in suits for taller men and a short rise in suits for shorter men. A high-rise pant is one in which the waistband sits higher on the body and a low rise sits low on the hips. Sometimes referred to as "stride."

rope shoulder: A heavily padded shoulder. Additional material inserted in the armhole seam along the shoulder results in the look of "roping," which elevates the top of the sleeve slightly higher than the shoulder pad area. This produces a distinctly dramatic look in the shoulder and was very popular in the 1970s.

rounded collar: A dress shirt collar style that has the points rounded off.

royalty: A percentage of the sales of merchandise paid to the licensor by the licensee for use of a highly recognizable name.

S

sack coat: A loose-fitting suit coat or sportcoat. Often associated with early traditional British menswear, the sack suit forms the basis of today's tailored garments.

sample store: Most typically a single-store operation that offers manufacturer and designer samples at reduced prices. Sizes are most often limited to those sizes in which samples are made.

Savile Row: A street in London's West End that is the home to some of London's oldest and most renowned custom tailors. The word is synonymous with high-quality tailored apparel. See also *bespoke*.

school tie: A small, repeated representational tie pattern. Originally, the tie represented affiliation with a particular school, and the school crest was the pattern used. Today, the interpretation has broadened to include representational patterns such as golf clubs, sailboats, birds, and so on. These patterns often represent the interests of the wearer. See also *club tie*.

seconds: Factory rejects that are defective in either piece goods or construction.

set-in sleeve: A tailored sleeve treatment where the sleeve cylinder is "set in" to a preformed armhole. This results in vertical seams on both the front and the back of the suit or sportcoat.

Seventh Avenue: The heart of the garment district in New York City.

shank: The neck of a button that is created by the thread it is sewn on with. The neck thread is wrapped to decrease wear and to make the button stand up. This avoids a pinch to the coat front when the coat is buttoned.

shawl collar: A softly rounded lapel with no gorge seam. It is found in more forward styles of sportcoats, in formal wear, and in smoking jackets. See also *notched lapel*, *peaked lapel*, and *gorge seam*.

shirt-tail hem: A deeply curved hem line on a shirt. When tucked into a pant waistband the shaping of the hem reduces bulkiness.

short run: A shorter manufacturing period within which a small number of similar items are manufactured. Smaller numbers of manufacture may result in lower efficiency and higher costs.

single-breasted: A coat front that has a single button or single row of buttons along the center front opening. This is the most common style of coat opening. See also *double-breasted*.

single-needle tailoring: A method of manufacture using single-needle sewing machines that produces higher-quality, smooth flat seams. It is typically a more expensive method of manufacture than using double-needle sewing machines. This method is used in better make shirts.

six-plus make: A "six-plus" make garment is the highest quality of construction in clothing. It signifies the highest percentage of handwork in manufactured garments. See also *make* and *grade numbering*.

slip-on shoe: A shoe lacking grommets and shoelaces. The foot slips into the shoe, as with a loafer.

soft shoulder: See *natural shoulder* and *Ivy League*.

skirt: The bottom circumference of a coat. See also *sweep*.

slash pocket: See *besom* and *inset*.

soft news: An entertaining, light-hearted approach to the news. Often associated with life-style issues and interests.

special order: An order of merchandise by a retailer to a manufacturer for a specific customer. This often occurs when a customer desires a garment that the store has in stock, but not in his size.

specialty store: A retailer that carries limited lines of merchandise or may specialize in selling one of a very few types of goods. These stores offer select merchandise and heightened levels of service.

split raglan: A sleeve style associated with outerwear. It has a slanted, raglan seam on the back and a vertical seam that looks like a set-in sleeve on the front. This armhole treatment allows for the ease of forward movement as in a raglan sleeve, yet has a more tailored look from the front. See also *raglan*.

split-size sleeve: Shirt sizing that can accommodate two sleeve lengths. The shirt barrel-style cuff has two buttons that can be adjusted to make a tighter cuff, thereby controlling the additional fullness of a too-long sleeve length. The ticket reflects a size like 15 x 32/33, indicating that the shirt will accommodate sleeve lengths of 32 inches or 33 inches.

split yoke: The method of cutting the yoke on the shirt back, resulting in a vertical seam dividing the yoke in half. This allows for better shaping in the shoulder area and is a more expensive method of shirt manufacture.

sponging: A process of preshrinking wool fabric. See also fabric glossary in chapter 10.

sportcoat: A coat that is sold as a separate unit. It is typically less formal than a suit.

sport shirt: A more casual form of the dress shirt, it may have two breast pockets or no pockets, and be long or short sleeved. The styling may include decorative details such as epaulets, flaps on the pockets, and sleeve straps. Fabrics vary more widely than with dress shirts and may range from solid colors to large and brightly colored plaids. Collars are most commonly button-down, English spread, and straight point. See also *dress shirt*.

sportswear: A classification of apparel that includes the subcategories of activewear and spectator apparel. It is the classification that involves the greatest amount of change in color, texture, and style as well as range in pricing.

stays: Slim, rectangular, plastic, or metallic inserts that help to keep a straight-point collar crisp. Most shirts have removable stays, which slip out of the collar for laundering. Other shirts incorporate the stays in the shirt interlining and are washable.

stock-keeping units (SKU): A numbering system used by a company to identify an item. Most often used in conjunction with computer inventory systems.

stock pattern: The standard pattern used by a manufacturer to make production apparel.

store brand: Merchandise that is offered by a retailer and available only through that organization. Often called "private label," the retailer frequently specifies the design of the items and produces it through contractors. See also *private label*.

straight-point collar: A collar that uses stays to maintain a crisp straight point. Used on dress shirts and some sport shirts.

stride: See *rise*.

studs: The decorative closures for formal shirts that are inserted into buttonholes on both sides of a formal shirt front.

suit: A coat and pant of matching fabric that are merchandised on the same hanger in the clothing department. See also *nested suit*.

suit separates: Coats and pants of the same fabric that are designed to be worn together, but are merchandised separately. They can be worn as a suit or as separates.

suspenders: Adjustable straps that pass over the shoulders to hold up pants. They eliminate the need for a belt.

sweep: The bottom circumference of a coat. See also *skirt*.

T

tab collar: A dress-shirt collar that is held firmly in place by small fabric tabs on the underneath side of the collar. It keeps the tie neatly in place.

tapered shirt: A box-cut shirt that has had the side seams angled to produce a slimmer silhouette and less bulkiness through the waist.

tailcoat: A formal evening coat with tails that start at the waist and taper toward the back of the knee, vented for the full length from the waist. The coat is short in the front and does not button. It is the "full-dress" coat and worn only for white-tie occasions. See also *cutaway, full dress,* and *white-tie.*

tailor: An individual with the skill to custom make apparel and to alter manufactured apparel to properly fit a customer. See also *custom tailor.*

tear sheet: A copy of a page from a publication. Usually represents an advertisement.

three-piece suit: A nested suit that includes a matching vest. See also *nested.*

throat latch: A fabric or leather extension that has a buttonhole. Positioned on the left side of the collar it would attach to a button underneath the right side and hold the lapels closed during cold weather. Also referred to as a wind tab.

topcoat: A lighter-weight version of an overcoat. It used to be worn as a transition coat from winter to spring. With heated cars and mass transportation, topcoats have exceeded overcoats in sales nationally for winter weather. See also *overcoat.*

topstitching: Decorative stitching along the lapel, collar, and pocket/flap edges. See also *bluff edge* and *pick stitching.*

tourney waist: A beltless pant style associated with golf pants. It often incorporates a stretch waistband to allow for ease of movement during a golf swing.

trade publications: Printed matter that addresses hard news, needs, and interests of the garment, retail, and affiliated industries. Formats may include newsprint-type journals, flyers, association trade journals, and magazines. The mainstay trade publication of the menswear industry is *Daily News Record (DNR).*

trench coat: Sometimes called a "spy coat," the classic trench coat is a tan-colored fabric that is belted and has epaulets, yokes, and decorative detailing. It gets its name from the coats officers wore in World War II.

Truman fold: A manner of folding a linen or cotton pocket square that produces a flat horizontal line running parallel with the top of the coat breast welt. Named after former President Harry Truman who often wore a pocket square in this manner.

tuxedo: A semi formal suit with satin lapels and a satin stripe down the side of each pant leg. May be single- or double-breasted, and is to be worn with a special formal shirt.

U

unconstructed: A coat that has very little in the way of padding, interlining, or lining. In the 1970s the "leisure coat" was a popular unconstructed style.

unfinished pant: A dress pant that is merchandised with a raw bottom on the legs. This pant must be hemmed or cuffed according to the desires of the customer. Suit pants are sold unfinished. See also *prehemmed.*

unisex: A term used to connote a style that is appropriate to both male and female.

universal product code (UPC): In product pricing, the barcodes that are used to identify and communicate information to a central computer.

V

vent: A slitlike opening in a garment, such as a sleeve vent or a back coat vent on the skirt of a coat.

video catalog: A catalog produced in video format for home view selection of merchandise. Usually directed toward the ultimate consumer, it allows the viewer to see apparel worn by models in action.

W

waistcoat: Another term for a vest. The term waistcoat today is most often used in conjunction with formal wear. It may be single- or double-breasted, and is worn under a coat.

wardrobe consultant: An individual who assists clients in wardrobe development. The individual may evaluate existing wardrobe in the home or may assist the client with retail purchases. A wardrobe consultant usually offers more extensive services than the personal shopper. See also *personal shopper*.

wear test: The testing by a manufacturer that entails actual wear and care of a garment by an individual. This often results in higher quality of merchandise manufactured.

western style: Detailing that may include arrowheads, contrast color topstitching, scalloped pockets and yokes, and shoulder gun patches. Garments may be cut to fit closer to the body.

white tie: The highest level of formality in evening dress. When an invitation specifies white tie, it is expected that male guests will wear tailcoats, or full dress. Women often wear ball gowns. See also *full dress* and *tailcoat*.

Windsor collar: A dress-shirt collar with a wide point spread. It was originally worn by the Duke of Windsor and was designed to be worn with the full, Windsor knot.

Windsor knot: A large triangular knot that is to be worn with a shirt that has a wide point spread. Popularized by the Duke of Windsor.

wind tab: See *throat latch*.

wing collar: A stiff, standing collar band with folded tips. This style is most often associated with the formal shirt worn with tuxedo or full dress.

wing tip: A traditional tie shoe that has a distinctive wing shape sewn on the toe. Leather is often cut with zig-zag edge and has perforated areas.

wishbone hanger: A sturdy wooden or plastic hanger that has a slight shaping to the upper edges. The shaping curves forward much like the curve of the shoulder and helps to maintain the shape of a coat. Wishbone hangers also include a special bar to hold the pant of a nested suit securely.

X

x-make: The grade level representing a totally machine-made garment. See also *grade numbering* and *six-plus make*.

Y

young man's cut: A suit that has a more highly suppressed waist than the average cut. The young man's cut typically has a 7-inch drop. See also *drop* and *athletic cut*.

INDEX